THE OMEGA FILES
SECRET NAZI UFO BASES REVEALED!

Branton

PRIVATE LIMITED EDITION
Global Communications

THE OMEGA FILES
by Branton
With a Prologue, **The Enemy Within,** by Ivan Fraser
Edited by Timothy Green Beckley
This edition Copyright 2008 by Global Communications/Conspiracy Journal

All rights reserved. No part of these manuscripts may be copied or reproduced by any mechanical or digital methods and no exerpts or quotes may be used in any other book or manuscript without permission in writing by the Publisher, Global Communications/Conspiracy Journal, except by a reviewer who may quote brief passages in a review.

Revised Edition

Published in the United States of America By
Global Communications/Conspiracy Journal
Box 753 · New Brunswick, NJ 08903

Staff Members
Timothy G. Beckley, Publisher
Carol Ann Rodriguez, Assistant to the Publisher
Sean Casteel, General Associate Editor
Tim R. Swartz, Graphics and Editorial Consultant
William Kern, Editorial and Art Consultant

Sign Up On The Web For Our Free Weekly Newsletter
and Mail Order Version of Conspiracy Journal
and Bizarre Bazaar
www.ConspiracyJournal.com

Order Hot Line: 1-732-602-3407
PayPal: MrUFO8@hotmail.com

The Omega Files

PROLOGUE

The Enemy Within - the Illusion Without

by Ivan Fraser

WHO BENEFITS?
TERRORISM AND DOUBLESPEAK
WHO DOES NOT BENEFIT?
INCONSISTENCIES ABOUND
PAVLOVIAN REACTIONS PREPARATION
VESTED INTERESTS
RELIGIOUS HYPOCRISY
LIES AND SPIN
SETTING UP THE SCAPEGOAT
FOOD FOR THOUGHT
KNOWN IN ADVANCE - THE PROOF
THE AMERICAN DREAM
FOR TOMMOROWS

The Omega Files

On September 11th 2001, the world was numbed by not only 'the largest terrorist attack', but also the biggest media event, in history.

Hollywood, it seems, has come true!

Within minutes, they were comparing the attack on America with Pearl Harbour; the 'big screen' and still fresh in the minds of millions. 'It's like a movie,' was the initial response of millions of stunned onlookers.

What the movie did not reveal, however, was that - like the sinking of the Lusitania, which brought America into World War I, Pearl Harbour was no sudden unannounced terrorist attack - Roosevelt knew of the coming attack from intelligence sources but did not evacuate the naval base; instead, it was allowed to go ahead in order that this could be used for propaganda purposes to allow him to graciously go back on his promise to the American people that they would not be drawn into another war.

Increasingly, big-budget War and Disaster movies have been appearing in our movie theatres over the past decade, including the likes of Independence Day, Armageddon, Die Hard…etc.

Luckily, we've all seen these cracking yarns - they are now a part of our collective psyche - and therefore we know instinctively how to react to such dramatic situations. We react in the way the movies taught us, don't we? We don our uniforms, enlist, cry 'God Bless America' and go looking for someone to kill. We go to fight to protect the freedom of our great country and that of the entire 'civilised world'. We place our total trust in the authorities, the military and the political leaders. Remember how the President saved us in Independence Day? Didn't the great generals comprehensively whip the enemy after Pearl Harbour to protect the 'free world'?

If only we could send in Arnie, Sly, Tom Hanks and Will Smith. They've already sent in the USS Enterprise to sort out those evil aliens.

The Omega Files

Will the President nuke 'em like he did at the end of World War II? Will he unveil the astounding technology he's been saving for a rainy day? Or will they send in a lone hero to take 'em out in a victorious climax, just when everything looks as though it's all going pear-shaped? And will Bruce Willis keep his vest on?

God, I'm proud to be an American today!

What do you mean, I'm not American? We're all Americans now. The tv told us that we are all part of the civilised world. The 'good' against the 'evil'. And we believe them, because that's exactly how it is in the movies.

Saddam, bin Laden, Gaddaffi...pussies, the lot of 'em.

It's time to kick ass!

WHO BENEFITS?

Let's be honest, the whole thing reeks like a bucket of dung: the more you stir it, the worse it smells.

Like many people, I sat spellbound in front of the tv - flicking back and forth between several US News channels - while planes crashed and buildings crumbled, and as thousands of people tragically lost their lives. The sensation that 'this is a movie' did not start to subside until a few days after the attack.

Within minutes of the story breaking, they were talking about Islamic terrorists and, more precisely, Osama bin Laden. It was all coming thick and fast; a confusing and horrifying barrage on the senses. For many, it was like being at the movies, or being caught in a dream. One's sense of reality suddenly crossed the border into a netherworld where it merged for a while with that mental state which is usually reserved for fantasy and entertainment.

I have to admit that as all the chaos was unfolding, and as the only information I had at my disposal was from the likes of CNN and Sky, I seriously considered the possibility that this was an attack by Islamic fundamentalist terrorists, seeking to destabilise the Western world. But when the follow-up attacks which should have occurred at the height of the chaos failed to happen - when the real strike should have occurred - I began to wonder.

I asked the same questions I always do about events on the world stage. I asked 'who benefits from this', and I asked 'what if we are being told the

The Omega Files

opposite of the truth'? What sense will the answers to these questions reveal about what has happened?

Looking at who benefits, it's all the same old faces and institutions that this magazine has documented for years, so I will not bore you with too many details about them. The interconnected names, related subjects and historical precedents to this are complex and numerous. Anyone new to these subjects really needs to look at the back-issues of this magazine to see how it all fits together.

Even so, this article must look at not only the most pertinent factors involved in the terrorist attack, but also to certain related issues, some of which do not, at first, seem to bear much relevance - at least superficially. In order to understand single events such as this it is imperative to see it in context with the wider picture.

Beyond the 'who', is also the 'what'? Again, to the readers of this magazine, the answer should be fairly clear.

There is an agenda in place to centralise world power into the hands of the few through the monopolisation and centralisation of business, politics and other forms of material power. The 'One World Government', the 'One World Bank', the 'New World Order'...phrases all too familiar to those who have been following this unfolding saga.

For years we have been warning about the potential implementation of fundamental infringements on personal freedom, compulsory microchip Ids for everyone, collection and storage of information regarding every aspect of our lives, closer monitoring through electronic media, restrictions on free speech and protest, erosion of the power of the individual and of the individually-minded collective, whilst magnifying the power of the select few in key positions, etc. etc. And more than this, we have been warning that in order to achieve this, situations need to be manufactured which will scare us all so much that we will ask for, or even demand, that such measures are put in place.

It is no coincidence that such measures and more are have been and will be advanced as a result of the recent attack. Now 'we' are at war - they say. Fear and paranoia is rampant. But we are not sure who to fear exactly. We know it's coming from Islamic areas - they say. Although this attack has all but been officially blamed on Osama bin Laden, they tell us that real enemy is still essentially 'unseen', thus requiring a planned long-term war - a new

The Omega Files

kind of war' - to eradicate global terrorism.

Fear is always magnified when the source is unknown, or uncertain; and people in fear are rendered so insecure that they will give up their minds and freedoms to those who will step forward to guide and protect them.

Over 100 years ago, a document which accurately described the course of the proceeding century was uncovered. The Protocols of the Learned Elders of Zion documents with stunning accuracy the techniques subsequently used by the world controllers in their march towards the establishment of the New World Order. As I showed in my article Proofs of an Ancient Conspiracy (Truth Campaign issue 16), the Protocols were not an isolated case of forged propaganda, originating in pre-Communist Russia, but were merely restating an agenda which has been documented throughout history since at least the middle of the first millennium BC when the Law was first laid down in the book of Deuteronomy:

...seven nations greater and mightier than thou [are to be delivered into the Judahite's hands], and: Thou shalt utterly destroy them; thou shalt make no covenant with them...ye shall destroy their altars, and break down their images, and cut down their groves, and burn their graven images with fire...for thou art a holy people unto the Lord thy God; the Lord thy God hath chosen thee to be a special people unto himself, above all people that are on the face of the earth...Thou shalt be blessed above all people...And thou shalt consume all the people which the Lord thy God shall deliver thee; thine eyes shall have no pity upon them...And he shall deliver their kings into thine hand, and thou shalt destroy their name from under heaven; there shall no man be able to stand before thee, until thou have destroyed them... Thou shalt surely smite the inhabitants of that city with the edge of the sword, destroying it utterly, and all that is therein...etc.

Furthermore...Thou shalt not lend upon usury to thy brother...unto a stranger [non-Jew] thou mayest lend upon usury...And all the people of the earth shall see that thou art called by the name of the Lord; and they shall be afraid of thee...thou shalt lend unto many nations, and thou shalt not borrow. And the Lord will make thee the head, and not the tail; and thou shalt be above only, and thou shalt not be beneath...etc.

These are but a minute fraction of many examples of the nature of the destructive 'master-race' mentality displayed by these so-called 'men of God' in but one book in the Old Testament.

The Omega Files

The other books of the Torah, written in the wake of Deuteronomy are equally ominous for the Gentile nations. For example, Exodus 23:22 explicitly states God's promise to his people:

If thou shalt indeed...do all that I speak, then I will be an enemy unto thine enemies...and will destroy all the people to whom thou shalt come.

And one of the main observances demanded of God, for which his reward will be utter destruction of the enemy, was written in Deuteronomy 12:2:

Ye shall utterly destroy all the places, wherein the nations which ye shall possess served other Gods.

The following is but one of many passages from the Protocols which can be equally applied to today's political situation:

The intensification of armaments, the increase of police forces - are all essential for the completion of the aforementioned plans. What we have to get at is that there should be in all the States of the world, besides ourselves, only the masses of the proletariat, a few millionaires devoted to our interests, police and soldiers.

Throughout all Europe, and by means of relations with Europe, in other continents also, we must create ferments, discords and hostility. Therein we gain a double advantage. In the first place we keep in check all countries, for they will know that we have the power whenever we like to create disorders or to restore order. All these countries are accustomed to see in us an indispensable force of coercion. In the second place, by our intrigues we shall tangle up all the threads which we have stretched into the cabinets of all States by means of the political, by economic treaties, or loan obligations. In order to succeed in this we must use great cunning and penetration during negotiations and agreements, but, as regards what is called the "official language," we shall keep to the opposite tactics and assume the mask of honesty and complacency. In this way the peoples and governments of the goyim, whom we have taught to look only at the outside whatever we present to their notice, will still continue to accept us as the benefactors and saviours of the human race.

(Protocols 7:1-2)

The Omega Files

TERRORISM AND DOUBLESPEAK

Xenophobia, especially towards those of Arab descent is rapidly on the increase. The message from the governments and media is to be vigilant of strangers; to be suspicious of those we don't know and about whose backgrounds we are uncertain, as they may be terrorists in our midst.

We have a world of increasing population; a huge proportion of which are not contributing significantly to the global economy - the globe which is considered by the self-appointed elite few to be their personal fiefdom - but instead are consuming and draining the resources of those same elite few; the elite few who exist to profit from and control the masses. These unproductive millions are what Bertrand Russell called the 'useless eaters'. They are concentrated in places like Afghanistan and Pakistan and in other the Third World areas where there is also a large number of Islamic factions who have no desire to be part of the 'Western Utopia' which is unfolding daily in front of our eyes; Islamic factions who refuse to play ball with the Illuminati's military-industrial complex.

Slowly, over the course of the past century, many of the 'useless' eaters have been turned into 'useful eaters' through being coerced into providing cheap labour - often slave labour - for Western-based companies, or have been diligently raising cash crops to sell cheaply to the West in order to raise the money needed to pay off loans they were forced to take from the Western bankers.

Gradually, the independent nations of all races and religions are becoming serfs to the Western global feudal system - the New World Order.

Today, nations all over the world - even those who oppose the West's capitalist tyranny, such as the Muslim nations - are binding together in alliance with the West in a common cause. Such nations and factions which hitherto posed a real threat to the New World Order agenda have now taken significant steps to come under the wing of the very same force. The leaders of such nations - the New World Order puppets - have used the excuse provided by the terrorist attack to move from being covert agents of the New World Order to being overt agents. Aided by the threat of war, the people of such nations have been persuaded to join the One World Government almost overnight.

The New World Order is eliminating its opposition by intimidation, force and absorption. The Establishment is very quickly scaring the world into accepting its agenda. In a great reversal of logic, it is using a deliberate covert strategy of terror to combat what it overtly describes as 'terrorism'.

For, what is a 'terrorist'?

...a person who uses or favours violent and intimidating methods of coercing a government or community.

(Concise Oxford Dictionary)

By definition, then, the so-called 'free' Western power bloc has become the largest terrorist organisation in history. But then, those who have been keeping abreast of the activities of the New World Order know that already. And we knew this long before September 11th 2001.

In future, terrorism will be defined purely as actions taken against the New World Order bloc, whilst 'on-side' terrorism will continue to be classed as a righteous struggle to protect the 'free' world.

One of the most significant terrorist organisational cells in the New World Order agenda has been Israel. A state which itself is little more than an army of occupation created from mass warfare, bloodshed and the violent imposition of an ancient religious-political agenda known as Zionism.

Zionism has just received a massive boost through recent events in America. A hundred years ago, the biggest opposition to Zionism and the Judaic agenda was the Western Christian-based power-bloc. Since that time, the West has increasingly conceded to the agenda. By simply being part of the so-called 'democratic' West, by voting for our governments, we are effectively pro-Zionist, whether or not we realise it. And that is how we are seen by the enemies of Zionism..

Today, the biggest enemy of Zionism is Islam. Israel is 'on-side'. The US-led coalition is saying 'anyone not with us is against us'. Anyone threatening the coalition will be an automatic enemy of the 'civilised world'. The chances of Israel gaining total control over Jerusalem has just increased many-fold, which is what must be for Zionism to realise its central aims. In the immediate aftermath of the bombing in America, Israel began the rhetoric and propaganda campaign to lend their full support to the USA and took the opportunity to increase their assaults on Palestine in order to give the clear message that Israel is the USA's closest ally. A week later, Palestine was called to a cease-fire by Arafat and Israel responded by doing the same. Of course the newspaper headlines reported that Israel had declared peace upon Palestine, as though this was an Israeli initiative. Which all smacks of pro-Israeli propaganda, and the cease-fire itself is more likely to be a propaganda exercise than an act of respect for the dead, considering the amount of bloodshed and hatred generated between the two sides throughout the last century.

Over one hundred years ago, the Protocols of the Learned Elders of Zion outlined the clear, cold subversive and brutally pragmatic political methodology which world government is utilising today to steer the direction of the world:

It must be noted that men with bad instincts are more in number than the good, and therefore the best results in governing them are attained by violence and terrorisation, and not by academic discussions. Every man aims at power, everyone would like to become a dictator if only he could, and rare indeed are the men who would not be willing to sacrifice the welfare of all for the sake of securing their own welfare.

What has restrained the beasts of prey who are called men? What has served for their guidance hitherto?

In the beginnings of the structure of society, they were subjected to brutal and blind force; afterwards - to Law, which is the same force, only disguised. I draw the conclusion that by the law of nature right lies in force.

Political freedom is an idea but not a fact. This idea one must know how to apply whenever it appears necessary with this bait of an idea to attract the masses of the people to one's party for the purpose of crushing another who is in authority. This task is rendered easier if the opponent has himself been infected with the idea of freedom, so-called liberalism, and, for the sake of an idea, is willing to yield some of his power. It is precisely here that the triumph of our theory appears; the slackened reins of government are immediately, by the law of life, caught up and gathered together by a new hand, because the blind might of the nation cannot for one single day exist without guidance, and the new authority merely fits into the place of the old already weakened by liberalism.

(Protocol 1:3-6)

So does this mean that the completion of the Judaic agenda or the Christian Apocalypse, through mass bloodshed, is upon us? Consider the following:

The Omega Files

Our State, marching along the path of peaceful conquest, has the right to replace the horrors of war by less noticeable and more satisfactory sentences of death, necessary to maintain the terror which tends to produce blind submission. Just but merciless severity is the greatest factor of strength in the State: not only for the sake of gain but also in the name of duty, for the sake of victory, we must keep to the programme of violence and make-believe. The doctrine of squaring accounts is precisely as strong as the means of which it makes use. Therefore it is not so much by the means themselves as by the doctrine of severity that we shall triumph and bring all governments into subjection to our super-government. It is enough for them to know that we are too merciless for all disobedience to cease.

(Protocol 1:24)

Realistically, there should be no apocalyptic war. The West is far too powerful. We have enormous destructive capabilities and technologies which dwarfs those of the Islamic world. We only need to remember the so-called 'war' in Iraq in the '90s to see with what ease even a major Arab power can be defeated. It all depends on how protracted the elite want it to be. This could potentially be ideal for the eugenics operation, to trim back on the 'useless eaters' and to end the opposition to the Zionist Illuminati agenda once and for all.

To triumph, the Illuminati agenda must keep us all in a state of fear, and the means to do this is through the fear of the perceived enemy - real or imagined. Just as in George Orwell's 1984, it is not so much the direct military power of the State, but more the imagined unseen terror which lurks behind every unknown face, which keeps the masses subservient to the government; to the point where the people actually come to fully embrace the ideals of their masters who are those very unseen terrorists themselves:

It is from us that the all-engulfing terror proceeds. We have in our service persons of all opinions, of all doctrines, restoring monarchists, demagogues, socialists, communists and utopian dreamers of every kind. We have harnessed them all to the task: each one of them on his own account is boring away at the last remnants of authority, is striving to overthrow all established form of order. By these acts all States are in torture; they exhort to tranquillity, are ready to sacrifice everything for peace: but we will not give them peace until they openly acknowledge our international Super-Government, and with submissiveness.

The Omega Files

(Protocol 9:4)

Of course, there is more to this than Zionism. At the end of the day it is all about power and control funnelled into fewer and fewer hands. There are plenty of individuals who want to be on the winning side, whatever religion, race or creed should 'triumph'. It is a sickness in the very core consciousness of man. A survival instinct gone cancerous. We need to see it as a common problem, to which religious and political agendas are mere symptoms and tools used to manifest domination of the masses by the self-selected elite few.

I think the most likely outcome of this will be less of an out and out global war, but more of an excuse to clamp down in the areas of freedom and to implement massive centralisation of power; to tidy up loose ends and restrict or disable individual and organised resistance to the New World Order programme. The elite don't want an apocalyptic war. Things are going too well for them as it is. But they do need massive propaganda (mind-control) opportunities which they have an excuse to back by force, preferably with the general support of the masses.

Wars are extremely profitable to the economies of the winning side. The winning side is always the Illuminati. The major global banks never lose. They loan countries of both sides of the conflict enormous amounts of money to arm themselves and they keep those countries afloat for as long as deemed necessary during times of crisis. When the war is over, the victorious side is left with staggering debt to the international banks, whilst the defeated side is left with reparations. Finally, both sides are left with a need to take loans from the same banks to rebuild their countries and economies.

Another interesting question to ask is 'who does not benefit?'

WHO DOES NOT BENEFIT?

Apart from the thousands of grieving families across the world, whose lives have been shattered by this wanton slaughter, and all people of the world whose freedoms are further eroded, perhaps the most significant factor in this whole examination is that those who supposedly carried out the attack, have benefited least.

It is certainly not to the benefit of the Islamic world, whether extremist fundamentalist or not. The overwhelming condemnation and almost global unity which was inevitable following such an attack will make it impossible

The Omega Files

for an Islamic victory against Western capitalist states. No-one has yet come forth to proclaim responsibility or to state the cause for which the terrorists willingly laid down their lives. So ultimately, there is very little logical sense in a religious or political terrorist organisation carrying it out in the first place. Are we supposed to believe that people will willingly sacrifice themselves to a cause and not proclaim that cause; not take the opportunity of having the entire world's attention; to remain silent - even deny it?

We are certainly supposed to take for granted that Islamic terrorists are wholly responsible for this. In the few days following the disaster, the US news reported that the date of the attack is highly significant to Islamic terrorists because it fell on the 31st anniversary, to the day, of the first major airline terrorist hijack in which 3 planes from TWA, Swissair and BOAC had been hijacked by Arafat's Palestinian Liberation Organisation activists. The event and the organisation it spawned became known as Black September. So someone was making the point very strongly that we should be looking towards Islamic terrorists, from the outset.

Still, nobody from the Islamic world has admitted responsibility for the recent attacks. How curious to set up all the signals, and yet refuse to take the opportunity to publicise their cause to the entire world!

In the early '70s, the CIA had its own agent as chief of intelligence in the PLO, named Ali Hassan Salameh, as well as the covert support of Arafat. Are we expected to believe that intelligence gathering and spying has so crumbled since then that we were so unprepared for the recent attack in America?

However, all is not as it would appear. The hijacking of the planes actually occurred on September 6th and were blown up on September 12th.

Why was the media making the point that September 11th was such a significant day to Palestinian terrorists? Was it just concocted to ensure that people would look no further than Islamic extremists and consider no other option; to ensure that our minds would already be well and truly made up at the earliest possible opportunity, in order to avoid anyone considering any other options? The 'enemy' was effectively identified and served up on a plate by the media before the world had time to recover from the traumatic shock of what had just occurred - the point at which minds are far more easily manipulated than in times of peace and security - when we were still dissociating from reality because of the traumatisation of our minds!

The Omega Files

The lying did not end there. Fox News, on their website, were keen to draw parallels with Islamic terrorism in an article entitled, 'September Anniversary of Several Past Attacks, Events', which reported that:

September marks the anniversary of several noted political events and terrorist attacks.

On Sept. 11, 1922, a British mandate was proclaimed in Palestine, despite Arab protests. It lasted until 1948, after the United Nations authorized a partition of the territory and the state of Israel was established.

Again, this simply is not true. The mandate was basically an official policy recognising 'grounds for reconstituting their national home in that country'. It was approved by the Council of the League of Nations on July 24th 1922, having spent years on the drawing board. The date at which the mandate actually came into force was September 29th.

Fox News also just happens to be part of a larger media empire which includes 20th Century Fox, the very company which produced such propaganda/mind control exercises as the movie Independence Day.

Let us consider what the Protocols of the Learned Elders of Zion have to say about the covert use of the Press:

In the hands of the States of to-day there is a great force that creates the movement of thought in the people, and that is the Press. The part played by the Press is to keep pointing out requirements supposed to be indispensable, to give voice to the complaints of the people, to express and to create discontent. It is in the Press that the triumph of freedom of speech finds its incarnation. But the goyim States have not known how to make use of this force; and it has fallen into our hands. Through the Press we have gained the power to influence while remaining ourselves in the shade; thanks to the Press we have got the gold in our hands, notwithstanding that we have had to gather it out of the oceans of blood and tears. But it has paid us, though we have sacrificed many of our people. Each victim on our side is worth in the sight of God a thousand goyim. (my emphasis)

(Protocol 2:5)

We must compel the governments of the goyim to take action in the direction favoured by our widely conceived plan, already approaching the desired consummation, by what we shall represent as public opinion, secretly promoted by us through the means of that so-called "Great Power" -

the Press which, with few exceptions that may be disregarded, is already, entirely in our hands.

(Protocol 7:5)

In other words, what the press expresses as public opinion, becomes public opinion and is orchestrated that way to implement the desires of the hidden hand which pulls the strings from behind the scenes. The same can be said for the tv and movie propaganda created in the form of 'entertainment'.

INCONSISTENCIES ABOUND

The Islamic world faces a potentially catastrophic retaliation from the West and its Allies. The suicide attack on New York and Washington could very probably be a suicide attack by many thousands of Muslims, who will ultimately also suffer the consequences of the actions of these supposedly extremist few.

What kind of terrorist or 'freedom fighter' deliberately carries out an operation which they know will lead to the exact opposite outcome of that which they profess to be fighting for? What kind of religious or political terrorist, opposing the Zionist Illuminist Capitalist One World Government hands over the perfect opportunity to them to have carte blanche to impose everything it has ever dreamed about imposing, which includes wiping out themselves in the process?

Furthermore, given the scale of the operation and the opportunity for mass destruction and disruption of the West which was presented to these terrorists, why didn't they do any more than they did?

Certainly the US and the Western economy has been disrupted, for a short while at least, but why was the target in New York only the World Trade Centre?

Why did they not destroy Wall Street? If they wished to plunge the Western economy and the Zionist banking system into chaos, why did they hit the WTC and leave the hub of the banking world untouched?

Could the answer be that the operation was not intended to cause maximum chaos, nor even masterminded by those outside the West? Only that it should appear so?

I think we have to be courageous enough and open-minded enough to

The Omega Files

consider this very real possibility.

Consider elements in the run-up to this event. Until a few years ago I, as I am sure many people did, thought that racial and religious tensions here and around the world had receded somewhat. Certainly racially motivated events in this country had not been headline news for a long time. Then suddenly, especially after the Stephen Lawrence affair, the race issue was everywhere in the newspapers and on tv. Increasing numbers of reports of racially-connected events - riots, common assault, murders and bombings - began pouring from our screens. Not only that, but simultaneously, the tv was inundated with programmes about Nazis, warfare, disasters, the Holocaust etc. etc. Programmes shown recently such as Jon Ronson's Secret Rulers of the World took every opportunity to link anti-New World Order sentiments and activism with extreme right-wing Nazism and especially with what they call 'anti-Semitism'. The fear of being associated with such taboo organisations is enough to keep most people from openly expressing their opinions, and is a convenient tool used by the masses to police themselves by denouncing and ostracising the outspoken few.

A year ago, the Arab-Israeli conflict escalated when renewed Middle East aggressions created an opportunity for the extremist Jew Ariel Sharon to become head of his nation. Since which time, conflict between Palestinians and Israelis - Muslims and Jews - has escalated.

At the same time, we in Britain were prepared for an emergency situation and overt militarisation of our land by the Foot and Mouth crisis which was manipulated into being and further manipulated to maximise the amount of fear and disruption, as well as the mental agitation and trauma which has ensued. All of which has created the atmosphere of preparedness for increased control, loss of freedoms and acceptance of a visible military presence, where previously we had expected to see none.

Britain, though shocked into submission by the foot and mouth crisis had, by this point, already made significant in-roads towards the Orwellian nightmare of the police state. Increasing draconian laws have been aided for a long time by the media-led call for massive numbers of surveillance cameras on the streets of our cities and towns - as a response to increasing propaganda in the media highlighting the fear of crime. The idea of mass surveillance as a good thing has subtly been popularised by voyeuristic television 'fly-on-the-wall' documentaries and game shows such as the enormously popular Big Brother.

What was once considered to be a futuristic nightmare feared by the masses is now a reality desired by the masses. The next stage in Britain is planned to be the introduction of compulsory ID cards, more surveillance etc.

And on and on it goes.

PAVLOVIAN REACTIONS

Despite the fact that the Islam terrorist issue is all about Zionism and the West's (especially America's) support and aid for Zionism, the media remains almost silent about this issue.

I am writing this article a week after the attack on America and I have yet to see one news programme or documentary discussing the issue of Zionism!

As usual, we need to consider what they are not telling you, as much as what they are.

No doubt, people expressing such views as I have here will be seen as 'traitors' by some. Links will immediately start firing in the minds of the programmed masses between expressing these views and Nazism, anti-Semitism, racism, anti-Americanism - 'dangerous subversives' and 'mad conspiracy theorists' the lot of us. And that is exactly how the majority have been programmed to react.

Interestingly, the programmed preconception in recent years, in Britain, has been that those waving flags and proclaiming a pride in British culture, were associated with such subversiveness in the programmed minds of so many British people. Which has always been an entirely bizarre attitude, considering that, at the same time, we have been encouraged to accept other cultures, learn about them, respect them and see us all as 'one' people. Ethnic carnivals, religious celebrations, 'black pride', 'Native American wisdom' etc. have been very trendy and 'right on' in recent times. Of course, there is absolutely nothing wrong with that. Other cultures have a great deal to teach us and the more we know about each other, the better we can communicate and truly understand our common humanity and respect our differences. However, there is a common unconscious perception that it's okay and right to extol the virtues of other races and cultures and their religions, whilst being suspicious and prejudiced against those extolling being white or celebrating white culture. Such illogical attitudes - which is almost a kind of self-loathing - are manipulated states of mind which can be used to control the masses in uncertain times such as these.

While current conflict lasts, as it did in the previous wars and conflicts, and as it is currently in America, patriotism will be extolled. Racial hatred against Arabs will be tolerated - at least by many British people, if not by 'officialdom'. Intolerance will be tolerated. Though, because the plan appears to get the Islamic world on-side, we could also see an increase in calls for racial tolerance and integration etc. as a result of inevitable racial and religious unrest - overplayed to the extreme to further the agenda. In war time, sudden reversals of attitudes and new Pavlovian reactions occur, as the masses react to the provided stimuli that is carefully engineered by the world's elite. That is how quickly and easily minds and attitudes can be changed depending on the deliberately - but superficially - shifting focus of the New World Order agenda.

By even hinting that Zionism may have played a central role in this whole affair, one may be condemned by reflex action in the eyes of the 'civilised world'. In such times as these, by criticising one's 'ally', one becomes the 'enemy'. But we must be honest and courageous enough to speak the truth openly, or things will never change.

It is so mind-bogglingly easy to control the masses through such propaganda!

PREPARATION

We have we been deliberately prepared, for many years, through the media, movies and orchestrated dirty tricks campaigns, for the moment when the 'great and the good' would step forward to defeat the 'evil in our midst'. Events such as these always follow a period of psychological manipulation.

For example, the hugely successful movie Independence Day contained so many of the overt and subliminal factors we have recently witnessed in the terrorist bombing and its aftermath:

1. The world is threatened by alien terrorists. For ET terrorists, read non-Western alien terrorists. An unknown force from 'outside' managed to strike from within. These were subliminal archetypes of what actually unfolded.

2. The attack was sudden and unexpected, plunging the 'civilised' world - as represented by New York and Washington - into a burning chaos.

The Omega Files

3. The strikes came from the sky and resulted in spectacular explosions, destroying well-known world-famous landmarks.

4. The scenes move from New York to Washington.

5. The movie includes a direct hit on the Whitehouse; something which was initially feared to be a target. As in the movie, the Whitehouse was evacuated.

6. Although the movie focussed on the strikes on America, the aliens were also off-screen - striking the entire world at the key capital cities; thus necessitating a global unification, a joint offensive against the enemy, which is exactly what has been called for and implemented following the terrorist attack on America. Subliminally, we have been led to react by associating an attack on the US with an attack on the whole world. Of course this has been facilitated by choosing a target in which thousands of individuals from over thirty countries worked every day.

7. Who ultimately pulled off the operation as leader of the 'free world'? The President of the USA - the superman of the piece; entirely honest, brave and upstanding. How like the media portrayal of GW Bush.

There are also further subliminal elements in this movie worthy of mention. Such as, who provided the 'spiritual' guidance? It is the Jewish father who conducts a Jewish prayer session, done in Hebrew. Not a Christian or Muslim, Hindu or whatever else religious/spiritual message is played in the movie (with the exception of a brief Christian wedding scene). When one of the attendees points out that he is not Jewish, the message he receives from the Jew is that 'nobody's perfect'. Rather than what we would have expected from the archetypal Christian, which would have been something like, 'it doesn't matter, God loves all His children, no matter what faith', we get typical Judaic religious bigotry and racial/religious supremacy, passed off as humour (according to Judaism God is purely a Jewish deity and only Jews are the chosen ones, while the Gentiles will eventually be enslaved and ruled by the 'chosen' at Yahweh's chosen time).

In the movie, who saved the day? The New York Jewish American super-intelligent boffin, interestingly named David Levinson - i.e. David 'son of Levi' - clearly a name with loaded ancient Judaic messianic significance.

Considering that Jews make up only approximately 3% of Americans, the Hollywood movie/propaganda machine and interconnected News media

The Omega Files

machine is overwhelmingly controlled by Jewish magnates, producers and media moguls. Key positions in the US Administration have been dominated by Jews, Clinton's Administration in particular was noteworthy for being almost entirely Jewish. Their portrayal of Muslims and their pro-Zionist propaganda is hardly surprising therefore.

If the British political parties were comprised on 90%-plus Asians, or any other particular non-British racial or religious grouping, I am sure the British people would have something to say about unfair representation of interests in Parliament. But strangely nobody seems to bat an eyelid about a small minority interest being the vast majority controlling body in US politics.

Unsurprisingly then, in Independence Day, like 99.9% of the American movies which serve as propaganda and mind control tools for the Illuminati, there was no Muslim hero or victim portrayed. More often than not, the Muslim - if represented at all in a major movie - will be portrayed as the bad guy, usually the terrorist, such as in major Hollywood movies as True Lies, The Siege, Executive Decision...etc. (the latter of these were, incidentally produced with the co-operation of the Defence Department of the USA).

Another main hero of the movie is the black American pilot. This is a man who is first seen in bed with a single mother who is also a stripper. The subliminal message here being, the best people are unmarried single parents who work in sleazy jobs. There is only one normal married couple portrayed in the entire movie, the President and his wife (who is dead by the end of the movie anyway). The Protocols and Talmud are very clear about the hatred of Christianity. The Protocols express a plan to erode Christian nations to destabilise the (once) Christian Western world and replace (once) strongly held Christian values with ultra-liberalism, drunkenness and what was then defined as general degeneracy. Nowhere is this more obvious than in the Soviet Union, where the most popular teatime show is a no-holds barred uncensored run down of the day's traumatic deaths, interspersed by naked weather girls, whilst alcoholism is at an all-time high, the porn industry is enormous and the country is largely run by gangsters, some of whom are in official government positions. However, such deliberate decimation of culture is also to be seen having been inflicted upon many non-Christian cultures such as the indigenous American, African and Australian peoples.

The white American 'have a go hero' farmer interestingly played a vital

The Omega Files

role in the victory by making a suicide aeroplane assault on the alien ship, thereby facilitating the 'good guys' in their fight against 'evil' enemies from beyond. He too is a single parent, this time the father of several mixed race children, and is also a drunk.

These are the new types of role models in the New World Order.

The point I am making here is not that it is wrong to be single, unmarried, black, Jewish or a stripper etc. per se. Rather that unrealistic scenes are repeatedly portrayed as the norm, and in this case the norm for the best of us - the heroes, the role models we aspire to. It is a message which is constantly preached by the entertainment media, and we have to consider just why this is?

Like the movie Pearl Harbour, special and disproportional efforts are made to push forward the racial elements in the stories. Pearl Harbour in particular - being supposedly an account of real events - is guilty of misrepresentation, over-emphasis and over-sentimentalisation of the racial issues it portrays and has been widely criticised for it. Whereas Independence Day, which as a work of fiction can hardly be criticised as such, has barely a scene in the movie involving more than one person in which Jews and black people and those of mixed race are not involved. Again, this is not to highlight anything being wrong with being black or of mixed race etc., it is to highlight the relentless promotion - overt and covert - of the 'norm' society which does not actually exist, but which is being created in the West and around the world.

Why is this significant? Firstly, as I said, there are conspicuously no Muslims, when in fact there are hundreds of thousands of Muslims in New York alone. Moreover, having become a multicultural and multiracial Western world which is enormously different from the Europe and America which existed a century ago, the elite can use this as a weapon. The cry 'we are all One World now' cannot be contested. And One World requires a One World Government. Thus multiculturalism and multiracialism, as it is being manipulated to be (rather than as it would naturally develop otherwise), is a great tool for the New World Order agenda. As we have seen many times, criticism of the New World Order is easily turned around by the likes of the ADL and JDL etc. to racial and religious issues, whereby those exposing the agenda are accused of being racists and bigots, anti-Semites and Nazis etc.

No doubt, many people reading this now will have automatically reacted

The Omega Files

in self-righteous indignation at what they think I have just said and will now be denouncing me as a 'racist bigot' and 'anti-Semite'. Already the inner predators and the decades of Illuminati programming will be distorting what they have read, firing up all kinds of emotional responses. To those people, I suggest you re-read what you think you have read and see how easy it is to be programmed.

Just to be sure the message permeates the predators, let me say that I have no hatred towards people because of their racial or religious background. I do not blame non-indigenous peoples for settling in other countries in order to try and establish a better life for themselves and their families. Neither do I class others as inferior or less worthy, based upon their race or religion.

The artificial promotion of the multiracial and multicultural society by the hidden government is not a matter of altruism or philanthropy. It is used to increase the proportion of 'minorities' in an indigenous society in order to:

a. gradually erode the indigenous culture and any strengths it may have had in its pure state - which is also the what happens to those ethnic cultures that establish themselves in another land. Gradually, the various cultures living in close proximity will become largely homogenised into a single culture. In the intermediate stages differences are still very much apparent, however, and can be manipulated to:

b. divide and conquer through orchestrating racial and religious tensions into opposing sides which can be played off against each other, having also served to:

c. erode national and religious loyalties, which are so divided between non-indigenous races and religions that any national united opposition to the NWO agenda is significantly diminished. Eventually, as well as a single world government and currency, there will emerge a single world religion which will unify the current religions and unite the world's opposing religious factions.

d. Perhaps most pertinent to the current situation: artificially cultivated multiracialism facilitates the ease with which foreign subversives can be planted inside a country to destabilise it to the advantage of another country or an alien religious or political movement. This is exactly how Judaism and Zionism has risen to world dominance since the spread of the organisation from Eastern Europe to Western Europe and into the US, where

The Omega Files

it is now disproportionately a majority power-bloc. Thus is enabled the placement of agents in positions of power - often as apparent representatives of their own ethnic group - whilst in fact representing primarily their own branch of the NWO - different appearances, same agenda.

The agenda of multiracialism and multiculturalism is perhaps one of the aspects of the agenda which is most difficult to understand and accept. Having been born into such a world, it is taken as the norm. People in general don't think beyond their own time and impose their current values upon other times, if they do consider them at all. They therefore fail to appreciate that this time is not the product of a natural evolution of freedom-loving 'good' overcoming the 'evil' of the past; it is the product of a war of attrition on the minds of the masses by a manipulative coalition of many generations of a self-appointed elite.

This agenda has been operating not for a few generations, but for thousands of years. It advances almost imperceptibly slowly, therefore; except at times such as the present, when the agenda becomes more apparent. The same agenda outlined in the Protocols of subverting nation states was also written in the Jewish Torah and has been in operation for at least 2,500 years. By small steps are great journeys made.

Gradually, the world has become a collective of states in the New World Order, led by British and American 'imperialism', which eventually dissolves into multiculturalism, whereby Western capitalist business can be easily established in those countries that now rely on their 'allies' and business counterparts for economic stability. Military and political alliances are forged and strengthened. Coalitions such as the EU, NATO etc. are created and eventually a single power bloc emerges from what used to be independent nation states. Any states left outside of this 'great beast' are then intimidated, bombed, terrorised into submission, or are economically disadvantaged or isolated and therefore are forced into a merger with the rapidly emerging single World Government.

Recent events in America are the direct result of the ancient agenda of subversive globalisation and the destabilisation of nation states, their cultures and their leadership.

The goal is to have a single World State, peopled by individuals of a single culture, economy, religion and politic. The future Utopian state will be much as HG Wells predicted in his novel The Time Machine. A world populated

The Omega Files

by shiny happy docile people living an ideal lifestyle without a single original thought in their heads, who read no books and have no idea of their true history; and who are entirely unaware that below their feet they are being farmed as food for the elite controllers who stay out of sight, hiding in the shadows. These elite creatures - called Morlocks in the novel - are parasites who have mind controlled the shiny happy ignorant population - conditioned them - to respond to the signal on cue and offer themselves willingly to their hidden 'gods'.

Race and religion are major tools of the Illuminati and it is imperative that we understand these issues in order to appreciate the bigger picture.

It is purely such manipulation of these issues by those who wish to control others that I am highlighting here. Being of another ethnic origin does not make one inferior to a person who is white and vice versa. We are simply different that is all - we are One family made up of children many different personalities. We should respect and appreciate our differences. Unthinking programmed ultra-liberals, radicals, politicians, 'trendies' etc. who insist we all conform to the idea that we are 'all the same' are insulting the respective indigenous cultures and races of the world and are playing right into the hands of the Illuminati. Neither does one have to be a racist or anti-Semite, or hate anyone to appreciate one's own culture or race or nation, if that is what one wishes to do. Neither do we have to conform to racial or religious stereotypes, if that is our choice. But we must be sure that our choices are actually our own, and come from an informed basis, rather than being implanted by mass propaganda.

Following the Jewish faith does not mean you are a willing agent of the New World Order agenda. People will often be automatically drawn into siding with 'their own' organisations, unaware of how they are simply supporting the New World Order agenda. This way, a manipulated racial or religious 'problem' will gain large support from those particular communities and the desired pre-planned 'solutions' will be easily implemented with mass support. Exactly this has occurred in the USA, following the attack, wherein masses of Americans who have previously criticised the President, or simply did not care very much either way about US politics are now waving their flags and yelling their support for the current government and its policies. The majority of Jewish people are as manipulated as anyone else, and by the same force as everyone else. We mustn't forget how willing the Zionists are to sacrifice their own in the belief that the 'end justifies the means'.

The Omega Files

Christians and Muslims are no exceptions when it comes to being sacrificed and manipulated by those who bear the appearance of being 'one of us'. Just look at how Jewish, Muslim and Christian leaders all over the world have pledged support to the US recently, despite some of them being previously - at least officially - opposed to the US and its policies.

It's time to step outside of the conditioning and put aside the false taboos and 'politically correct' shackles of the mind. Our attitudes and decisions must be based on truth and information shared openly and lovingly.

We are watching a movie, people. We are watching actors on a world stage.

The constant media propaganda subliminally programmes us to accept the One World agenda and makes us fearful of criticising it. So powerful is it that it can turn us against ourselves to the point where we will fight against our own best interests to uphold causes which are little more than illusions. It paints a false picture of reality and repeats it over and over again, until that image is actually manifest as reality. The attitudes and behaviours portrayed on the screen become the attitudes and behaviours expressed by the masses.

Art imitating life? Or deliberately manipulated art creating reality to ancient religious and political agendas?

VESTED INTERESTS

Independence Day is just one example of how much subliminal programming we are exposed to by the 'entertainment' media. A comprehensive list of examples would take many pages.

Considering how controlled Hollywood is by Jews, it is not surprising that there is a severe lack of Islam in the movies, except to portray Muslims as the 'bad guys'. The following is a brief overview of just how Jewish US movie and entertainment industry is, consider the following (although the following lists may be a few years out of date, they serve well enough to make the general point):

* The Walt Disney Company, is the largest movie corporation. Chairman and CEO is Michael Eisner,

* The Disney empire includes several television production companies: Walt Disney Television, Touchstone Television, Buena Vista Television), its

The Omega Files

own cable network with 14 million subscribers, and two video production companies.

* The Walt Disney Picture Group is headed by Joe Roth and includes Touchstone Pictures, Hollywood Pictures, and Caravan Pictures, Miramax Films (run by the Weinstein brothers).

* In addition to TV and movies, the corporation owns Disneyland, Disney World, Epcot Center, Tokyo Disneyland, and Euro Disney.

* AOL/Time Warner, Inc. The chairman of the board and CEO is Gerald M. Levin.

* Time Warner's subsidiary HBO is the country's largest pay-TV cable network.

* Viacom Inc. is headed by Sumner Redstone (born Murray Rothstein). It produces and distributes TV programs for the three largest networks, owns 12 television stations and 12 radio stations. It produces feature films through Paramount Pictures, headed by Sherry Lansing; and also owns Blockbuster video stores.

* Viacom's publishing division includes Prentice Hall, Simon & Schuster, and Pocket Books.

* Viacom is also the world's largest provider of cable programming, through its Showtime, MTV, Nickelodeon, and other networks.

* Rupert Murdoch's News Corporation, owns Fox Television Network and 20th Century Fox Films. Murdoch is a Gentile, but Peter Chernin, who heads Murdoch's film studio and also oversees his TV production, is a Jew.

* The Japanese Sony Corporation, whose U.S. subsidiary, Sony Corporation of America, is run by Michael Schulhof. Alan J. Levine heads the Sony Pictures division.

* New World Entertainment is owned by Ronald Perelman, who also owns Revlon cosmetics. The chairman at New World, is Brandon Tartikoff - formerly head of entertainment programming at NBC.

* DreamWorks SKG is run by David Geffen, former Disney Pictures chairman Jeffrey Katzenberg, and film director Steven Spielberg.

* MCA and Universal Pictures, are both owned by Seagram Company Ltd. The president and CEO of Seagram, the liquor giant, is Edgar Bronfman,

The Omega Files

Jr., who is also president of the World Jewish Congress.

* Disney, Warner Brothers, Sony, Paramount (Viacom), and Universal (Seagram) accounted for 74 percent of the total box-office receipts for the year to date (August 1995).

As is the case with Hollywood, so it is with American news media. Consider the following:

* American Broadcasting Companies (ABC), Columbia Broadcasting System (CBS), and National Broadcasting Company (NBC) are all controlled by Leonard Harry Goldenson and staffed all the way down by hand-picked Jews.

* The Newhouse media empire owns 31 daily newspapers, including Cleveland Plain Dealer, the Newark Star-Ledger, and the New Orleans Times-Picayune; the nation's largest trade book publishing conglomerate, Random House, with all its subsidiaries; Newhouse Broadcasting, consisting of 12 television broadcasting stations and 87 cable-TV systems, including some of the countries largest cable networks-the Sunday supplement Parade, with a circulation of more than 22 million copies per week; some two dozen major magazines, including the New Yorker, Vogue, Madamoiselle, Glamour, Vanity Fair, HQ, Bride's, Gentlemen's Quarterly, Self, Home & Garden....etc.

* The New York Times, the Wall Street Journal, the Daily News and the Washington Post (run by Katherine Meyer Graham) are all Jewish controlled.

* Time under AOL/Time Warner - see above), Newsweek (run by the Washington Post), and U.S. News & World Report (owned and published by Mortimer B Zucherman) are the most significant US news magazines.

* The three largest book publishers: Random House, Simon & Schuster, and Time Inc. are owned or controlled by Jews

* Western Publishing has more than 50 per cent of the children's book market. Its chairman and CEO is Richard Bernstein.

* The White House press secretary Ari Fleischer is also a Jew.

Surely such monopoly on politics, news media and entertainment by such a minority is ludicrous? Of course it is. But then, it's a ludicrous world, isn't it?

RELIGIOUS HYPOCRISY

In its state of media-manipulated trauma, the world has handed over its

The Omega Files

mind and heart to the World Government and is asking it to impose its agenda. We have given George W Bush power beyond measure. The man who was raised for the post of US President from the start. A man so deeply damaged by his upbringing - like so many presidents and officials - that he should be in therapy - certainly not leader of the so-called 'free world'. 'Dubya' is the product of a long chain of paedophiles, murderers, war-mongers, mind controllers, and yes, terrorists.

The religious world is no exception when it comes to mass manipulation. Many Muslims are now calling for a so-called 'holy war' and are playing straight into the hands of the pro-Zionist Illuminati. The Christian nations, rather than extolling the peaceful message of Jesus, are at the forefront of the cry for revenge (often disguised as a cry to destroy 'evil') - paying mere lip-service to the central tenets of the message given by the 'Prince of Peace'.

I was intrigued to see the so-called 'Christian' memorial service at St Paul's Cathedral on Friday 14th of September. The final hymn to be sung was 'The Battle Hymn of the Republic', following which, the Archbishop (with an impressively straight face) told the congregation to 'go in peace'. What amazingly monumental hypocrisy!!! Subliminal programming for the masses.

'Glory glory Hallelujah.' Reminds me of the old wartime song, 'Praise the Lord and Pass the Ammunition'. The propaganda is in full swing: overt and covert. Even the Queen managed to squeeze out a few tears on cue. 'God save our gracious queen', came next. If there is one person on this earth who is less likely to need saving, then I couldn't name them.

However, I was heartened somewhat by the fact that what appeared to be half of the congregation at St Paul's did not take part in singing the Battle Hymn. Many seemed rightly confused and uncomfortable by the occasion. They were there to pay their respects, seek guidance and a message of hope and peace in their chosen religion, but were instead being coerced into raising their voices in praise of a 'righteous' 'holy' war. Just one example of how opposing sides can be manipulated into the same destructive mindset.

The phrase, 'Crusade against terrorism', has already been used by the Western alliance. Are we really going to repeat the Crusades all over again? It would seem so, given the attitude of the US government in their desire to attack not only the terrorist organisations themselves, but also anyone who they decide has allied with them. Are we going to witness another mass slaughter in the name of the Lord?

The Omega Files

How similar to the attitude of the Catholic hordes who slaughtered the Cathars during the Albigensian Crusade under the cry, 'Kill them all. God will know his own!'

Afghanistan is not the Taliban. The Taliban are an extremist terrorist occupying power in Afghanistan. The people of Afghanistan are living under desperate conditions and constant fear as the result of wave after wave of terrorism and warfare against them stretching back into history. Many are starving, weak, depressed and desperate. And yet, the West has planned military action against Afghanistan under the excuse that it is going to take out the Taliban and their leaders, who are unlikely to be there when they arrive.

And who is it within the US government that are calling for severe retaliatory action? While Secretary of State Colin Powell is at pains to urge restraint and care, his (Jewish) Deputy Secretary of State Paul Wolfowitz has been calling for early wide-ranging strikes against numerous targets across the Middle east and in Asia, including Iraq. US (Jewish) Secretary of Defence Donald Rumsfeld was described by one official as looking like 'something out of Nightmare on Elm Street. Rumsfeld's policy on the invasion of Afghanistan is quite clear, and his attitude to the whole affair could perhaps be gleaned from his statement: 'I think of this in the sense of self defence, and there is nothing that inhibits the United States of America from defending itself.'

In Britain, Blair's foreign policy advisor just happens to be Sir David Manning, once ambassador to Israel and NATO. Whilst British Ambassador to Washington is Sir Christopher Meyer.

Keep stirring the bucket of dung and before long even the least sensitive of noses must detect the stench.

LIES AND SPIN

Don't expect the media to proportionally represent the anti-war pro-peace sentiments which so many of us have, though. The media machine, in times of war, is primarily a propaganda tool to programme the mass psyche in the direction intended by the elite.

Who can forget the CNN newsreel of a handful Palestinians celebrating the news that America had been hit by a terrorist attack, which was aired within hours of the event? Undoubtedly, this single piece of footage, played over and over again, caused great distress and anger at the entire Islamic world at the point at which the world was in a state of mental trauma and turmoil. Jonathan Dimbleby chaired a debate on ITV that same week and asked a Palestinian representative about what she thought of the scenes shown on tv of 'thousands' of Palestinians celebrating the strike on America.

They say 'truth is the first casualty of war', and this charade was no exception.

Firstly, the scenes shown on tv were not of 'thousands' of celebrating Palestinians. That was the only such footage to be aired, over and over again, thereby magnifying the impact and creating the illusion that there were thousands of demonstrators. Secondly, there was absolutely no evidence within that footage that these people were specifically celebrating the attacks on the US.

Most chillingly, however, it appears that the newsreel was not even shot that day!

I recalled part of the newsreel, but could not place it, until I saw a story reported on the internet that someone had saved news footage of the 1991 invasion of Kuwait. The report stated that this same news footage was broadcast then, and the Palestinians filmed were in fact celebrating the arrival of the Allied troops at the beginning of the Gulf War. (I have yet to confirm this and would appreciate it if anyone has any firm evidence that this is the case.)

True or not, such deception by the major News Media should not surprise us. There are plenty of precedents. Prior to the Gulf war, fake news footage had been released for the very same reason: to whip up the masses against the identified 'enemy'. Stories of abandoned premature babies left on floors, while incubators were looted by Iraqi troops etc. was guaranteed to send your average American into a state of vengeful hysteria. But it was later revealed to be nothing more than pure invented secret-government-backed media propaganda. The 'nurse' who reported this was discovered to have been none other than the daughter of the Kuwaiti Ambassador to the US.

SETTING UP THE SCAPEGOAT

Other propaganda techniques have been used recently also. One Intelligence ploy which was notably once used to set up Lee Harvey Oswald for the murder of John F Kennedy seems to have been played in this current situation. The technique is to set up staged events immediately prior to the main event involving those who will later be blamed, in order to ensure that plenty of evidence is available to pin the blame directly and quickly on whomsoever the Establishment has pre-decided should be the scapegoat. In Oswald's case, he was 'seen' prior to the JFK assassination in various places acting suspiciously and provocatively in order that key witnesses would later be able to easily identify him as buying equipment and shouting his mouth off concerning his political views. The evidence suggests that these high-profile appearances of Oswald prior to the assassination were not actually Oswald at all, but were CIA look-alike operatives putting on a show in preparation for the main event. Of course this made him appear guilty and the case virtually closed against him in the public mind before he had even been arrested. Shortly thereafter, he was conveniently assassinated by CIA/Mafia stooge Jack Ruby.

In the case of the so-called WTC bombers, one individual, identified as a hijacker, was a man named Mohamed Atta. This man was described as 'a citizen of the world, travelling on a passport from the United Arab Emirates...living in Germany'. Although already suspected by German authorities of taking part in terrorist activities, his passport and visa were not suspended and he was able to travel freely between Germany and the USA. Though he was a student in Hamburg, he had plenty of money. He was able to write a cheque for $10,000 for flying lessons in Florida. That must have made an impression! In December 2000 he paid $1500 for a 6-hour Boeing 727 flight simulation at SimCentre Inc. in Florida. The instructor, Henry George, recalled: 'Looking back at it, it was a little strange that all they wanted to do was turns...most people who come here want to do takeoffs and landings.'

A tad cheesy, one might think? But it works as a piece of convincing circumstantial evidence as far as the gullible public are concerned.

As Conan Doyle was so ingenious in demonstrating in his novels about the great detective Sherlock Holmes - 'facts' often point in the opposite direction to the truth, and often the lazy and naïve detective will plump for the most obvious conclusion and think no further - nor even laterally - at where the evidence actually, ultimately leads.

The following comes from MSNBC's internet homepage report on September 24, entitled 'Bush: "We're at War"':

The Omega Files

At the time, Atta aroused no suspicion. When he turned in his rent-a-car in Pompano Beach, Fla., on Sept. 9, before heading north on his suicide mission, he reminded the dealer, Brad Warrick, that the car needed to be serviced. "The only thing out of the ordinary," Warrick recalled, "was that he was nice enough to let me know the car needed an oil change." Atta and several friends were regulars at a Venice bar called the 44th Aero Squadron, decorated in the motif of a bomber-squadron bunker, complete with sandbags. "I never had any problems with them," said the owner, Ken Schortzmann. They didn't want to be bothered, but didn't drink heavily and flirt with the waitresses, like some of the other flight students. Atta seemed to be the leader. "He had a fanny pack with a big roll of cash in it," said Schortzmann.

Last week Atta and two of his buddies seem to have gone out for a farewell bender at a seafood bar called Shuckums. Atta drank five Stoli-and-fruit-juices, while one of the others drank rum and Coke. For once, Atta and his friends became agitated, shouting curse words in Arabic, reportedly including a particularly blasphemous one that roughly translates as "F-k God." There was a squabble when the waitress tried to collect the $48 bill (her shift was ending and she wanted her tip). One of the Arabs became indignant. "I work for American Airlines. I'm a pilot," he said. "What makes you think I'd have a problem paying the bill?"

'Ah,' cries bumbling police detective Lestrade, 'the case could not be clearer. All the evidence points to these chaps. They were seen with plenty money; known terrorist links; plane flight simulation lessons. An open and shut case if ever I did see one Mr 'Olmes.'

It is at this point that Holmes points out the inconsistencies that Islamic extremists, prepared to die for their religious/political beliefs must surely be the last people to visit a bar and drink five vodkas, considering their ban on alcohol! Then to make such a ruckus and blaspheme against the God they were prepared to die for, just before they were about to dispatch themselves into his arms? To believe that would be incompatible with sanity! What kind of super-terrorist network, with the power to evade global Intelligence detection, employs a bunch of drunken rabble-rousers who would prove to be so incompetent as to draw so much public attention to themselves prior to pulling off one of the most secret and significant strikes in the history of world terrorism?

The Omega Files

I, for one think this all sounds far too implausible and convenient. Cattle-fodder for the masses. Gravy for the brain.

The same report went on to say:

Although investigators now suspect that Atta may been the leader of his cell, it is not clear if and when he was, in effect, "triggered." The pattern of bin Laden's terrorism is to insert operatives into a country where they are "sleepers," burrowed deep into the local culture, leading normal lives while awaiting orders.

Here we appear to have some actual truth mixed with subtle spin. Atta could very well have been, and probably was, a 'sleeper' agent. More than likely he was 'triggered', not as a willing participant in a holy war for Allah, but as a CIA mind-controlled assassin, programmed to play his part in drawing attention to himself, before plunging his plane into the WTC.

Those people around the so-called 'civilised' world, especially in the US, who are caught up in this charade, playing their part in preparing for war, need to ask themselves just why it is that such a thing could happen? Why does someone sacrifice their life and those of thousands? What has the USA ever done to anyone to attract this kind of action?

Well, the list is as long as your arm. The USA and its allies have been the largest terrorist organisation in history. They have destroyed countless millions of lives in their struggle for power. They have oppressed the Islamic nations as they have oppressed and parasitised the rest of the world. Would it really be such a surprise that some of those oppressed people would actually wish to fight back? If that is indeed what actually occurred?

Those with an open-mind need to think a bit further and consider the probability that this has all been an inside job from the start. The Intelligence community is not so incompetent as to have allowed this to happen through ignorance. They certainly had masses of data immediately following the event! Enough to make numerous arrests and identify the major players. Aided, of course by the sloppy trail conveniently left for the FBI to sniff out, such as leaving Korans in public places, having air-flight manuals left in cars, and hiring vehicles in their own names etc. Surely, signs would have been apparent beforehand if such an incompetent crew had been responsible?

Osama bin Laden is the obligatory 'bad guy' in the same vein as Oswald,

The Omega Files

Sirhan, McVeigh etc. A CIA-trained agent - a Saudi Arabian heir to a fortune - used to help organise and fund the covert war against the Soviets in Afghanistan in the late 1970s onwards. Did he really ever cease to be a CIA operative? Whether or not he was involved in the terrorist attack on America remains to be seen. Perhaps we will never know for sure.

FOOD FOR THOUGHT

An event of such magnitude, with such fundamental implications for global freedom, if deliberately orchestrated by the elite, would not have been planned in the weeks prior to the event. It would have been on the agenda for a very long time indeed. Who knows how long?

Was it known as long ago as August 1997 when it almost appeared as though the mother of the future heirs to the British throne was about to announce her engagement to Dodi Al Fayed? Should this have occurred, Diana and her children would have been related to an Arab Muslim with known links to terrorism! Al Fayed was a cousin of Adnan Khashoggi, of the Saudi Royal family, a known CIA asset involved in arms sales to Iran. It is even possible that Diana may have been willing to convert to Islam.

Is it possible that recent events in America are intrinsically connected to what happened in Paris in 1997? Was the Establishment eradicating a future embarrassment, as part of the equation which seems to have so many complex inter-linking factors pointing a huge finger of suspicion at our usual suspects?

Another factor which never gets a mention in mainstream media is the strange fact that, despite the Royal family being the head of the Protestant Anglican Church (Protestantism being essentially a more Judaised, more Old Testament focussed, form of Catholicism), every male child is circumcised by a rabbi!

It is noteworthy to mention in this connection, that, following tradition of the Royal House of England, which requires circumsicion of all male children, it was the Jewish Mohel of London rather than the Royal Physician who was called to circumcise the son of Princess Elizabeth. The following news item from a British newspaper will be of interest:

Crown Prince Charles Circumcised by a London Mohel

London (JTA)-Crown Prince Charles, son of Princess Elizabeth and heir to the British throne, was circumcised in Buckingham Palace by Rabbi Jacob

The Omega Files

Snowman, official Mohel of the London Jewish community.

One contact of mine wrote to Rabbi Malka - a highly respected Mohel of the Jewish community - and asked why the Royals are being circumcised by a rabbi, considering the fact that the circumcision is considered to be a sacred covenant between Jews and Yahweh. His reply was basically as above. However, another contact of mine, who had engaged a local rabbi on this very same question was told that he did not understand Malka's logic and agreed that a rabbi should only perform such a ritual on Jews, given the clear religious significance of the ritual.

Without wishing to appear to be going too far over the top with speculation in all this, surely it is a reasonable question to ask why the children of the head of the Church of England are being initiated by a rabbi into one of the most sacred Jewish rituals? Do the heads of the Church of England actually follow a religion other than that which they appear to. Are the British Royal family secretly practising Judaism, as opposed to Christianity?

If so, this would add extra weight to the argument that Judaism and Zionism, and the interconnected network of secret societies and elite families which incorporate this faction of the New World Order establishment, is likely to be behind, rather than the 'victims' of such events as we saw in America on September the 11th, and in Paris in August 1997.

Islam is the greatest enemy and biggest threat to Zionism in the modern age. For the Zionist aims, as recorded in the Bible, Talmud and Zohar, to be fulfilled, then Islam must be rendered impotent, enslaved or destroyed. Jerusalem must be returned entirely to Jewish hands.

Here, perhaps it is important to reiterate that Islamic terrorism is all about their opposition to Zionism and what they see as the West's allegiance with it. The Protocols are well known amongst the Islamic world and taken extremely seriously by many Muslims. Although, if you were to ask your average American citizen if they know what lies behind acts of Islamic terrorism, I doubt if he or she would be able to tell you. It seems, however, that your average citizen, who relies heavily on the tv news for information on such affairs, is not going to get to know about this from that particular medium. One would think that in the aftermath of the attack, and during the round-the-clock coverage of the event and related issues,nthat someone would think to air a few shows on the reason behind the thing, and perhaps even the odd historical documentary to keep the citizens informed of just why

The Omega Files

they have suffered so enormously.

Rather than this, the world has been subjected to a barrage of war-mongering propaganda, emotional manipulation, avoidance of essential issues, and outright lies by the mainstream media. Surely the 'land of the free' stands for freedom of information and freedom of thought? Surely to be truly free, society requires an informed population? Surely the people deserve informative and accurate reports of the central issues?

The cynical words of the late great American comedian and social commentator Bill Hicks are so relevant today. In his message to Americans that they are unable to see past the government propaganda, he informed them: 'You are free...to do as we tell you!'

KNOWN IN ADVANCE - THE PROOF

What further evidence do we have as proof that this terrorist attack was no sudden unforeseen event? At least as early as 4 days prior to the attack a number of investments in the City of London were mysteriously dropped, as though certain investors were privy to the knowledge that an event was imminent that would cause massive losses on the Stock Market (although recent reports have suggested - perhaps too conveniently - that the actions were instigated by the terrorists themselves as bin Laden is known to invest in the Stock Markets):

Richard Crossley, an analyst at Teather & Greenwood, a City broker, said that he had tracked suspicious short selling and share dumping in a swath of stocks badly affected by the terrorist attacks.

He said that on the Friday before the attacks, more than 10 million shares in Merrill Lynch, the US investment bank, were sold compared with 4 million on a normal day. He added that exceptionally high volumes of retail and leisure stocks had also caught his attention.

"Before the attacks there was no pattern to this phenomenon," he said. "The shares that were sold were doing very well and someone was selling them in very large quantities with no real reason." Mr Crossley believes that someone with inside knowledge of the attacks could have been making money on its expected outcome for up to three weeks before the terrorists struck. "What is more awful than he should aim a stiletto blow at the heart of Western financial markets? But to profit from it. Words fail me," Mr Crossley said.

The Omega Files

(The Times London September 18)

And the Intelligence agencies of the world had no prior knowledge of this attack? Give me a break!

Consider also the fact that the US, long before the terrorist attacks, had already planned and begun to implement an attack against Afghanistan and the removal of Osma bin Laden! What a coincidence too, that this was all planned in advance to take place at exactly the time the so-called 'response' to the terrorist attack is going ahead! The following piece of news was not reported by the mainstream tv media and probably is one of those few reports which seems to get into the press and subsequently ignored, despite being of major significance.

A former Pakistani diplomat has told the BBC that the US was planning military action against Osama Bin Laden and the Taleban even before last week's attacks.

Niaz Naik, a former Pakistani Foreign Secretary, was told by senior American officials in mid-July that military action against Afghanistan would go ahead by the middle of October.

Mr Naik said US officials told him of the plan at a UN-sponsored international contact group on Afghanistan which took place in Berlin.

Mr Naik told the BBC that at the meeting the US representatives told him that unless Bin Laden was handed over swiftly America would take military action to kill or capture both Bin Laden and the Taleban leader, Mullah Omar.

The wider objective, according to Mr Naik, would be to topple the Taleban regime and install a transitional government of moderate Afghans in its place - possibly under the leadership of the former Afghan King Zahir Shah.

Mr Naik was told that Washington would launch its operation from bases in Tajikistan, where American advisers were already in place.

He was told that Uzbekistan would also participate in the operation and that 17,000 Russian troops were on standby.

Mr Naik was told that if the military action went ahead it would take place before the snows started falling in Afghanistan, by the middle of October at the latest.

He said that he was in no doubt that after the World Trade Center bomb-

The Omega Files

ings this pre-existing US plan had been built upon and would be implemented within two or three weeks.

And he said it was doubtful that Washington would drop its plan even if Bin Laden were to be surrendered immediately by the Taliban.

(George Arney, BBC News, 18 September, 2001)

Naik also informs us that the Taliban and bin Laden were warned of the planned strikes two months before the terrorist strike against New York and Washington.

The warning to the Taliban originated at a four-day meeting of senior Americans, Russians, Iranians and Pakistanis at a hotel in Berlin in mid-July. The conference, the third in a series dubbed "brainstorming on Afghanistan", was part of a classic diplomatic device known as "track two"…

…"I told the Pakistani government, who informed the Taliban via our foreign office and the Taliban ambassador here."

The three Americans at the Berlin meeting were Tom Simons, a former US ambassador to Pakistan, Karl "Rick" Inderfurth, a former assistant secretary of state for south Asian affairs, and Lee Coldren, who headed the office of Pakistan, Afghan and Bangladesh affairs in the state department until 1997.

According to Mr Naik, the Americans raised the issue of an attack on Afghanistan at one of the full sessions of the conference, convened by Francesc Vendrell, a Spanish diplomat who serves as the UN secretary general's special representative on Afghanistan. In the break afterwards, Mr Naik told the Guardian yesterday, he asked Mr Simons why the attack should be more successful than Bill Clinton's missile strikes on Afghanistan in 1998, which caused 20 deaths but missed Bin Laden.

"He said this time they were very sure. They had all the intelligence and would not miss him this time. It would be aerial action, maybe helicopter gunships, and not only overt, but from very close proximity to Afghanistan. The Russians were listening to the conversation but not participating." (my emphasis)

(extracted from article: Threat of US strikes passed to Taliban weeks before NY attack - by Jonathan Steele, Ewen MacAskill, Richard Norton-Taylor and Ed Harriman. The Guardian, September 22,

2001)

The Omega Files

Even if, at the very outside chance, the terrorist bombing against America was actually a pre-emptive response to planned military action by the US against Afghanistan and bin Laden, rather than a deliberate inside job by the US-led New World Order, either way one looks at this situation the US government caused this tragedy!!!

All that baloney about there being an Intelligence break down has to be utter tripe!

THE AMERICAN DREAM

While the American people are shocked grieving, running telethons, gathering in the streets to proclaim their support for their 'great' leadership and the plan to rid the world of 'evil', the fact that their own government is responsible for their tragic suffering is ignored.

The pain and unbridled truth is that the general populous of America are gullible and naïve. They are brainwashed into their illusory mindset that America is the 'land of the free', whilst America is in fact the very evil empire they believe they are opposing. Those same masses of programmed Americans are not only the victims of this terrible event, but are also the cause of it. It is they who give their support to the tyrants who control their country and the world through terrorism and deceit. Without their support in thought and deed, this whole charade could never work.

For all of our sakes America WAKE UP!

You are the global terrorists!

You are not the 'land of the free'. Your government is not the protector of freedom and governor of 'right' in the world. You do not stand for 'liberty and justice for all'. You stand for exploitation and slavery, greed and injustice.

And what you sow, so shall you reap!

The people who have suffered and died in New York and Washington were not all totally innocent victims of an unprovoked terrorist assault. Yes, the rescue services showed great courage, putting their own live before those of others - many of whom died bravely in the course of their duty and deserve the enormous praise and respect they have been given in the aftermath of the disaster. However, the WTC is a major cog in the machine of global exploitation and terrorism. Where on Earth do you think all of that money and property which is processed every day through the WTC comes from? It comes from the exploitation of the planet, the people, the animals, the environment. In order for America to be 'free' and prosperous, millions upon millions of people and animals have suffered and died horrendously, and continue to do so in numbers far greater, every day, than were killed in the strikes on New York and Washington! Are they not also worthy of our tears and respect, our love and aid? Do they not also have the right not to be terrorised, raped, starved and killed - by us?

You Americans who believe in the utter crap which you are fed from birth in the way of propaganda - and thankfully there are many Americans who do not buy it and are not part of the sad and sordid affair I am outlining here - have played your part in creating this whole sorry mess.

Until now, you have been relatively untouched. You have lived a life of relative comfort and prosperity - like most of us in the West - and have been insulated and disassociated yourselves from the harsh reality of what actually occurs in the real world. Now you have tasted first hand the bitter reality, the pain and heartache of terrorism, war and suffering on your own doorstep, consider those areas around the world in which suffering and exploitation, hunger, war and fear is the daily norm. And realise that in the great majority of cases it is because America and its allies in the Western military industrial complex have either caused it or allowed it to happen in order that a) the so-called 'free' world can prosper, buy bigger and better things, live a more luxurious life etc, and b) the few ultra-powerful self-appointed elite can maintain their secret tyranny.

It is your own government you should be directing your anger at now, America. You need to address the cause and not the symptoms of this sickness. As do we all in the 'First World' nations outside America, to whom much of the above applies equally. As far as the elite are concerned, 'ignorance is bliss'. So they cultivate us like plants, keeping us in the dark and feeding us bullshit. They keep us servile by giving us what they have cultivated us to believe we want and need. Because while there are full bellies, there are empty minds.

FOR TOMORROWS

It seems that the true 'evil' Empire is about to get even stronger.

It is time to take a bigger view; to look at our own selves and attitudes; to examine our own reactions to all this and try to put fear in its place. Because

The Omega Files

fear feeds the flames. The flame of the spirit burns brightest without fear. Love is the flame of the spirit.

Through fear, people will enlist their minds and bodies in the war against humanity and our freedom, while believing they are fighting for it.

The best way to see this whole charade is in reverse. It makes more sense that way when one understands that the elite and the consciousness which controls them works in reverse.

When they say 'hate', we should think 'love'.

When they say 'move fast', we should apply the brakes.

When they say 'them', we should think 'us'.

When they extol 'freedom', we should consider just exactly what they mean by that, and see that what they actually mean is enslavement.

It is so easy to get caught up in the movie and play the role dictated to us by those who are experts in manipulating our emotions and thoughts.

We are so much better than that. We are able to reason and check our base emotions with logic and spiritual insight.

Imagine if nobody decided to play the parts allotted to them? With no audience participation, what would happen to the show?

Recently, we have seen how people, given enough reason, can come together in a common cause. The bravery and dedication of the New Yorkers, who have tirelessly dedicated themselves to aiding in the rescue attempts should be an inspiration to us all. The resilience of all those affected and the ability, in times of crisis, to open arms and hearts for the common good, shows us that we are not incapable of drawing on our strengths and humanity to try to make the world a better place. As well as grief, hate and fear, I have seen great love and kindness displayed by the American people. Rising from the ashes of the sadness, however, has also been the coming together of a nation of individuals who recognise the need for freedom, justice, unity and a spiritual light in all of our lives.

'Why do we need a war to feel good about ourselves?' asked Bill Hicks.

Perhaps a greater indictment on the state of humanity is to be found in the answer to the question: why, after so many centuries of seeing the results of hatred and fear, war and destruction, do we still need people like

The Omega Files

Bill Hicks to ask such questions?

Those who ignore the lessons of history are doomed to repeat them.

Those who allow others to think for them will forever be puppets of anyone ruthless enough to manipulate them.

What does it take to wake up the love which is inside everyone of us and to finally put aside the fear and hatred and ignorance?

My fiends, we are at war. But the war is not a new one. The 'enemy' is not terrorism. It does not lie 'outside'. It is not 'alien' - whether ET or human. The war is being fought on a spiritual level. It is the eternal war between the light and dark aspects of our very souls. The enemy is within.

We mustn't let propaganda confuse the issue and divert our attention towards red herrings and inappropriate reactions. We mustn't let religion or politics dictate our lives and cause us to ignore the battle we face every day to overcome the base elements of our consciousness which too often dictates our responses to life's challenges.

We are our own Devil. We are our own God.

We create our own reality by our thoughts. We allow our own inner predators - our own inner demons - to blind us to the Truth and to therefore create the reality which the predators desire.

The predators hide in the primordial brain, the part of the mind which we developed in our evolution through the reptile stage. It is reactive and unemotional, like the reptiles we evolved from. It serves to keep us alive by controlling the primal need for sex, food, territoriality, fight or flight. It is cold-blooded and without reason.

We have the power to keep this aspect of ourselves in check with our higher senses of awareness, reason, intellect and spirituality.

Those world leaders who have been dominated by this reptilian aspect of themselves have manipulated mankind into being their willing prey by magnifying their cunning and intellect whilst destroying their own spirituality. They are now trying to manipulate the rest of the world into reacting against implanted ideas - stimuli designed to re-programme the mind. They have reversed reality. They have convinced us that it is in our best interest to become their slaves, by convincing us we are free. They have conditioned our responses and enchanted us with their fake religions and politics. They

The Omega Files

have used every weapon available for their own ends and have assaulted our minds on every level.

And still the world is captured, spellbound. While we await Jesus, God, Allah, Yahweh, the ETs, the 'glorious revolution' etc. to come from 'above' and save us, we sit like rabbits in headlights, and as the car ploughs forward the real impending danger remains unseen and ignored.

There is nothing 'out there' which is coming to save you. There is nothing 'out there' which you don't already have inside you.

Everything you have seen and will see and imagine you may see one day 'out there' is a huge guiding finger pointing right back at you. Stop watching the finger.

We have an infinite number of tomorrows to get this right. How many of them are we going to waste repeating all our yesterdays?

The Omega Files

THE OMEGA FILES

by Branton

INTRODUCTION

If, as the late J. Allen Hynek claimed, over 1 in 40 people have been abducted and 'processed' by the 'alien/secret government' agenda — or 1 in 10 according to more recent sources — then you are bound to know SOMEONE who is an abductee and KNOWS it. This information is for THEM.

For those who are not "UFO Abductees", the information in this file is nevertheless vital and applicable, and may one day save your life!!! If you believe that information about "Aliens" is only for those who have lost all touch with reality, then PLEASE accept that information in this document that you CAN accept, and pass over the rest, at least for now. Your future may depend on it. As I have said, this information may save your life.

This file contains the most intricate and intimate details of a global conspiracy which seems to be rooted in an alien - military - industrial collaboration which is intent on bringing all freedom-loving peoples of this world under its control, through the implementation of a global government which has commonly been referred to as the 'New World Order'.

We have pulled no punches and are laying everything out on the table in regards to the New World Order agenda as I and those who have contributed to this document perceive it. If you are one who is easily offended, then be warned. Most of you who read this will realize that you may have personally supported in one form or another — albeit unknowingly — certain religious, economic, or political organizations which are on various levels being controlled by those forces that are working towards the implementation of the New World Order.

Those who have contributed to this file have not compromised nor held

The Omega Files

back on what they perceive to be the truth in regards to this conspiracy. We make no apologies, since we feel that this agenda has already been responsible for damaging this American Republic in ways that most cannot even begin to comprehend, and will continue to be a threat to its very existence and prosperity until this 'enemy' is forever purged from our nation and those traitors responsible for violating our national security and 'selling out' this Constitutional Republic of the United States of America are brought to justice.

Consider this a declaration of WAR against those eco-political forces and their draconian backers who would destroy our prosperity and freedom for their own fleeting material gain. So with no further introduction, we repeat the words of Louisiana District Attorney and JFK assassination investigator James Garrison, who boldly stated before leaving this world... "LET THE TRUTH BE TOLD, THOUGH THE HEAVENS FALL!"

Chapter 1 .... The Beginning

Chapter 2 .... Nazi Bases In Antarctica

Chapter 3 .... Nazi History

Chapter 4 .... Nazi History II

Chapter 5 .... David Emory's Talk Radio (On NAZIs)

Chapter 6 .... How The United States Lost The Second World War

Chapter 7 .... The Group That Has No Name

Chapters 8-10 .... Covert War, Origin of the Group, Goals for the N.W.O.

Chapters 11-14 .... Groups Operation, Groups Funding, Destruction of America, The Coming Chaos

Chapters 15-16 .... Mind Control Techniques, U.S. Military Officers —Shackled by U.N. Forces

Chapter 17 .... Admiral Byrd and Operation High Jump

Chapter 18 .... Hitler Escaped!

Chapters 19-22................................... Polar Defenses, German Space Base, South Atlantic, Rand Corp.

The Omega Files

Chapters 23-24 .... German Flying Disc, Falkland Island War

Chapter 25 .... German Economic "Miracle"

Chapter 26 .... Sam Russell's 'Open Mind Forum' Program

Chapter 27 .... Civil War Is About To Begin In The United States

Chapter 28 .... Mind Control Projects Out Of Atlantic

Chapter 29 .... Rockefeller: Mass Murderers

Chapter 30 .... Arco, Eastlund And The Roots Of HAARP

Chapter 31 ....Testimony Of Charles Hamel

Chapter 32 .... War Of The Caverns

Chapter 33 .... The United Nations In The United States

Chapter 34 .... F.E.M.A. Federal Emergency Management Agency

Chapter 35 .... The Bavarian Illuminati

Chapter 36 .... The Final Invasion Of The United States

Chapter 37 .... Countdown To The 1997 Northern Showdown

Chapter 38 .... Conclusion And Philadelphia Phase II

PROLOGUE

THE OMEGA FILE

1. THE BEGINNING

"...Another figure has an EVIL face... 'HE LOOKS LIKE A GERMAN NAZI. HE'S A NAZI... HIS EYES! HIS EYES. I'VE NEVER SEEN EYES LIKE THAT BEFORE!!!" The above quote was made under regressive hypnosis by one of the first publicized 'UFO abductees', Barney Hill who — along with his wife Betty — claimed to have been abducted by grey-skinned entities from a space craft which apparently originated from the Zeta II Reticuli star system. The Grey alien abductors were obviously working with the human military officer who was encountered by Barney. This military officer was ap-

The Omega Files

parently a full-fledged Nazi, although this incident took place over 15 years after Europe had 'supposedly' been de-Nazified. This quote can be found in the paranormal encyclopedia "MYSTERIES OF THE MIND, TIME & SPACE", p. 1379.

Those who are familiar with the connections between Nazi's and UFO's may find the following document easier to accept than those who have never been introduced to the reports of secret Nazi aerial disk experiments, much less reports of their secret collaboration with the so-called Grey aliens years before the corporate-fascist infiltrators and sympathizers within the U.S. Intelligence Agencies began making their own treaties with these same serpentine 'aliens'. Much information has been released about an 8-Level underground base under Camp Hero near Montauk Point, Long Island where full-fledged Nazi and CIA agents have apparently been working on sophisticated time-space manipulation experiments, as well as microwave mind-control experiments aimed at large populations, which are — according to researchers Al Bielek and Preston Nichols — being carried out to a greater degree than ever before under the cover of the Alaskan 'HAARP' project. It has been stated that unusual frequency broadcasts were detected all over Los Angeles prior to the L.A. Riots of 1992 shortly before the riots broke out, and there were inferences that the L.A. Riots were part of an "Operation Garden Plot" trial-run to establish martial law in America on the pretext of preventing a potential race war throughout the country.

The Montauk Projects, in collaboration with Brookhaven National Labs; the I.T.T. corp. [which is largely owned by the German Krupp family who built munitions plants for Adolf Hitler and which, according to Al Bielek, has terminal accesses to the "Alternative-2 black budget underground network" under some of its major facilities]; and the Bavarian THULE society [which provided most of the financial backing for the 'Montauk' or 'Phoenix' projects]... have — according to numerous sources including abductees — been working very closely with Orionite and Draconian 'Reptiloids' and 'Greys' based within an underground facility surrounding DULCE, New Mexico. This information comes from Preston Nichols, Duncan Cameron, Al Bielek, and Peter Moon... all of whom claim to have had some connection to the Montauk projects, although in most cases CIA mind-control technology was used to induce an alternate personality in the workers there as an assurance that the secret activities remained concealed. The Reptiloids in Alpha Draconis and Rigel Orion claim that they originated on earth in pre-

The Omega Files

historic times and were part of a bipedal reptilian or saurian race [like the cunning velociraptors?]. Now they are here to take back 'their planet' from the human race. In order to accomplish this, they are using multi-levelled deception and propaganda — mostly through 'channeled' information and through information conveyed to 'abductees' — to convince humans to capitulate themselves over to aliens 'guides' and thus allow the aliens access to their minds and in turn to our society in general.

This same tactic, according to various contactees [Billy Meier, Jefferson Souza, Israel Norkin, Maurice Doreal, George Andrews, Thomas Castello, Alex Collier, etc.] has succeeded on many other colonial worlds that the 'Greys' have conquered, and it has also worked on this world to the extent that they have taken control of much of the 'underground black budget empire' — a vast network of interconnected underground military-industrial bases and cities that have been constructed with the assistance of TRILLIONS [yes, I said TRILLIONS] of dollars siphoned from the American economy via taxes, drugs, organized crime, etc., money which has literally gone 'down the tubes', leaving our economy in a state of chaos. From this point and onward throughout this file, when the term 'Military-Industrial' complex is used, we are not referring to the U.S. Military in its entirety. In fact you could say that there is a definite and a violent conflict which is growing between what might be referred to as the "Military-Industrial-Executive" complex and the "Military-Congressional-Electorate" complex... Americans are being carefully groomed as an economic slave society to serve the underground 'Master Race' WITHOUT their/our knowledge. Prices continue to rise, yet income continues to fall farther and farther behind. The change is almost imperceptible, like the proverbial frog in the pot [you know, if a frog is thrown into a pot of boiling water it will immediately jump out, yet if it is put into a pot of cool water and the heat is gradually increased, it will remain in the pot until it boils to death].

The alien-fascist underground continues to rely on our continued gullibility and ignorance to keep its empire scam going. One of their most guarded secrets of all, and one that they must protect at all costs, is that the Nazi's really didn't loose World War II. I know this may sound incredible, but read on. The joint reptilian-fascist underground empire, complete with massive 'concentration camps' which make those in Nazi Germany pale by comparison, has chosen America as its major target because the Americas are the last bastion of freedom on earth. The 'takeover' is more-or-less com-

The Omega Files

plete within the underground systems, however numerous attempts to implement a joint Draconian-Fascist dictatorship in America have failed because of heavy resistance and support for a Constitutional form of government. God and the 2nd Amendment are really the only forces standing in the way of a complete takeover. This has prevented the 'outer world' from succumbing to this draconian invasion. Now that their secret is beginning to be exposed throughout the media in TV series' such as DARK SKIES, they are desperate. Their window of opportunity is closing and they must act fast, before the alien-manipulated military-industrial-complex comes under the control of the 'patriots', and the 'alien' technology in their possession is commandeered by TRUE Americans. This would mean that everyone — not just the mind-controlled 'elite' — will have access to interplanetary technology, which in turn would mean that freedom-loving Americans would eventually come to the defense of those interstellar cultures who have fallen under the oppression and control of the Draconian-Orion imperialists. Many of those living on other worlds within this sector of the galaxy are descended from colonists who originally had their ancient genesis here on planet earth! I know this sounds incredible, however the reason for this will be explained later on.

Many of these are of pre-Scandinavian or 'Nordic' heritage, and are for a large part peaceful and ethical beings. Now let me reiterate that I am not trying to imply that ALL of the 'Nordics' who are encountered in 'starships' [or UFO's] are non-Interventionists and wish us all the best. There are many collaborators who have joined with the interventionist-collectivist Draconian and Orionite forces, and many others who are under the direct psychological control of more malevolent 'aliens'. Neither am I trying to imply that ALL Reptiloids are out to destroy us. It may be more realistic to use the term INTERVENTIONISTS as opposed to NON-INTERVENTIONISTS, in spite of whatever species an 'alien' is a part of. There is a third group who we might refer to as the COLLECTIVISTS who, because of their all-inclusive nature, are being torn between the Interventionists and Non-Interventionists. Several contactees have stated that the non-interventionists are centered in an alliance of mostly humanoid cultures in the Pleiades and Andromeda constellations; whereas the interventionists are centered in an alliance of mostly reptiloid cultures in the Draconis and Orion constellations. The fact is that most of the leading interventionists are reptiloids whereas most of the leading non-interventionists are humanoids. If we apply this to the third chapter of the book of Genesis, then it would seem that the 'serpent' race is a 'wild'

The Omega Files

reprobate race which is ruled by base animal or predatory instincts. Since the reptilians have or did have in the past a limited degree of individual choice and since they are connected to the 'racial memory', this is to some extent their collective fault. However mankind must accept some of the blame because — being created in the 'image' of God [possessing a conscience?] and possessing a soul, which the reptilians themselves lack [save for the some of the so-called genetic 'hybrids' or 'hu-brids'] — mankind was originally created spiritually superior to the serpent race, or at least they/we WERE spiritually superior to them in the beginning.

In other words man was given charge over the physical creation, something the angels themselves could not do because they were not created as material beings. And yes, they were also given charge over the most cunning and intelligent of all of the 'beasts', the 'serpent' race [Genesis 3:1]. If we are to accept the symbolic and/or literal interpretation of Genesis chapter 3, then it was the rebel angels who moved upon the serpent race and acted through them to deceive and destroy mankind's connection to the Creator or the Source of all LIFE. Once this connection was broken, the Divine supernatural flow was broken at the human level, and a creation which formerly had enjoyed perfection and harmony began to turn WILD. The **Luciferians** may have appealed to the jealousy that the serpent race harbored towards mankind, considering that mankind had been given a higher status in the scheme of things than their own race possessed, and once the Luciferians offered to give them power over humankind [sorcery] and over the creation [technology] in exchange for allowing the rebel angels to incarnate through their race, the reptilians accepted. In so doing however the serpent race for the most part lost their individual identities and became the absolute physical 'puppets' of the fallen angels. The descendants of these degenerate beings [Genesis 3:15, which I believe has a duel physical AND spiritual interpretation] constitute a large majority of the occult-technological manifestations which we know today as "UFO encounters".

Only today the "serpent" comes in the form of a "Grey Alien" and the "forbidden fruit" is offered in the form of grandiose promises and occult-technology which will supposedly give the 'elite' human recipients 'god-like' powers over their fellow human beings. Now you might say that I've lost touch with reality, that I've been reading too much science fiction, or have gone off the deep end of theological and eschatological speculation. Well, just consider this. IF a hostile alien force exists, would it not be logical

The Omega Files

for them to infiltrate powerful agencies on earth and use the influence of those agencies to relentlessly pound into the minds of the masses that those who believe in aliens and starships are lunatics, fools, imbeciles, and paranoids who have lost all touch with reality and should be consigned to mental institutions? That is EXACTLY what they would try to do, in spite of MASSIVE evidence to the contrary that such a reality DOES exist. One of the major deceptions which the 'Draconians' have used to subvert humanity, especially intelligence agencies, is the idea that THEY — the aliens — genetically created the human race and placed us on this planet, and therefore they are our 'gods'. And so, powerful individuals with whom the aliens interact — and who have been given promises which sound too good to be true, because they ARE, in exchange for their cooperation — have opened the door for the alien infiltration and infestation of all levels of our society. That is, the infiltration of our society by collectivist-interventionist reptilian-based entities known as the 'Greys' and 'Reptiloids'. And the ancient black gnostic 'serpent cults' of Bavaria, Germany were ready and willing to enter into a 'marriage of convenience' with these draconians because like the aliens themselves, they also wished to rule the planet. The aliens needed the global economic and fraternal connections of the 'Bavarian' secret societies, whereas the human 'elite' needed the alien mind control technology. The Bavarian elitists agreed to a certain percentage of the planet once the 'New World Order' was implemented.

Some 'contactees' such as Maurice Doreal claim that the reptiloids in prehistoric times lived in the Antarctic region, when it was a subtropical zone, and that they were subsequently driven underground and off the planet by a race or pre-Nordic humans whose lost and long-forgotten civilization now lies buried deep beneath the sands of the Gobi desert. Some of these scientifically advanced 'Nordics' migrated westward and eventually gave rise to the tribes who would in the course of time lay the foundations for the Scandinavian nations, whereas others went underground into a subterranean realm called 'Agharti', located generally below central Asia and the Gobi. Millions of Buddhists know the legend of Agharti, but they consider it sacred knowledge and are careful about revealing the 'secret of secrets' to skeptical Westerners. World travelers such as Nicholas Roerich in his book "SHAMBHALA" and Ferdinand Ossendowski in his work "BEASTS, MEN AND GODS" had gained the trust of these natives and detailed the legends of 'Agharti' in a humble and respectful manner. According to ancient Agharian crystalholographic recordings which Doreal's 'Blond' friends — from an un-

The Omega Files

derground colony below Mt. Shasta, California — showed him within an ancient repository vault beneath the Himalayas, these ancient 'pre-Nordics' waged a war for the surface of the planet and later an underground war against the 'serpent' races which had taken residence within a system of massive multi-leveled underground caverns beneath the southwestern slopes of the Himalayas and the Indian subcontinent.

These caverns were and are known by Hindus as the realm of 'Patala', or 'Snakeworld', where the 'Nagas' or serpent people dwell in their capital city of Bhoga-vita. Many Hindus considered the 'Nagas' to be 'demons', whereas others were prone to worshipping them. Aryan-Hindu legend tells of at least two entrances to the Nagas underground 'world', one of three worlds spoken of in Hindu cosmology. One entrance is believed to be Sheshna's well in Benares, India and another is located in the mountains surrounding Lake Manosarowar, Tibet. Both the 'Reptiloids' and 'Nordics' eventually left the planet, leaving the ancient remains and ruins of their cultures within the underground caverns. Similar ruins as well as current operational bases reportedly exist on and beneath the surface of the moon and Mars, along with signs of the ancient wars that the humanoids and reptiloids fought for control of the solar system before both species discovered how to manipulate hyperspace and began sending explorers and colonists to other nearby starsystems. The humanoids eventually colonized the Lyra, Pleiades, and Andromeda constellations as well as others; whereas the reptiloids colonized the Draconis, Orion, and Reticulum constellations, among other systems. The stories that contactees tell of the devastating battles and galactic massacres — in almost every case initiated by the collectivist-interventionist reptiloids/greys — between the two galactic superpowers are integral although controversial elements within the annals of Ufology. Now the 'war' is coming 'back home' one might say, in that 'Mother Earth' in addition to being the original home world is also perhaps the most strategic world in the galaxy when one considers its centralized location and the profusity of genetic materials, water, chemicals, minerals, flora, fauna, etc., in great abundance and variety. The 'Draco-Orion' Empire agents — who according to some contactees are operating within the comet-planetoid 'Hale-Bopp' and other numerous 'asteroids' in this system in order to conceal their activities — are here to build an army of human mind-servants [via abductions, mind control implants, etc.] who they can program with alternate identities which are activated during abduction experiences.

The Omega Files

They realize that Terrans possess an inherent warrior instinct-passion and a potent 'metagene factor' resulting from a mixture of many racial lines which can produce specialized genetic abilities within individuals... instincts and abilities which the Grey-Reptiloid interventionists believe would be better harnessed and subverted than challenged. They intend to use these programmed abductees as 'human shields' or weapons in the ancient war against their enemies in the 'Andro-Pleiadean' Federation, who incidentally maintain a massive underground basing system centered below the Death Valley region of California. This 'base' was originally established around 2500 B.C. by ancient navigators from Greece and India who discovered vast caverns within the Panamint mountains. According to Paiute American indian legends these "Hav-musuves" were dressed like Greeks and had constructed vast cities of "marble beauty" within large cavern systems deep beneath the Mojave desert regions, cities which some Paiute chiefs had seen with their own eyes. The "Havmusuvs" later developed an aerial technology once the inland sea which filled Death Valley in ancient times — and connected it to the Pacific Ocean — disappeared. At first this 'silvery flying canoes' which appeared in the skies around 1000-2000 B.C. were small, possessed wings, and moved with a loud 'whirring' sound. Later models were larger, wingless, and more silent. More sophisticated craft appeared that could travel between worlds, and later between stars, and as a result of their discovery of the secrets of 'Hyperspace Travel' they were able to colonize other worlds and star systems.

The manipulation of Hyperspace was incidentally also a part of the Philadelphia/Rainbow projects of the 1940's and Phoenix/Montauk projects of the 1980's. Creating a hyperspace field is not as difficult as one might think, and essentially involves the electromagnetic generation and manipulation of magnetic and anti-magnetic fields. It is the concise 'focusing' of such fields in order to accomplish certain tasks without disastrous side-effects which is where things become complex. The Andro-Pleiadean Federation forces based under Death Valley were reportedly in contact with Nikola Tesla — through whom they guided the Navy's Philadelphia Experiments behind the scenes. Forty years later the Draco-Orion forces based under Archuleta Mesa had established contact with Dr. John von Neumann, who was director of the Montauk Projects on behalf of the [Nazi] Thule Society. The betrayal of the Navy's Philadelphia/Rainbow Technology to the Thule Society's Phoenix/Montauk Projects was accomplished by a joint CIA/NSA-SIRIAN-DRACONION "double agency" called the "Black Monks", who were

The Omega Files

involved in BOTH the Philadelphia AND Montauk projects. This agency was brought under the psychological control of the Draconian - Bavarian collaboration and became an instrument for the infiltration of these outside forces into American intelligence agencies, and in fact all levels of American society. As for the Phoenix [Montauk] and Philadelphia [Rainbow] projects, these are reportedly being carried out separately by 'Nazi' and U.S. Navy intelligence, respectively, as late as the 1990's and this has resulted in what might be referred to as a time-space war between the Andro-Plieadean-Navy backed "Philadelphian" agents and the Draco-Orion-Nazi backed "Phoenician" agents.

There are even rumors that Nikola Tesla's death may have been faked, and that he escaped and joined a secret "Marconi" scientific underground colony somewhere in South America. If such rumors have any basis in fact, then what interaction if any they may have had with the secret 'Nazi' bases in South America remains a mystery. In addition to the above, according to contactee Israel Norkin, Draconian and Orionite agents have been infiltrating the so-called "Ashtar" collective lodges based in Sirius-B, and have apparently commandeered a segment of the implant-based electronic collective "hive mind" for their own use, masquerading as "Ascended Masters" to facilitate an easy assimilation of Sirian cultists into their agenda. Other Sirians were able to see through the deception and, joining forces with the 'Federation' [Andromedans, Pleiadeans, Tau Cetians, Procyonese, Koldasians, etc.], they began to break away from the Ashtar collective's cultic stranglehold and develop their lost personal sovereignty and commenced to wage a relentless civil war against the Orion-Sirian collaboration, driving them from the system. The Sirian resistance to the collaboration may have had its roots among those patriotic Sirians who remembered the devastating wars which had been fought in the past against the Orionites over which side would serve as the overlords for this immediate sector of space [21 star systems including Sol]. NOW the epicenter of the entire galactic battle is gravitating towards the Sol system as the Draconians, Orionites and their human collaborators are arriving here en masse to support a New World Order agenda which will serve as a power-base through which they can once again re-group their forces.

Apparently planet earth, the original 'home world', is the KEY. If the Draconians and Orionites can impose a fascist New World Order on the planet, ruled by a human elite who are completely sold-out to their agenda,

The Omega Files

they believe that they can use planet earth and the New World Order as a base from which they can destroy forever their enemies in the Federation. According to Preston Nicholes, Federation agents from the Andromeda and Pleiades constellation 'beamed' into the Montauk base under Camp Hero at the northernmost tip of Long Island, sacrificing their lives in an attempt to sabotage the projects there and prevent what they believed to be a very real and potential space-time disaster of apocalyptic proportions, which was being precipitated by fascist and alien scientists who were playing god by experimenting with the elemental forces of the universe. This might have been on the same scale of, or even worse than, the space-time disaster which was precipitated by an ancient antediluvian?] race, leaving a 'rift' in the time-space continuum in what has become known as the Bermuda Triangle. Several thousand young people, according to Preston Nicholes, Peter Moon and Al Bielek, have reportedly been abducted by the CIA-Nazi-Grey collaboration and have been taken to the Montauk base for 'programming' and release. Several thousands more children who were part of the Montauk Projects — before they were sabotaged in 1985 only to be reestablished at a later date by the CIA/NSA — were abducted permanently and used in time-space dimensional window and mind control experiments. Most of these children, who were usually 'street kids' or 'homeless kids' who would not be 'missed' as much as the children of more wealthy parents — were 'lost' in the other dimensions as a result of these experiments.

So then, according to some there is absolutely no doubt that — as they did within the underground facilities of Germany — the 'Nazis' and the 'Greys' are collaborating to this day from underground bases beneath Camp Hero [Montauk Point, Long Island]; Area 51 [Nellis Air Force Base, Nevada]; Dulce [Archuleta Mesa, New Mexico], and a massive underground facility below the Denver International Airport. This latter facility, according to 'inside' sources, is being prepared to be used as the New World Order control-center for America. Aside from the many anomalous stories that have surfaced from the D.I.A., there are bizarre accounts of strange tunnels and seemingly useless equipment at the Airport — 'useless' that is unless one intends to confine and transport large numbers of people to deep underground concentration camps which are rumored even now to be active and occupied by unfortunate men, women and children who have mysteriously 'disappeared' from outer society. Many Americans know on an unconscious or intuitive level that something has gone terribly wrong with their country, and the aliens/fascists are desperately trying to turn this frustration inward

The Omega Files

in order to further destabilize American society. An abused society will take out their frustrations on whatever they 'perceive' to be the source of the abuse. And in many cases the true abusers or oppressors will escape justice by carefully creating 'scape goats' who are 'framed' in order to receive the collective wrath of the nation... whether that scapegoat is in the form of a Lee Harvey Oswald, a Sirhan Sirhan, a Tim McVey, an Aldrich Ames, etc.

Although such men may have been 'programmed' to do what they did, they are certainly NOT the ones who are ultimately responsible. Are we headed for an impending war with an "underground empire" that was jointly established by Aliens and National Socialists who were given refuge within the Military-Industrial complex following the end of World War II? Area-51, the Montauk base, the Denver International Airport base, and the Dulce base seem to be the MAJOR North American centers of activity for the collaboration between the agents of the Bavarian Black Nobility cults [who have ruled vast financial empires in Europe for over 1500 years] and the alien 'Greys' — although there are other bases located in other parts of the world as we will see... one of them being a joint Nazi-Alien network reputedly existing beneath the mountains of Neu Schwabenland, Antarctica — possibly the very staging-base from where the 'aliens' who abducted Betty and Barney Hill operated. Another — the "M.A.L.T.A" or "Montauk Alsace-Lorraine Time Archives" base — is reportedly located in the Alsace-Lorraine Mts. near the border of France-Germany, and yet another 'Dulce type' base is said to exist near Alice Springs / Pine Gap Australia.

2. NAZI BASES IN ANTARCTICA

We will now examine the various claims of Nazi bases in Antarctica, which as we have said, may very well have been the point-of-origin of the 'Nazi-Grey' craft that Barney and Betty Hill encountered during their abduction experience. The historical facts are evident. Beginning in 1838, long before the end of the Second World War, the Nazi's commenced to send out numerous exploratory missions to the Queen Maud region of Antarctica. A steady stream of expeditions were reportedly sent out from [at the time] white supremacist South Africa. Over 230,000 square miles of the frozen continent were mapped from the air, and the Germans discovered vast regions that were surprisingly free of ice, as well as warm water lakes and cave inlets. One vast ice cave within the glacier was reportedly found to extend 30 miles to a large hot-water geothermal lake deep below. Various scientific teams were moved in to the area, including hunters, trappers, col-

The Omega Files

lectors and zoologists, botanists, agriculturists, plant specialists, mycologists, parasitologists, marine biologists, ornithologists, and many others. Numerous divisions of the German government were involved in the top secret project. This is where the mainstream historians leave off, as only revisionist historians will dare consider the implications of the rest of the story... After all the data was gathered, deep underground construction teams came pouring into the renamed "Neu-Schwabenland". They came on cargo ships, military transport ships, and submarines. The cargo ships coming from South Africa were protected by a host of killer-submarines and military ships. This might explain the intense Nazi war efforts in North and South Africa. Any ship that even came close to the shipping routes from South Africa to Antarctica were destroyed by German U-boats to protect the secret.

After all the goods were brought, the VIPs and scientists started to show up with a compliment of ULTRA, a highly specialized Nazi SS team like our MJ-12. ULTRA has always been in control of Antarctica. ULTRA is the name of a secret alien interface agency in the NSA. Remember that the NSA has connections to both the Nazi S.S. and the Dulce base. According to contactee Alex Collier, the upper level members of the NSA-ULTRA group are cloned replicates or have been so heavily implanted, virtual cyborgs, that they could be considered as being barely human — automatons who are remotely controlled by the Greys' group ego or group mind. It is also noteworthy that ULTRA is also the NAME OF the Above Top Secret CIA-NSA-Alien base under the Archuleta plateau and peak northeast of DULCE, New Mexico. This might also explain Valdamar Valerian's insistence that early newspaper clippings just prior to the outbreak of World War II imply that "the Germans" were "all over" New Mexico exploring caves and mines, buying up property, and engaging in all sorts of mysterious activities. Could Antarctica be the real power behind the New World Order? If the Nazi bases still exist in Antarctica then they would no doubt still have secret contact with the Bavarian cults which sponsored and were an integral part of the Nazi party, like the Bavarian THULE society for instance. It is interesting that the re-united East and West Germany is paving the way for the 'unification' of Europe. For instance, all economic bar-codes must be processed through Germany, Germany is trying to impose enforced nepotistic career restrictions where one's career is determined by the family one is born into, a British news agency spoke of investigations of the Bavarian secret service who were reportedly smuggling weapons grade plutonium into Germany from a nuclear black market operation they had established in the former Soviet States, the

The Omega Files

Illuminati has its base in Germany [Bavaria], and Germany has been the most active country in the international drive for Internet censorship and control.

In other words, Democracy seems to be dying a painful death in Germany, IF it ever really existed there in the first place. As for Neu Schwabenland, the construction and secret projects in Antarctica continued throughout the entire course of the war. Just before the end of the WWII, two German provision U-boats, U-530 and U-977, were launched from a port on the Baltic Sea. Reportedly they took with them members of the antigravity-disk research and development teams [ULTRA], and the LAST of the most vital disc components [much of this technology and hardware had been transported to the base during the course of the war]. This included the notes and drawings for the latest saucer or aerial disk designs, and designs for the gigantic underground complexes and living accommodations based on the remarkable underground factories of Nordhausen in the Harz Mountains. The two U-boats duly reached the new land of Neu-Schwabenland where they unloaded everything. When they arrived in Argentina several months later, their crews were captured. It seems as if they were either counting on the formerly German-friendly Argentineans to allow them access, or it could have been that they intentionally allowed themselves to be discovered for misinformation purposes, i.e. — "yes... we are the last two renegade German subs. We've been trying to hold out but...oops, you caught us... the war's finally over!" The crews of these U-Boats were of course interrogated by U.S. Intelligence agents who had suspected the existence of the Antarctic base. Whatever the Nazi soldiers tried to tell them, apparently the Americans were not convinced... especially considering the subsequent and ill-fated U.S. Navy backed military actions against the Nazi's "Last Battalion" in Antarctica in later years under Admiral Richard E. Byrd, who arrived at Antarctica with an entire military armada and provisions to last 6 month.

However the the entire expedition lasted only 8 weeks, with only approximately three weeks of actual full-scale Antarctic operations. The Antarcticans were desperate following the war, and knew that a confrontation was imminent. Much effort was put into developing secret weapons projects to defend their new underground Empire, which no doubt was constructed with the 'help' of a large number of expendable slave laborers transported from the concentration camps of Europe. The major base-city of Antarctica became known as the NEW BERLIN, or by the code-named "Base-

The Omega Files

211". The actual beginnings of German interest in the polar regions may date back BEFORE the earliest U.S. Navy polar expeditions. For instance one segment of NOVA related that the remains of Capt. Charles Hall of the ill-fated POLARIS expedition, one of the first American ventures to the North Pole, were discovered in an ice grave by a subsequent polar expedition. It seemed that when the body was examined it was found to contain poison. It was also discovered by searching the records that the cook [who would be in the perfect position to administer poison] and the first mate on the Polaris expedition were German Occultist spies! Remember that the German secret societies of Bavaria, which had helped to precipitate the first and second world wars, date back to ancient times when — following the occupation of Egypt — the [un] 'Holy Roman Empire' military forces based in Germany, the seat of government for the H.O.R.E, brought back from Egypt the black gnostic "serpent cults" which later gave rise to the Bavarian Illuminati, the Bavarian Thule Society and a host of other lesser known satanic racist cults which gravitated around these. Could the occultist spies who sabotaged the POLARIS expedition have been attempting to protect a secret hidden deep within the polar regions? Could this secret have had something to do with an ancient collaboration between Bavarian satanic cults and reptilian-based aliens?

A German Polar researcher who we will identify only as 'Stefan' reveals that the 'historical' beginnings of German interest and research into the Antarctic or South Polar region itself began in 1873 when Sir Eduard Dallman on behalf of the newly founded German Society of Polar Research discovered new Antarctic routes with his ship 'GRONLAND'. "...Dallman discovered the "Kaiser-Wilhelm-Inseln" at the western entrance of the Biskmarkstrasse along the Biscoue Islands. Exploring the polar regions, the Germans were already at this time quite innovative, for the 'GRONLAND' was the first steamship to see the Antarctic ice at all. "Within the next 60 years 2 further expeditional thrusts took place, and two complete expeditions were fulfilled, namely 1910 under Wilhem Filchner with his ship 'DEUTSCHLAND'; and 1925 with the special designed polar expedition ship, the 'METEOR' under the command of Dr. Albert Merz. "During the recent years before WWII the Germans claimed to hegemony about parts of Antarctica and the wish to possess [their] own base grew stronger. At this time the Antarctic was not safe due to international treaties like today and a pragmatic proof of Germany's claim by a single strike to the south pole on the eve of the war seemed to be the best option. Hitler himself was anxious for a

The Omega Files

foothold in the Antarctic and such a claim could be used pretty well for the National socialistic propaganda and a further demonstration of the uprising "Superpower Germany". On the other side a new provocation of the Allies had still to be avoided for some time. Germany was — at this time — not completely prepared for the coming war. "As a matter of fact, the idea of a semi-civilian expedition in cooperation with the German national airline company, the 'LUFTHANSA' grew up. A civilian covered expedition with truly military and strategical background, a highly political charged balancing act. The command on this strike was given to the polar-experienced Captain Alfred Ritscher, who had already led some expeditions to the North Pole and proved courage and skillness in critical situations.

The selected ship was the 'MS SCHWABENLAND, a German aircraft carrier used since 1934 for transatlantic mail delivery by special flight boats, the famous 'Dornier Wale'. These 'Wales' were mounted on steam catapults on the deck of the ship and could be started and refueled this way easily. This circumstance should proof very well during the expedition. "The 'SCHWABENLAND' was prepared for the expedition on Hamburg's shipyards, which cost the huge amount of 1 Million Reichsmark, nearly a third of the complete expedition budget. "Meanwhile, the crew was prepared and scheduled by the German Society of Polar Research precisely. This society also made the sensational step to invite Richard E. Byrd, the most famous American Antarctic researcher. On the mid of November 1938 he arrived in Hamburg and showed the crew and a clearly selected publicity of 84 persons his new Antarctic dokumentation movie in the Urania of Hamburg. Byrd, who had flown across the south pole as the first human in 1929, was already at this time a living legend, a national hero to the Americans and most of the polar researchers. In 1938 he still was civilian. This invitation to the Germans could have been a typical irony of history, for nearly ten years later exactly this Richard E. Byrd — then in the rank as US NAVY admiral — got the instruction to destroy the secret German Antarctic base 211. To do this, he was given the command of the biggest military force on the Antarctic ice ever seen, 13 ships and nearly 4000 men staff. That mysterious operation which is said to have ended in a catastrophical failure. "The 'NEUSCHWABENLAND' left the port of Hamburg on December 17th 1938 heading to the Antarctic on a precisely planned and determined route and reached the ice on January 19th 1939 at 4° 15′ W and 69° 10′S. The following weeks on 15 flights the 'PASSAT' and the 'BOREAS' flew across some 600.000 square kilometers and made with their special designed German "Zeiss

The Omega Files

Reihenmessbildkameras RMK 38" more than 11.000 pictures of the area.

The old Norwegian maps from 1931 on these areas were renewed, for they proved to be fake. [Could not be different, because the Norwegian expeditions before did never go so deep into the ice from the used Northern landing point]. Nearly one fifth of the whole Antarctic area was scanned this way, thus documented for the first time and simultaneous claimed to be German territory. To stress this claim on the outside too, the two planes dismissed several thousands of drop-flags, special metal poles with expedition's insignia on them, the 'swastika'. The whole territory now got the still valid name: 'NEUSCHWABENLAND', referring to a south German region [which is actually not far from me here]. "Interestingly, the Expedition seemed to have discovered ice-free areas with even lakes and small signs of vegetation in the mid of the Antarctic. The geologists said that this phenomenon was due hot sources in the ground. Concurrent, the landings points where marked with "prick-flags". "Notes: Some newer historians reduce the discovered area to an amount of 325.000 square kilometers. Do not trust these numbers, I have copies of the original flight maps here, revealing the number 600.000 in ancient letters. What could be the reason to reduce this number? "Most parts of 'NEUSCHWABENLAND' were renamed according to the Antarctic treaty in 1957. Look out for "QUEEN MAUD LAND"., "PRINCESS MARTHA COAST", "PRINCESS ASTRID COAST". On the older maps you will still find the original names. Yet, until today still many of the mountains in the northern Antarctic area carry German names like: "M_HLIG-HOFFMAN-MOUNTAINS", "WOHLTAT-MOUNTAINS", etc. These names were given according to leading Berlin bureaucrats who enabled with their policy the expedition's targets. "In the mid of February, the 'SCHWABENLAND' again left the Antarctic. It took two months back to Hamburg and Ritscher carefully used this time to organize the results, maps and photos.

Captain Ritscher surprised by the results of the flights, immediately planned after the arrival a second, fully civilian, expedition in use of lighter airplanes with skids. Facing the beginning of WWII, these civilian (!) plans were said to be given up somewhere on October 1939. "Yet, what about the military and strategic option achieved by this strike? Was it wasted resources so far? Today, all historians agree in the fact that WWII was not accidentally started but pretty well planned from the early 30's and even before. At least since 1933 (incidentally the same year when one of the first 'official' treaties between the Greys and Bavarian Intelligence was initiated — no doubt with

The Omega Files

more than a little help from the secret societies operating there - Branton) the whole German dictatorship tried to gain war fitness within a decade or earlier. In all — and I really mean all — aspects of life: military, 'civilian', economic, social, private, resourcing, engineering, foreign policy, and so on, in all aspects the Germans were put straight on their way to war more or less obviously. Pointing to this only aim, the National socialists abused the typical kind of German correctness and missing sense for rebellious scrutinizing. Nothing was left to chance! And this same method was used in the Antarctic issue, which in my eyes NEVER ended with Ritscher's return [in] 1938 but went on during the WWII. "Unfortunately, at this point all valid information has vanished. What is left is a scattered puzzle of hints, testimonies and reports which go up to the fifties and which we partially can not verify anymore. So IF the Germans WERE able to build up an Antarctic [underground] base on the results of Ritscher's expedition, this would be one of the really best covered secrets in German history. No question, German engineers HAD the knowledge to construct something like that as the huge underground establishments of the Nordhausen complex in the Harz as well as Kahla complex at Thuumlringen and many more prove. Does this remind you Americans of something???

The pattern somehow is the same: A lying government / dictatorship and a frightened, blind-held folks willing to obey and believe in what they are fed up with...[see Roswell]. "So, what we did in Part II ... was the attempt to restructure chronically those parts of the puzzle we could gather within some months of research on this topic. Nobody can say that the following really happened, so you might see it as speculation first. Yet, we HAVE tremendous parallels on several sources from which we can only say this one thing 100%ly: THEY COULD NOT HAVE KNOWN OF EACH OTHER! "What follows now is the attempt of a chronological collection of the events and their conclusions as far as they are known to us today. They all lead to the establishing of the Antarctic base 211 at the end of war by means of German submarines and flying saucers and to the [failed ?] attempt to destroy it by the US Navy in 1947. (Note: The following are brief descriptions or synopsis' of information and documentation which 'Stefan' has in his possession, yet which we will not quote in their entirety here. - Branton): "— Evaluation of the anti-gravity propulsion of a nearly 100% functional flying saucer going down in the 'Schwarzwald' in the summer 1936. "— Alternative hypothesis: Self-developing this propulsion by experiments of German scientists basing on Viktor Schauberger's anti-gravity experiments. "— First unmanned

The Omega Files

flights with the new [re-]built propulsion. A very special section of the "Reichsluftfahrtbehoumlrde" gets the project under its control with the aim to build up anti-gravital fighters and troop-carriers. The project's name is 'HANEBBU' [some sources also call it the 'VRIL' project]. The prototypes are numbered in ascending order.

The project has many setbacks in the first years due to the massive electro-magnetic disturbances and their interaction with conventional electric components. Although the propulsion can be handled and used principally, it seems to be nearly impossible to "drive or fly" these prototypes in sharper angels than 90, thus not usable as fighters. Additionally normal navigation systems referring somehow to magnetic fields were completely useless and special magnetic independent navigation instrumentation designed, the celestial guidance system: "Meisterkompass" and "Peiltochterkompass". "— Further secret German expeditions to 'NEUSCHWABENLAND'. As landing points, there could have been used two of the three marked landing bays north-west of the "HLIG-HOFFMAN MOUNTAINS" close to 3° W and 70° S. Those were already documented as 'landing bays' by Ritscher. "— Starting the assemblage of the Antarctic base 211. Simultaneously a second secret base is build up on a high plateau in the South American Andes. [Argentina ?] "— Necessary items for the erection of the bases are continuously transported on submarines. Note: German submarine commanders are highly experienced in the Arctic waters due to the need of delivery of material and people to Germany's northern Arctic bases and civilian research stations. In fact at least 20 well documented operations have taken place along the Arctic until 1945 by means of these submarines. Some of these operations, especially the later ones, had to be carried out under extreme conditions and with the permanent threat of contact with the enemy. Besides, on their way to the south pole, researchers discovered somewhat like a straight deep submarine trench fitting pretty well for the necessary transportation's. "— The 'HANNEBU' series has left the stadium of prototypes and brought up to 19-25 ships in 2 [or even 3] sizes. "HANEBU I" is a small vessel, "HANNEBU II" a more sophisticated, larger one. Some reports even hint at "HANNEBU III", which was designed as a mothership. If this third type has become reality, there existed only one single ship. So, the overall transport capacities are still very limited, due to a quite small diameter of the disks.

Additionally production of ships gets more and more difficult, because

The Omega Files

the Allies managed to cut of Germany's raw materials more and more. Yet 'HANNEBUs' managed to disturb some allied bomber raids over Germany. Note: Every allied bomber pilot in the [latter] years of the war knew the mysterious threat of the so called "foo-fighters" appearing and vanishing with incredible speed and causing bright-orange light phenomenon's and paroxysmal instrumentation failures on all electric and magnetic parts of the bombers. In no source a direct attack by these "foo-fighters" is mentioned, they seem to play a completely defensive role on the late air war over Germany. (Note: see the movie, THE BATTLE OF THE BULGE, which correctly implies that the Germans were on the verge of developing a whole range of incredible new aerial weapons, and needed to prolong the war for a few more months in order to get their new jets, etc., into production, and the Battle of the Bulge was a part of this plan. However just as these new weapons were about to go into mass production the German military failed to fully succeed in their battle plans to buy more time and prolong the war for a few more months, and the Allied invasion of Germany began. That particular victory may have been closer than most of us would dare to believe. If the 'Nazis/Antarcticans' are planning for another planetary takeover, then this time they may have an alien force working with them. Could the abductions and implantation's by 'aliens' be a joint CIA-Nazi-Alien project to implement electronic mind control programming on millions of people throughout the nations in preparation for the attempted implimentation of an electronically-controlled New World Order dictatorship? - Branton) "— The enormous pressure of the Allies force the Germans to give up the big secret underground facilities in Eastern Germany. The Allies themselves seem to be pretty well informed on these facilities and overall eager to capture them.

The Germans flee and leave back much material of the 'HANNEBU' project. Their attempt to rebuild the construction zones in the middle of Germany fails. The war is nearly over. "Quotations: "... I have seen enough of their designs and production plans to realize that if they [the Germans] had managed to prolong the war some months longer, we would have been confronted with a set of entirely new and deadly developments in air warfare. " — Sir Roy Feddon, chief of the technical mission to Germany for the Ministry for Aircraft Production in 1945. "When WWII ended, the Germans had several radical types of aircraft and guided missiles under development. The majority were in the most preliminary stages, but they were the only known craft that could even approach the performance of objects reported to UFO observers... " — Captain Edward J. Ruppelt Chief of the US Air Force Project

The Omega Files

'Bluebook' on 1956. "Notes: "— A last convoy of submarine vessels leaves German Harbors with direction to Antarctica and Andes. It is the overall successful attempt to escape the Allies' clutches. Among this last convoy there are the U 530 [Captain Otte Wehrmut] and the U977m [Captain Heinz Schaumlffer]. "— The last visual contact with U977 was on April 26th at Christiansund. Schaumlffer's crew did not reveal anything about the submarine's destination or load. The vessel vanishes now for nearly 4 months, before the crew delivers a completely empty vessel to Argentinian Officials. "— In the same way, leading NS-Officials and technicals are evacuated from Berlin/Potsdam with the HANEBU fleet heading to the meanwhile COMPLETED (?) base 211. The overall transport capacities are quite limited. "— The submarine convoy achieves in the southern Atlantic Sea a sea victory over an Allied unit trying to stop it. This event is under wraps until today. "— Germany's capitulation [to the Allies] 17 August 1945. "— Some submarine crews who are not willing to live in the base or who perhaps can't be admitted to the base travel to Argentine and hand over their completely empty submarines. "— Among those are the documented cases of U530 and U977.

High US NAVY officials immediately traveled down to Argentine and started severe interrogations on the crew. Scgaumlffer repeatedly denied to have brought anyone or anything to anywhere. Although most of the crew are unwilling to tell what really happened, it is possible that these interrogations deliver important information about the location of the base. (Note: One source has claimed that the information the interrogators received involved the escape of Adolph Hitler, Martin Boorman, Eva Braun and a major segment of the Nazi leadership — not including those who were 'sacrificed' to the Nuremberg trials after the war — to the South Polar base. This source claimed that these interrogations ultimately LED to the military action against the entrenched Nazi forces in Antarctica under the command of Navy Admiral Richard E. Byrd. - Branton). Yet for us, it remains very mysterious what the crew really did after the official capitulation on May 1945, for they confessed to have heard it soon on their own radio. When Schaumlffer came free, he immediately traveled back to Argentina to stay there with some fellows for the rest of his life. (Note: Others claim that a large number of 'Antarcticans' have infiltrated South America via Argentina, and in turn North America — where the Nazi "UFO" forces have reportedly established several underground bases. They are reportedly working with "Paperclip" Nazis, members of various Bavarian fraternal cults, and Anglo-American corporate fascists above, in a plan to bring down America by creating a fascist

The Omega Files

revolution in the United States, like the one that brought the Nazi's to power in Germany. The concentration camps, thousands of train cars equipped with shackles, and executive orders for the implementation of martial law are already in place. - Branton) "— Until today more than 100 submarines of the German fleet are missing. Among those are many of the highly technological XXII class equipped with the so-called 'Walterschnorchel', a special designed and coated schnorkel enabling submarines in combination with their new developed engines to dive for many thousand miles. A 'trip' to the base without recognition becomes pretty possible with this technology. "— The US Navy tries to destroy the German base which did not surrender at the end of war. The operation is a disaster. The base remains functional, at least in parts. "— More than one year after the surrendering of U977 the US NAVY launches the biggest military operation in the Antarctic ice under the command of Admiral Richard E. Byrd.

This is the operation 'HIGHJUMP', including 13 ships, 1 aircraft carrier, 2 seaplane tenders, 6 two-engined R4D transports and 4000 men. The only official statement on the purpose of such a task force is the need for testing "new material under the extreme Antarctic conditions." The force starts up at the established US bases in the "ROSS SEA", then it moves up the western Antarctic coast heading toward the Northern Antarctic coast, 'NEUSCHWABENLAND' and building up a bridgehead on January 27th 1947 somewhere west of it. Officially the expedition is a big success because it delivers many new facts of the use of military equipment under extreme conditions. "— What is the need of such a big task force in this area? IF the expedition was such a success, WHY did Byrd already return to the US in February 1947? The operation was planned and equipped for a full 6-8 month duration. Did this expedition carry atomic warheads as some sources say? (Note: although the entire expedition lasted some 8 weeks as suggested earlier, some sources claim that the actual battle — once Byrd's forces had been divided into three main battle groups on the continent of Antarctica — lasted only 3 weeks. - Branton) "— Byrd flew in 1947 at least one time in a right-twisted circle across the whole territory 'NEUSCHWABENLAND' heading from southwest over the 'RITSCHER HOCHLAND' and the eastern areas to the Pole. On his return to the US, Byrd reveals in an [often quoted but nowhere validated] interview with a reporter that it was "necessary for the USA to take defensive actions against enemy air fighters which come from the polar regions" and that in case of a new war, the USA would be attacked by fighters that are able to fly from one pole to the next with incredible speed". (Actually this quote HAS been validated, as will be seen later on in this document - Branton).

Byrd has to face a secret cross-examination by US authorities. The US withdraws from the Antarctic for almost a decade. (Note: Another claim which has been made by certain investigators, although the original source is difficult to track down, was that upon returning to the States Admiral Byrd went into a rage before the President and Joint Chiefs of Staff and in an almost demanding tone, strongly 'suggested' that Antarctica be turned into a thermonuclear test range. - Branton) "— World wide mass sightings of UFOs. In the late 70's it becomes more and more obvious that many of these sightings are identical in some technical details with the 'HANEBU' series. This can be stated especially for the so called 'ADAMSKI' UFOs in the early fifties which somehow look very terrestrial, nearly in "fashion style" of this decade and somehow very different from the rest of flat-bottomed crafts. "— The International Antarctic year with large civilian research projects starts. The result is the Antarctic treaty in which all participants agree to avoid any military operations in this region in future times.

This treaty ends somewhere in the year 2000.

3. NAZI HISTORY

Following is a chronology based on research by Val Valerian of LEADING EDGE RESEARCH, regarding the secret 'Nazi' history pre and post World War II. In each code the first two numbers denote the year, the middle two the month, and the last two numbers the day of the month:

140000 - Adolph Hitler 'dreams' of Germany's greatness in the world. 240000 - American [Bavarian Illuminati backed] bankers form I.G. Farben chemical cartel in Germany. 280000 - T. Townsend Brown discovers electrogravitic capacitance effect. 291000 - U.S. undergoes economic collapse, planned by the Bavarian Illuminati. 300000 - Dr. Henry Coanda begins work on Lenticular Aeroform designs. 330000 - Adolf Hitler Takes power. All outstanding German scientists forced to work in Nazi laboratories. 340000 - Germans producing pilotless aircraft. 350000 - German research program on aerial warfare advances by spectacular leaps. 350100 - German experimental rocket research at Reinickendorf and Kummersdorf West. 350600 - American named Wilson [whose non-traditional theories on aerodynamics are rejected by the American government and established scientific organizations as unrealistic] comes to aid German aerial research pro-

The Omega Files

grams. 350622 - Research at Reinickendorf and Kummersdorf West in Germany moved to Thuringia. 360000 - Standard Oil Company [which later becomes EXXON] builds refinery in Germany. 370000 - Germans recover crashed disk. Work begins on German disk program based on recovered 'alien' technology. 380000 - Standard [EXXON] Oil sends I.G. Farben 500 tons of lead additive for gasoline. 390000 - Germans working on mini-television for bomb / rocket guidance. 390802 - Germany and Soviets sign PACT against Poland. (Note: The Communist dictator Vladimir Lenin was originally an agent of the German government who was smuggled into Russia from Germany by train to incite the Bolshevik Revolution. Lenin, no doubt speaking for his Bavarian masters, stated that : "First WE will TAKE Russia, next we will CAPTURE the nations of eastern Europe, then we will TAKE the masses of Asia. Finally, we will surround the United States and that last bastion of freedom will fall into our hands like over-ripe fruit." In spite of this treaty, Hitler invaded Russia to the absolute devastation of Stalin. It may have been that the Jesuit advisors who worked within the Nazi S.S. according to Edmund Paris, put pressure on Hitler to invade Russia because the Roman church considered the Greek Orthodox church of Russia to be its enemy, after having broken away from Rome in earlier times and declaring itself an independent force. - Branton) 390901 - Germany invades Poland. 390901 - Soviets invade Poland. 410000 - Germans test Schriever-Habermohl Model I prototype flying disk or lenticular aircraft Model II in 1944. 410600 - Germany successfully tests Schriever disk design. 410800 - I.G. Farben tests Zyklon B gas. 420000 - German 'fireballs' harass allied pilots and aircraft. 420225 - [German?] UFOs appear over Los Angeles. 1,430 rounds fired against them. Some on the ground killed or wounded by unexploded anti-aircraft shells. 430000 - CIA's Allen Dulles [Bavarian Illuminati] cuts a deal with Nazi SS intelligence. This would eventually lead to a massive infiltration of the CIA by Nazi S.S. agents, who would in turn begin a global program of toppling third world governments and replacing them with their own fascist puppet dictatorships. Germans complete research on alloy of magnesium and aluminum. 440000 - OSS agent Douglas Bazata receives contract on General George Patton's life. Feuerball aircraft constructed at aeronautical factory at Wiener Neustadt. Germans test Bellonzo-Schriever-Meithe designs based on Coanda disk. 440300 - Wilson replaces German saucer [rotor] propulsion with advanced jet propulsion. 440613 - V-1 rockets fall on England. 440720 - Attempted assassination of Hitler. 440906 - V-2 rockets fall on England. 441000 - Soviet Army advances through nations of

The Omega Files

eastern Europe. 441123 - Allied pilots run into 'fireballs' over Strasbourg. 450000 - Both L.F.A. at Volkenrode and center at Guidonia working on disk craft. Soviets gain some German disk data [and apprehend?] Dr. Guenther Bock. United States captures some German disk technology and scientists. British technical advisor discovers German plans for advanced lenticular aircraft. 450200 - Kugelblitz [crew-carrying Fireball] test flown in Thuringia, reached speeds of 1250 mph. 450216 - Kugelblitz tested near Kahla, disk-shaped, 1250 mph. Germans begin to transfer saucer projects to South Polar underground bases. 450223 - Perfected engines removed from Kugelblitz and sent to polar base. Kugelblitz, minus engines, blown up by SS personnel to prevent the design from falling into the hands of the Allies. 450225 - Workers at Kahla complex brought to Buchenwald and gassed so as not to reveal secret of Nazi disk projects. Kahla closed. Slavian slave-laborers from various underground facilities also taken to Karshagan and other camps and killed. 450400 - General Hans Kammler disappears from Germany. 450425 - Gen. Kammler joins Wilson and Gen. Nebe on U-977 bound for South Pole. 450507 - Germany 'surrenders'. 460000 - America turns 2/3rds of Germany's aircraft manufacturing over to Soviets. Nazis help form CIA operations division with Rockefeller assistance. Imported SS intelligence officers help form Radio Liberty and Voice of America. Gen. Hoyt Vandenburg becomes director of CIA. U.S. and Canada begin joint disk development programs in underground plants. 460726 - Truman signs National Military Establishment Act. Creates NSC, CIA. 470000 - CIA Mind-Control drug project begins at Bethesda Naval Hospital. German disks start flyovers over United States. National Security Act. CIA begins to monitor UFOs. 470100 - Operation Highjump begins at South Pole to find the German Bases. Military Commander Admiral Richard E. Byrd leads 4000 troops in reconnaissance over Antarctica, and encounters resistance from 'Aryan' [German/Austrian] saucer fleets. Apparent casualties on both sides. 470624 - Kenneth Arnold reports seeing 9 disks at 9200 feet and 1700 mph, 40-50' dia., shortly after his involvement with the Maurey Island / Tacoma investigation [six UFOs, and men-in-black, sighted] following which a reporter, and two Army G-2 agents carrying 'slag' samples to Wright-Patterson AFB, die mysteriously. Some of the same names connected to Maurey Island, Fred. L. Crisman in particular, mysteriously turn up years later in connection with the J. F. Kennedy assassination. Maurey Island later considered possible experimental test of Nazi - Project Paperclip - CIA antigravity craft, and the JFK assassination an apparent attempt to implement a fascist coup d'etat within

The Omega Files

the Executive branch of the U.S. Government. 470923 - Secret briefing to Gen. Schulgen from Lt. Gen. Twining says disks are real. 470924 - Covert operation 'Majestic-12' or 'MJ-12' is established by Truman to control the UFO [Nazi, etc.,] situation. 490000 - German disks again fly over United States. 490113 - [Nazi?] craft frequent sensitive installations in New Mexico. 500000 - Canadian Scientist Wilbert Smith states to Sarbacher that UFOs exist. German disks again overfly United States. Smith, a Canadian, reports that aerial disks are the most classified subject in the USA. 510410 - Truman relieves General MacArthur of his command and replaces him with Gen. Ridgeway, a CFR member. MacArthur earlier disobeys U.N. directives by initiating a secret attack on the Communist stronghold at Inchon [leading to a quick end of the war], after he and other military leaders suspected the pro-Socialist U.N. officials of betraying their battle plans to the North Koreans. Truman goes into hiding at Camp David for two weeks following MacArthur's return, fearing that the highest-ranking military general in the United States would arrest him for treason. After Truman fires MacArthur for his unauthorized military action, he receives much condemnation from confused and angered patriotic Americans who criticize Truman for his decision. 52-'55 - Rise in 'contactee' encounters. Many of the contactees such as George Adamski, William Dudley Pelley, George Hunt Williamson and others found to have pro-fascist ties with American Nazi movements [see: MESSENGERS OF DECEPTION, by Jacques Vallee], similar to the fascist ties and leanings of some of the 1990's 'Ashtar' UFO cults. Contactee Reinholt Schmidt and other Nebraskans claim encounters with disk pilots who speak and act like German soldiers. Schmidt claims 'they' take him to secret chambers below the Great Pyramids of Giza, where there are incidentally — according to some sources — tunnels leading down to ancient underground facilities maintained by an 'Ashtar' group called Kamogol-II or the 'Giza People', who have maintained collaboration with Orionite reptilian life forms for thousands of years. The Germans had an established alliance with these renegade 'Gizeh' Pleiadeans [Aldebarans] and Orions long before they were approached by the Greys in 1933. Since the Gizeh forces also maintained a collaboration with the Greys, the Bavarian cults were more-or-less in collaboration with them by proxy via their alliance with the Kamogol-II Ashtar Group. According to John Lear, these renegade Pleiadeans intentionally 'crashed' a disk in Germany that was packed full of technology, so that the technology could be used for the German war efforts to bring about planetary 'de-population' and restore the dominance of the 'Aryan' race, which

The Omega Files

this group of Pleiadeans believed themselves to be a part of. It was the Aryan races who brought Hinduism to India during the ancient Aryan invasion of the Indian sub-continent from the north. The Egyptian connection may have resulted from the claims made by certain ancient Egyptian scholars that the first Egyptians [and Mayas] were originally navigators from India. 520929 - NATO Exercise 'Operation Mainbrace' interrupted by [Nazi?] UFOs. 521104 - NSA: Presidential Executive Orders exempts NSA from all laws. National Security Agency imputed with even more power and influence than CIA.

530000 - Dwight Eisenhower becomes president. Eisenhower appoints Nelson Rockefeller to group on Govt. reorganization. It was Rockefeller, in collaboration with 'Nazi' agents, who assisted in the establishment of MJ-12, the NSA and CIA as fronts for Bavarian Intelligence, a 'secret government' within the Constitutional government. Many who have gotten close to the CIA's ultimate secret — that is the Nazi S.S. controlling factor — are murdered by CIA assassins. Allan Dulles, CIA Director, approves mind control project MKDELTA. Entire German-disk-duplication project goes underground. Thomas Townsend Brown gives Air Force demo of his electrogravity effect. NSA James Moseley comes up with 'Earth-made devices' theory. First government disk duplication projects succeed. Work with Canadian government on aerial disks continues. 550300 - NSC 5412/1 group formed. Planning Coordination Group. Nelson Rockefeller is head. 560000 - Captain Ruppelt published 'Report on Unidentified Flying Objects' and states that Germans have extremely advanced air vehicles. CIA memo authorizes use of drugs on inmates of prisons. 580925 - Victor Schauberger, implosion vortex scientist who developed several 'implosion' engines for Nazi lenticular or disk shaped aircraft, dies in Linz, Germany. 590000 - 'Avro VZ-9, System 606A' disc test flown. 600000 - Translator for Eichmann's boss becomes Reagan's personal secretary in California. Project Aquarius [NSA] initiated.

601204 - Dr. Henry Wang, German disk researcher, dies at 54 yrs old. 620000 - Many disks observed around DULCE, New Mexico. Nazi's may be involved there to some degree as well as CIA-NSA involvement and a multi-leveled base where antigrav, biogenetic, psi-warfare, and mind-control research is being carried out to the extreme. 630000 - Kennedy issues ultimatum to MJ-12 member Gordon Gray, says he's going to spill the beans on the whole mess [CIA disk projects, international drug trafficking, mind control, collusion with Grey aliens, etc.] and inform the public. Kennedy, having had to learn these facts from the RUSSIANS, discovers that the scenario is true

The Omega Files

and threatens to 'dismember' the CIA if they don't come clean and surrender to Congressional supervision.

631122 - President Kennedy murdered in a fascist coup d'etat attempt carried out by CIA agents, Mafia hitmen, and the overseers of MJ-12 [MAJI — or the BLACK MONKS]; their man Lyndon Johnson becomes President. 640917 - Government releases Warren Commission report to explain away Kennedy death. 671000 - Britain hit by wave of aerial disks. 691203 - Maj. Keyhoe gets ousted from his NICAP [Civilian UFO research organization] position by CIA infiltrators, and is replaced by John Acuff. 710600 - CIA 'critic' James E. MacDonald drives into desert and 'shoots himself.' 740000 - Gerald Ford becomes President. Nelson Rockefeller becomes Vice-president. (Note: Here is an alternative to a famous parable: "A fool and his money are soon elected"! - Branton) 75-'78 - Project Gabriel: Development of Sonic weapon derived from Nazi technology. 760000 - CIA document released, say Ultrasonics research lasted 20 years. Skull & Bones [a German-based cult] member George Bush becomes director of CIA. Dulce, New Mexico area begins to experience intense animal mutilations. The Dulce base is intended to be a major underground joint-operational control center for the New World Order in the West. A similar facility under the Pine Gap region near Alice Springs, in central Australia, is prepared for use as an Eastern control center. 770000 - Freedom of Information Act established, many subsequent documents released proving Air Force-CIA-NSA interest in [and development of] UFO's.

780000 - NSA employee provides CIA NICAP Chief Acuff with Classified documents. NICAP CIA Chief Jack Acuff sells NICAP lists to NeoNazi 'Samisdat' organization in Canada. 780619 - Carter issues unconstitutional Executive Order creating F.E.M.A. Later FEMA executive orders 'authorize' the suspension of the U.S. Constitution and Bill of Rights in event of a 'National Emergency'. 780908 - Researcher and scientist Paul Bennewitz discovers unusual aerial and underground activity in Jicarilla Apache Reservation near Dulce, N.M. [Archuleta plateau]. Also sightings of unusual 'atomic spacecraft', helicopter pads, black CIA [Nazi SS?] limos, black choppers, hundreds of armed special forces who disappear into the cliffs when approached, mini-lab vans, etc. 790000 - Thomas Edwin Castello takes photos/videos/notes and flees from his position as Head of Dulce Base Security, 6 copies of everything is made before he goes into hiding. His wife and child are abducted by agents before he can reach them however. He never

The Omega Files

sees them again. Castello describes earlier work as a top secret photo analyst during which he developed a role of film showing an 'Adamski' type craft with a 'swastika' on the side. 800100 - Peter Gersten secures two UFO-related documents from NSA under FOIA. Reference to 239 documents which could not be released because of 'national security' restrictions. 800800 - Intrusions by [Nazi?/Grey?] aerial disks at Manzano Weapons Storage area at Kirtland AFB, N.M., filmed by Paul Bennewitz. 801100 - Paul Bennewitz still being monitored by NASA with assistance from Fugate Miller. 801126 - SA Doty receives call from Senator Schmidt of N.M. Asks OSI's role in connection with Bennewitz. 820427 - NSA admits it has over 239 top secret documents which relate to 'UFOs'. 830409 - AFOSI agent [Kirtland AFB, NM] Richard Doty shows Linda Howe Presidential Briefing on UFOs. 830409 - Paul Bennewitz gets interviewed. Determines Dulce base location. 840000 - Rex-84 exercises [FEMA] test ability to round up people and confine. 840426 - Lt. Gen. Bond killed at Area 51 during disk test. 850000 - Livermore Labs begin to manufacture artificial blood for Dulce Facility [Los Alamos, Rand Corp., Dept. of Energy connections to Dulce]. 870000 - 'Dulce Papers' released — Data on Five entrances to [upper] Dulce lab is leaked. 871011 - Las Vegas paper reports on Area 51, DREAMland. 880325 - John Lear released public statement on status of affairs, referring to UFO's and CIA [Nazi] activity in the underground base at Dulce, etc. 880600 - Pres. Bush proposes converting unused military bases to prisons. 880700 - John Reynolds contacts Paul Bennewitz in New Mexico. John Lear attempts to contact Bill English about Grudge 13 report. 890000 - Project Excalibur: Develops earth-penetrating nuclear warheads to destroy underground enemy bunkers or bases. 890100 - William Cooper and John Lear issue indictment to the President. 890226 - William Cooper sends 536 copies of Indictment to Congress. 2 replies. 890517 - Roads to Archuleta Mesa above Dulce, New Mexico are roadblocked to prevent intrusion. 890927 - Researcher Greg Keith, in an article in THE WALL STREET JOURNAL, relates statistics that 2 out of 3 black children are aborted, and that 43 percent of all abortions are performed on black women. Keith accuses Margaret Sanger, based on her own admissions, of being a SOCIAL ENGINEER — one of many who have targeted Blacks, Jews, Eastern Europeans and other NON-ARYANS for reduction and extermination through population control, genocide, infanticide-abortion, sterilization, etc.

The Omega Files

4. NAZI HISTORY PART II

The following is a more detailed 'chronology' released by Leading Edge Research, with a few comments of my own added:

1793 — JOHANN ROCKEFELLER of GERMANY comes to the USA, probably the deadliest immigrant America will ever know. Not because he was a German but because he was a German RACIST with some very dangerous international banking cult connections.

1919 — Adolph Hitler joins the Thule Society in Germany. In the Thule Society, the 'black sun' played a prominent role as a 'sacred' symbol of the Aryans. The inner core within the **Thule Society are all Satanists**. (Note: Just what would motivate these Satanists in their agendas for global conquest? The answer is that they do not believe in an Almighty God, therefore they believe that they can get away with it. I'm afraid that these cultists are in for a rude awakening. This present file is evidence of that, since without the intervention of a "higher power" working behind the scenes through all of those who have contributed to this document, I can state with all confidence that you would not be reading these words right now. - Branton)

1932 — Adolph Hitler gains control of German society enough to force scientists to work in laboratories on advanced aircraft design. Aided by the implosion vortex technology of Victor Schauberger, and the technical expertise of scientists like Schriever, Habermohl, Ballenzo and Miethe, the Germans make extraordinary progress. There is evidence that they might have been aided by contact with Gray entities from inside the Earth and an 'Ashtar' connected group of humanoid aliens in Aldebaran.

1933 — A profusion of German 'tourists' swarm over the southwestern United States, buying land, checking mineral rights and also exploring caves and caverns. This was discovered during a background check on some of the cities [and newspapers] in New Mexico.

1934 — the vast Rockefeller financial empire, in an effort to back German racial superiority and eugenics, financially supports Nazi Germany in collaboration with Prescott Bush [George Bush's father]. In 1929 the German Ernst Rudin enacts German Sterilization Laws.

1939 — Operation Canned Meat begins, where the Germans stage an incident at the Polish border as a prelude to the invasion. As a result of newly acquired technology, the German scientific effort is pushed forward by leaps

The Omega Files

and bounds, and is developed at several underground research facilities at Reinickendorf, Kummersdorf and Thuringia. The earliest "pilotless aircraft" were produced in 1934, and had some moderate degree of success. The United States was quite aware of the German technical progress and sent an American named Wilson to Germany to "give technical assistance" and generally to keep an eye on German technology. It was probably by virtue of Wilson that the Germans never used their [anti] gravitational craft en mass in the war, for Wilson attained a high position in the German technical community, and switched propulsion methods from gravitational to advanced jet propulsion in an apparent effort to "get technology out there to fight the war". Because of this, German gravitational research remained in the labs and stayed in the R&D [Research & Development] phase until around 1941, when the Schriever/Miethe designs were successfully tested. It was clearly a situation where the war was going on faster than the Germans could technically develop their designs. Hampered by sabotage and deliberate technical misguidance from Wilson, as well as delays in metallurgical research which didn't result in an acceptable alloy of magnesium and aluminum until 1944, the Germans could only continue to harass allied pilots with the 'fireballs', pilotless craft developed and used since 1942 which emitted electrical fields that interfered with the operation of aviation engines.

1943 — General Reinhard Gehlen infiltrates Soviet intelligence. Gehlen forms a partnership with Allen Dulles [a Bavarian Illuminist and American 'Nazi'], which results in the creation of the CIA [and some years later the more powerful NSA] from a core of Nazi SS intelligence officers brought to the US under the auspices of Operation Sunrise, Overcast, and Paperclip.

1945 — The British discover German plans for advanced craft and joined the efforts of the United States to subvert the German program. Obviously those agents who would later become the core of the 'CIA' were not involved in this attempt to subvert the secret German projects, in that the CIA was originally established as a fifth-column for Bavarian intelligence operations in America. On February 16, despite allied efforts, the Germans successfully flew a crew-carrying version of the 'fireball' from the underground facilities in Thuringia. The craft had a top speed of over 12,500 mph. The craft was called the 'Kugelblitz'. The Germans in the scientific community knew the war was lost as early as 1942, due to signs of an imminent alliance between America, Great Britain and Russia. They decided to establish a plan for continuing the dream of the Third Reich in spite of the war.

The Omega Files

They decided that the establishment of a separate society founded on Nazi principles of genetic purity was the answer. The development of gravitational technology aided that plan. On February 23, the newest engines of the Kugelblitz were tested and then extracted from the craft. The 'shell' or 'casing' of the Kugelblitz, minus the engines, was blown up by SS personnel and the scientists, plans and engines were shipped out of Germany to the South Polar regions, where the Germans had maintained underground construction activity since 1941. Two days later, on February 25, the underground plant at Khala was closed and all the workers sent to Buchenwald and gassed. The Germans also sent their "Aryan elite" children and other elements of their society to the underground bases. General Hans Kammler, who disappeared in April 1945, was instrumental in the evacuation operation, as was General Nebe. There, the Germans developed a eugenic society that apparently is limited to a specific number of people. They're still there. Apparently they also maintain underground technical colonies in South America. On April 12, Roosevelt dies and Harry Truman, a high **Mason** as was Roosevelt, becomes President of the United States. On May 7, 1945, Germany surrenders. Both the Americans and Soviets gain access to elements of German disk technology and scientists which the German Nazi elite had neglected to eliminate before their hasty departure at the close of the war. The British Canadians also had access to some of the data that the United States had acquired, as well as some data directly from the German efforts. On September 20th, Wernher Von Braun and other V-2 colleagues arrive in Boston, Mass and are transported to White Sands New Mexico to work in the U.S. missile program (Note: Von Braun along with other 'Paperclip' Nazi SS personnel were at the 'treaty signing' event at Muroc-Edwards AFB in 1954 according to Dr. Hank Krastman, when the NSA officially entered into a pact with the reptilian Grays. Previous to this the Nazis [Bavarian Thule Society] and Scottish Rite Masons [Bavarian Illuminati] had established 'treaties' with subterranean-based 'Gray' and 'Reptiloid' species that were in turn in contact with others of their kind beyond the confines of planet earth - Branton). Over 1,000 Nazi S.S. scientists are transported to the United States by Bavarian cult members operating in high-level economic and political positions in America — the 'Corporate-Fascist' government — and are given false papers in order to work for the "U.S. government". These Nazi S.S. infiltrators continue to infiltrate the electorate government of the United States of America via their fascist 'parasitic' fifth column government centered around the CIA, NSA, AQUARIUS, etc.

The Omega Files

1946 — Bavarian-connected agents within the United States eco-political structure import German S.S. intelligence officers in an effort to form what later becomes the Central Intelligence Agency. This Agency, initially an "intelligence gathering" office, soon commenced to spreading its influence throughout the entire U.S. intelligence community to the point where it became the controlling influence over all intelligence efforts and in fact a "secret government" in and of itself. The influence spreads beyond the borders of the U.S.A. as the CIA engages in a 'covert war' against the world superpowers and third world counties, assassinating undesirable leaders and replacing them with fascist CIA-backed military juntas, etc. This was part of a plan that was formulated by Allen Dulles and Reinhard Gehlen in 1943, when a deal was cut with German intelligence to provide the "United States" with a viable intelligence operation as well as provide German intelligence agents with "a place to go after the war". A good inducement, indeed. Remember that the Nazi's were backed by American bankers who were/are members of the Bavarian secret society lodges, as were the Nazi's themselves. Did millions of Allies shed their blood during World War II only to be betrayed by traitors in our midst?

1947 — The Germans, having had two years to get it together after the war, started making flyovers of the United States in their disks, which had by then achieved a remarkable degree of development. This prompted the United States to undertake plans to ascertain both the exact location of the German bases at the Pole and their technical capabilities. In 1947, Operation Highjump was conducted around Antarctica in an attempt to locate the Germans. It was a failure. The Germans used their technology to thwart the efforts of the United States. It wasn't until 1958 during the International Geophysical Year that another major attempt to do something about the German problem was made. Various polar expeditions that occurred in between 1947 and 1958 had intelligence as part of their design, and also seemed to evoke activity from other forces and entities from inside the Earth. There also seems to be some evidence that the Germans made contact with alien forces from inside the planet in relation to their activities in Antarctica. In 1947, the United States decided that the problem with both THE GERMANS AND THE ALIENS was getting a little dangerous. It was necessary for the U.S. 'government' to implement severe measures in order to hide the truth of the alien presence. The German problem was easier to control as far as public knowledge was concerned. In September 1947, TRUMAN caused the National Security Act to be passed in order to hide the activities of the Government, the CIA, and

The Omega Files

the alien problem. Was Truman aware of the Nazi infiltration of the U.S. intelligence community? Whether or not this was the case, Truman did sign a 'treaty' with the 'Reptilians' as part of his involvement with the 33-plus degrees of Scottish Rite Masonry, whose International 'Bankster' members had financed the Nazis up until the point where Adolph Hitler had become too hard to control. Whether Truman was directly aware of the fact that his sponsors, the German-American Rockefellers, had financed the Bolshevik and Nazi revolutions, is uncertain. CIA mind-control projects began at Bathesda Naval Hospital in 1947, with data gained from German S.S. intelligence. Truman created a study group in order to 'control' the alien problem, at least half of whose original members were affiliated with Bavarian-backed international banking fraternities like the Council on Foreign Relations. This study group was called MJ-12, PI-40 or ALPHA-2. A series of National Security Council [NSC] memos removed the CIA from the sole task of gathering foreign intelligence and slowly 'legalized' direct action in the form of covert activities. The memos, including NSC-10/1 and NSC-10/2, established a buffer between the President of the United States and the activities that were going on, as well as providing a means for the President to deny knowledge of any covert activities. Of course, all of this was un-Constitutional. Unfortunately Congress did not know what was going on either, as these 'appointed' representatives of the military-industrial complex began to take control of the U.S. government away from the 'elected' Congressional-Senatorial representatives of the Constitutional government. In 1947, FIFTY PERCENT of the CIA was composed of Nazi S.S. intelligence personnel, mostly within the inner covert ops segments of the agency. (Note: If this is the case, then it would be logical to suggest that it is THIS fifty percent of the Nazi 'German'-ated CIA which interacts with the greys and reptiloids within the Dulce, Denver Airport, Area-51 and Montauk bases, etc. - Branton)

    1952 — Reinhard Gehlen and Allen Dulles are dubbed Knights of Malta by the VATICAN. (Note: According to THE SECRET HISTORY OF THE JESUITS, by Edmond Paris, a large number of Jesuits assisted in the development of — and occupied powerful positions within — the Nazi S.S. Could the mass-murder of the Jews and the Russian Greek Orthodox Serbians in Yugoslavia during World War II have been a continuation of the Vatican's INQUISITION against its enemies?. The ancient 'Babylonian Mystery Society' which has reportedly maintained a secret line of Pontifex Maximus leaders since the time of King Nimrod, has been using the so-called 'Holy Roman Empire' as a 'cover' for its secret activities — in affiliation with the Jesuit lodge which cre-

The Omega Files

ated the Scottish Rite as a tool for infiltrating Masonry — and has maintained a strong presence within the Nazi S.S. The unknowing lay members of the Catholic Church and of NEARLY EVERY MAJOR DENOMINATION on the planet which has been infiltrated by the gnostic Jesuit lodge and their hatchlings — the Bavarian Illuminati, Bavarian Thule societies, and the so-called Scottish Rite of Masonry — should not be blamed for this subversion of the global political-economic-religious systems, that is if they have no knowledge of the conspiracy. I REITERATE here and throughout this File that I am not personally against any individual members of errant or apostate 'control' structures who are being 'used' against their knowledge for internationally destructive agendas, but rather against the 'regressive' control structures themselves. THAT is our target. If one wishes to be a Roman Catholic or a member of any other religion, fine... however when that 'religion' begins to pry into the realm of economic and political CONTROL at the expense of the freedom of others, then these 'religions' must be willing to face criticism for involving themselves in these areas, and refrain from hypocritically crying "your attacking my 'religious beliefs'". When an organization becomes a political and economic force of CONTROL, it has CEASED becoming a 'religion'. How much more for 'religions' who profess to have faith in Jesus of Nazareth - the Christ - or Melchizedek... the same one who in His zeal had 'cleansed' the Temple of those who were using 'religion' to fill their own money bags. Some organizations have lost the 'right' to be called exclusively 'religions' and must now be classed as economic-political power-cult structures. No matter how well-intentioned humans are, if they place themselves ABOVE their fellow human beings, then there is the temptation to use their knowledge or position to CONTROL those below them. It is religious POWER STRUCTURES which divide humanity through "holy wars" and such, NOT individual 'believers'. - Branton)

1953 — Albert K. Bender's International Flying Saucer Bureau was closed down following work on a theory linking disks with Antarctica. Bender is visited by MIB [Men In Black] and persuaded to stop his research. These were apparently transdimensional humanoid 'MIBs' — although there have also been reports of MIB reptiloids, androids, and U.S. government agents who have themselves taken on the label of "Men In Black", possibly in imitation of the dark-clad alien intelligence agents who have threatened numerous UFO witnesses to remain silent. Eisenhower asks Nelson Rockefeller for help with the alien problem. This is where the idea for MJ-12 was born. It was probably a critical mistake in asking a member of the world financial

ized control group for help with the alien beings. Because of human nature, the true 'controllers' are those who control the world's wealth — the International Bankers — as they are able to buy-off the weak factions within all of the governments of every nation, including an 'apparent' Constitutional Republic like the United States of America.

5. David Emory's Talk Radio (On NAZIS)

The following are some of the subjects that radio personality David Emory has covered on his talk-radio broadcasts in California:

— The pivotal role that Nazi and fascist elements played in the assassination of President Kennedy... evidence that American and German "Neo-Nazis", the Gehlen spy organization and Nazi rocket specialists working under Werner Von Braun figured prominently in the killing.

— The support American industrialists and financiers gave to Hitler's Germany and how this affected the allied military policy during the war as well as the incorporation of the Third Reich's intelligence forces into the CIA at the conflict's conclusion.

— The SS origin of the Green Berets, the re-establishment of Nazi elements in West Germany after the war, as well as Nazi influences on Senator Joe McCarthy, Interpol and the Alger Hiss case.

— The pivotal role in the Cold War played by Hitler's most important spymaster and his Nazi Eastern Front intelligence organization... the Gehlen organization's incorporation into the CIA; its role in establishing Radio Free Europe AND the first Palestinian terrorist groups as well as Gehlen's personal political ideology.

— The evolution of American fascism from the 1930's to the present... attempts to overthrow President Roosevelt, suspend the constitution and establish a fascist dictatorship in the United States.

— The World Anti-Communist League... the composition and operation of this reactionary organization whose fascist elements have wielded tremendous influence in the operations of the U.S. national security establishment... the massive intersection between this organization and the network created by Nazi spymaster Reinhard Gehlen.

— Former Nazi SS Officer and CIA agent Skorzeny's role in developing the methodology of modern terrorism and training many terrorist orga-

The Omega Files

nizations... the connections of western [fascist] intelligence agencies to the Munich Olympics massacre of several Israelis in 1972. (Note: Munich, Germany is the capital of Bavaria, by the way - Branton).

— Evidence that the U.S. national security establishment may have been planning a fascist coup in response to a terrorist provocation... the "Rex 84" martial-law contingency plan and its implementation in response to a terrorist 'incident'. Rex '84 appears to stem from a contingency plan to intern black Americans in concentration camps.

— The Fourth Reich — the complicity of [fascist] elements of U.S. intelligence with international terrorists...

— The assassination program which eliminated the democratic leadership of Weimar Germany paving the way for Hitler's rise to power... the formation of the Nazi Party as a front for German military intelligence.

— The connections between the Third Reich and South African society. Particular emphasis is on the Broederbond [the Afrikaner elite society which effectively controls South Africa] and how that organization developed with help from Nazi Germany... how residual elements of the I.G. Farben chemical cartel helped the growing South African nuclear industry.

— Uncle Sam and the Swastika... documents the Third Reich as a historical outgrowth of the multi-national corporate capitalism. Focus is on the dominant role of American-based multi-nationals in financing and arming Nazi Germany.

— The Third Reich's extermination programs from the "mercy killing" of handicapped children to the Auschwitz death factory. The Nazi liquidation's are exposed as a direct outgrowth of the international eugenics and mental hygiene movements, both mainstream movements with important implications for contemporary society.

— The growing intersection of third reich veterans, Middle Eastern terrorists, European neo-fascists and European ultra-leftists in a new form of international fascism.

— Circumstantial evidence suggesting that then vice-president George Bush may have been involved with the attempt on the life of former President Reagan... the close connections between the family of convicted would-be assassin John Hinckley and the Bush family as well as Hinckley's Nazi background.

The Omega Files

— The Nazis: Anti-Semites on George Bush's Campaign... the participation of elements of the Gehlen organization, the World Anti-Communist League and the P-2 Lodge in George Bush's 1988 election campaign.

— The work of Mae Brussell, a political researcher whose research is the foundation of Mr. Emory's... the suspicious circumstances surrounding her death in 1988.

— Livin' In The USA: The Search for Nazi War Criminals. In 1985, the San Francisco Examiner listed ten Third Reich fugitives considered to be the "most wanted" of all war criminals... the fact that most of them worked for U.S. intelligence after the war.

— The role played by German neo-Nazis in the assassination of President Kennedy.

— Adolf Hitler's escape from Germany at the end of World War II using information contained in previously classified U.S. intelligence archives, accessed by a London Times journalist and discussed in a military history quarterly. The story was revealed to U.S. intelligence operatives during their debriefing of former Gestapo chief Heinrich Mueller prior to Mueller going to work for U.S. intelligence, employed Mueller because of his anti-Communist expertise. Confident that his situation with his U.S. sponsors-to-be was secure, Mueller disclosed that Hitler escaped to Spain after the war and that his place in the bunker [and the grave] was taken by a double who was a distant blood relative of the Fuehrer. Mueller's alleged death at the war's end has also been effectively de-bunked.

— The relationship between Arab Nationalist groups and the Third Reich analyzed... the cooperation between... American Nazi groups and the Nation of Islam under Elijah Mohammed and Louis Farrakhan.

— Richard Nixon's... efforts on behalf of Nazi war criminals living in America, his apparent role in the assassination of President Kennedy and that event's connections to the Watergate Scandal... Nixon's administration and the drug trade and Nixon's plan to stage a provocation at the 1972 Republican Convention in order to force a cancellation of the general elections that year and the establishment of martial law... an analysis of the international fascist political milieu that created Nixon and of which he was an integral part.

— Several elements of historical and operational continuity between

The Omega Files

the development of fascism prior to World War II and its resurgence over the last several decades. Comparing American scientific racism of the 1920s and 30s with current thinkers of that school... the profound influence of the American social legislation spawned by that racism on the Nazi racial laws that were the pretext for the Third Reich's extermination programs... the American 'prosecutorial' staff at Nuremberg who helped to exonerate numerous Nazi war criminals and who subsequently participated in the cover-up of President Kennedy's assassination... a possible fascist connection to the gun-control movement (Note: It is indeed curious that the American Psychiatric Association initially contained over 2,000 German 'immigrant' members following World War II. The APA also was/is involved in GUN CONTROL lobbying.- Branton), as well as a possible connection between that movement and the assassination of President Kennedy... the resurgence of Fascism in Italy and Germany stemming from the fascist elements left in place in these countries as a result of the laxness of individuals such as the American Nuremberg staffers. (Additional Note on the above - From the www.buildfreedom.com website we read: "A principle player in the 1974 foundings of both HCI [then called the National Council to Control Handguns] and the NCBH [National Coalition to Ban Handguns, now renamed the Coalition Against Gun Violence] was Ed Wells, who was A 25-YEAR VETERAN OF THE COVERT OPERATIONS DIVISION OF THE CIA... There was also a fund raiser for NCBH hosted by the man Nixon appointed as CIA Director, William Colby... HCI spokesman Greg Risch — incredibly — admitted that "SURE THERE ARE A LOT OF CIA PEOPLE IN IT [HCI]", and also stated that there are quite a few "EX-CIA WHO DONATE TO US." - Branton)

— Several reasons for American's lack of awareness of fascism, its history and its methodology: lowering American educational standards and the deliberate obfuscation of the historical connection between powerful industrial and financial interests and fascism. Both have significantly undermined contemporary understanding of the political forces which produced Hitler and Mussolini... details important episodes in the development of the French fascist forces that culminated in the Vichy collaborationist government of Marshall Petain. The role of French fascists in undermining France and contributing to the German victory of 1940 is one of many aspects of the history of fascism which has been deliberately obscured... the clandestine methodology of fascism, in particular the underground organizational structure of fascist movements and its effectiveness in subverting established democracies... the underground Nazi cells of contemporary Germany and

The Omega Files

their evolution from the cellular organization established by the Third Reich prior to its defeat... the Swedish fascist Per Engdahl, and his role in maintaining the continuity of fascism from Hitler and Mussolini to the present. The re-emergence of fascism in Austria and the Czech Republic... [and] international networking between neo-Nazis... collaboration between neo-Nazis and national intelligence services, and connections between neo-Nazis and 'respectable' power politicians... Liberty Lobby, an influential American fascist organization.

— America's importation of the Gehlen organization after World War II, the 1934 Fascist coup attempt against FDR...

HOW THE UNITED STATES LOST THE SECOND WORLD WAR — RFA37

"America didn't win the war. Adolph Hitler won world war II." — Guatemalan president Jose Arevalo, after being replaced by dictator Jocabo Arbenz in 1951 The following is a synopsis of an extensive investigative series by David Emory revealing a working hypothesis that during the Cold War, German fascism and the Third Reich did not disappear as is commonly believed but rather survived underground and achieved a very real political and economic victory over the Allies. In the aftermath of World War I, the German Nazis learned that anti-communism could be used to achieve strategic leverage over Germany's prospective enemies such as Great Britain and the United States. The Third Reich utilized this stratagem to establish Fifth Column movements in countries they had targeted for conquest. Those movements were composed largely of sympathizers who viewed the Third Reich as a bulwark against communism. The Third Reich sought to escape the full consequences of military defeat in World War II by playing the anti-Communist card again. When it became clear that the armies of the Third Reich were going to be defeated, it opened secret negotiations with representatives from the Western Allies. Representatives on both sides belonged to the transatlantic FINANCIAL and INDUSTRIAL fraternity that had actively supported fascism... Viewed by the Nazis as a vehicle for surviving military defeat, [this collaboration] involved a Hitler-less Reich joining with the [international financial cults of] U.S., Britain, France and other European nations in a transatlantic, pan-European anti-Soviet alliance (This has apparently led to their European Economic Community — later known as the European Community or E.C. — conquest of Europe via economic manipulation rather than through force. - Branton).

The Omega Files

The de-Nazification of Germany was aborted. Although a few of the more obvious and obnoxious elements of Nazism were removed, Nazis were returned to power at virtually every level and in almost every capacity in the Federal Republic of Germany. A Hilter-less Reich then was incorporated into the anti-Soviet alliance the Third Reich's leaders had envisioned - NATO. One of the central elements in RFA37, the Reinhard Gehlen spy organization, functioned as a Trojan Horse vis-a-vis the United States. By deliberately exaggerating Soviet intentions and capabilities in order to alarm the United States, the Gehlen organization greatly exacerbated cold-war tensions and manipulated them to Germany's advantage. Perhaps the most important effect of the Gehlen organization was to introduce "rollback" or "liberation theory" into American strategic thinking. Rollback was a political warfare and covert operation strategy which had its genesis in the Third Reich Ostministerium headed by Alfred Rosenberg. This strategy entailed enlisting the aid of dissident Soviet ethnic minorities to overthrow the Soviet Union. In return, these minorities and their respective republics were to be granted nominal independence while serving as satellite states of "Greater Germany." In its American incarnation, liberation theory called for "rolling back" communism out of Eastern Europe and the break-up of the Soviet Union into its constituent ethnic Republics. Lip-service was given to initiating democracy in the 'liberated' countries. Liberation theory was projected into mainstream American political consciousness through the Crusade for Freedom. This enormous CIA domestic media campaign not only established liberation theory as a dominant element in American strategic thinking but also projected European fascists associated with the Gehlen milieu into positions of prominence within the powerful ethnic voting blocks in America.

The Gehlen imports combined with domestic reactionary elements to form a powerful fascistic and ultimately triumphant political engine referred to in RFA37, as the "rollback" or "liberation milieu." RFA37 traces the evolution of this milieu and its influence on international and domestic political affairs. The liberation milieu cemented its triumph in American politics through the assassination of President Kennedy. The program highlights the roles of Gehlen-related elements and intelligence agents associated with the PETROLEUM industry (as in the Rockefeller-connected EXXON, ZAPATA and ATLANTIC RICHFIELD or ARCO oil companies - Branton) in the JFK assassination. Particular emphasis is on George Bush's connections to this milieu as well as the milieu's relationship to the defense industry, military intelligence and CORPORATE America. RFA37 analyzes the Reagan and Bush

The Omega Files

administrations as the realization of the goals of liberation theory as well as the fulfillment of National Security Counsel #68. NSC 68 was the blueprint for U.S. strategy during the Cold War. Heavily influenced by the work of the Gehlen organization, NSC 68 called for the destabilization of the U.S.S.R. through a massive military buildup by the U.S. The strategy sought to bankrupt the Soviet economy through an arms race and to promote agitation among the dissident Soviet ethnic groups by Gehlen-related intelligence elements. In addition, the document called for an accompanying propaganda blitz in the United States to convince the American people to support the military buildup as well as the suppression of political dissidents. The Reagan and Bush administrations instituted the principles of NSC 68 and accomplished the aims of liberation theory. The realization of those goals also did enormous damage to the United States.

The cost of bankrupting the Soviet Union, turned the United States into the world's biggest debtor nation, severely damaged its infrastructure and crippled its competitive economic advantage internationally. In addition, the United States badly compromised its democratic institutions during the Cold War, possibly beyond repair. RFA37 hypothesizes that the realization of liberation theory primarily benefited GERMANY rather than the United States. Indeed, the recovery of Germany's "lost territories" was the goal of Gehlen's alliance with the western powers and was the raison d'etre for the Vertviebene groups. Founded by the SS and funded by the German government, the Vertriebene groups were part of the liberation milieu described above. (Note: Is it any coincidence then, that the true NERVE CENTER of the European Community or E.C. aka the 'New World Order' is GERMANY? - Branton). Their activity has increased dramatically since the end of the Cold War. The BND, the current German government intelligence service and the final incarnation of the Gehlen organization, has been extremely active in the newly 'liberated' territories where it has worked hand in glove with major German corporations and the various Nazi parties of Germany to realize Hitler's goal of a "greater Germany." A REAL-LIFE "ODESSA FILE"?: Confirmation of the above seems to have come from an anonymous individual who has released the following information — among other revelations — throughout the newsgroups via an anonymous news server... The following to me is reminiscent of the theme of the movie "THE ODESSA FILE", starring John Voight and set in 1963 West Germany: Newsgroups: alt.conspiracy.jfk,alt.mindcontrol From: an166618@anon.penet.fi Date: Sun, 11 Dec 1994 23:52:22 UTC Subject: JFK hit small part of conspiracy.

The Omega Files

7. MY 10-YEAR INVESTIGATION OF THE GROUP THAT HAS NO NAME

INTRODUCTION: The JFK assassination involved a much bigger conspiracy than Cuba or the Mob or the CIA or all 3 put together. It was planned, run and covered up by an international Group that has no name. I'm in the process of completing an investigation and expose on that Group's activities that I began in the early '80s. This investigation began after I encountered evidence of torture and mind control techniques among workers at a chemical plant involved in some litigation I handled in the late '70s. I'm posting this very short piece because I would like confirmation of those portions that can be corroborated before I complete the work. I do not seek to chat about it and I do not want anyone's approval or disapproval of the events or ideas. Unless you have been involved in it or are some sort of spook it's all going to sound very strange...

Based on the following very, very brief summary of a huge file on this subject, it seems apparent to me that you have each played a witting or unwitting role in treason. Those of you who think you have been serving a "better cause" should heed these words and THINK about what you have been doing to your country. For those readers who think mysterious forces are sending radio waves into their heads and bodies, or the like, please don't send responses or messages to me. On the other hand, if you've had flashbacks to violent events that you can't understand; if you recall your hands doing things that you didn't control; if you've awakened in a hotel room not knowing how you got there, read a newspaper story about a dead general or Congressman, recognized the picture and wondered if you were the one who did it; or if the phrase "remember to forget" has a great significance to you, you may want to read on & consider contacting me. [Contact must be through anonymous file server anon.penet.fi so that neither of us knows the other.

If it seems a worthwhile lead to me, I will reply by E-Mail to your anon id. Please do not contact me unless you use a password going through anon.penet.fi. I won't respond otherwise.] In 1983 I undertook to determine the reason for and the people responsible for the torture and behavior conditioning at the factory. Since then the investigation has broadened step-by-step into a much, much larger investigation. I cannot possibly recap the full story here. The initial course of the investigation has required over 400 pages of draft to adequately explain. So let it suffice to say that within the

The Omega Files

first 18 months I obtained identifications [photograph] from two independent witnesses of the principal torturer as Dr. Joseph Mengele. The same witnesses later identified [photograph] the man who was directing Mengele's activities as a person who was at one time the DIRECTOR of the CIA. Another key player in the Group's activities in Vietnam, the RFK hit, Watergate and various assassinations of American military and civilian leaders was one of that Director's highly-placed subordinates, who only recently left CIA.

This second CIA LEADER will be referred to in this piece by the same code name he used with my informant: Mr. Halloran. My primary sources for the mind control comments are in-depth, videotaped interrogations in awake states, as well as under deep hypnosis in conjunction with two hypnosis experts [one of whom has served as president of one of the internationally-recognized bodies in the field] of three witnesses. My primary source for the comments on the Group, its plans, goals, methods and history is one of the three above witnesses who appears to have been the illegitimate son of GEN. REINHARD GEHLEN resulting from the general's participation in the lebensborn program in 1942-43. He informs me that lebensborn continued well into the "70s, seemingly headquartered in FRANKFURT (Frankfurt is incidentally the traditional headquarters of the so-called Holy Roman Empire which ruled Europe with an iron hand during the Dark Ages. - Branton).

A significant part of the following account and the individuals mentioned in it is based on my informant's conversations with the man who appears to have been his father, Gen. Gehlen, in various parts of the Northeast & in Langley beginning in about 1953; briefings held by various spokesmen but mostly by the former CIA Director at the NY offices of a well-known (Rockefeller? - Branton) Foundation, which appears to be the American 'host' for the Group; and a list of the Group's members and agents that my informant was instructed to memorize during the period 1975-1987 in preparation for his intended role in the Group. In many cases it is not known whether the individuals' names were listed because they are 'players' or because they have been coerced into cooperation through blackmail or economic means or are associates of real 'players' who can control the named individuals. Thousands of names have been identified from virtually all walks of life, including such unexpected groups as the Nobel Committee [and] Vatican City... My informant states that over the years only a very, very few of the many thousands on the list have known the real plan and the real goals.

The Omega Files

8. THE COVERT WAR

A covert war has been waged against the people of this country and other countries for over 50 years. Some casualties of that war are people whose deaths are already suspect, but no one can quite put their finger on the real motive. John F. Kennedy, Bobby Kennedy, Martin Luther King. JFK by 4 marksmen, of which 2-3 actually got off shots, one of whom was a well-known French contract assassin headquartered in Madrid. (Note: these assassins would most likely include the 2 mafia hit-men behind the 'grassy' knoll and the 'tramps' who were assigned to pick up the spent shells; the CIA patsy Oswald in the Book Depository and another hit-man who shot from a building across from the book depository. Others allege that William Greer — the secret service limo driver — got off a quick shot with a handgun, which would make him the 5th gunman if we are to believe some scenarios. This would explain statements made by Dr. Charles Crenshaw, one of the original doctors who worked on JFK's body shortly after his death. On the April 2, 1992, segment of Geraldo Rivera's "NOW IT CAN BE TOLD", Crenshaw claimed that he saw Kennedy's head-wound and stated that Oswald could not have killed Kennedy as he was behind the President, whereas the fatal bullet wound came from the FRONT.

Crenshaw claimed that the bullet entered from the front and exited from the rear of his skull, leaving a large gaping wound 9-10 centimeters across. Although Texas law required an immediate autopsy in Dallas, the site of the crime, Crenshaw insisted that a swarm of Secret Service agents entered the hospital and demanded that the autopsy be performed out of state. It is interesting that the Secret Service of the U.S. and other countries are reportedly patched directly into the highest levels of Scottish Rite Masonry, or the Bavarian Illumiati. Dr, Crenshaw stated that several people he had known who had witnessed the President's wounds had died shortly afterwards under strange circumstances. He believed that the 'official' photos taken at Bathesda Naval hospital showing no ear exit wound were tampered with and that the whole affair was covered up. Branton). An assist on the job goes to an Oswald 'double' supplied by the KGB section headed in 1963 by a very high-ranking recent leader of the USSR. The 'double' killed Officer Tippit in plain view for no reason other than to implicate Oswald. JFK, by a security guard [Thane] & Sirhan, Sirhan [who was conditioned to kill and to forget both the kill and his control]. King, by someone unknown to us, but my source worked with 'Raul' [also used over 10 other code names] at CIA

The Omega Files

from 1967-83. 'Raul's' expertise for [the] CIA was the perfect "set-up" of innocent people in crimes. The MLK hit was the first and only time he did a set up in a political assassination. The whole Warren Commission seems to have been fixed, beginning with Warren and 3 other members of the Commission, all of whom my informant identified as agents of the Group. Every witness who could shed light on the Kennedy murders has been systematically hunted down and murdered. [I seek information from those who were in it. I believe I already know one who was. You might know something about it if you recognize the code name BLACKHAWK. If so, think about it.] Other victims of assassination by the Group whose names will be recognized include Franklin D. Roosevelt, Marilyn Monroe, Mahatma Gandhi, Anwar Sadat & Olof Palme. There have been many thousands more.

9. THE ORIGIN OF THE GROUP

The precursor of the subversive Group seems to have been formed in the first quarter of the century, we think in connection with the formation of the Federal Reserve. At first it appears to have been little more than a group of the world's leading investment and merchant bankers seeking world-wide control of money supply. But by about 1932 it developed into a scheme for a New World Order, in which there would be total control of human behavior by a world government. They sponsored Hitler through two of their most important German members: Paul von Hindenburg and Franz von Papen. By the 1930s the key players seem to have included Hess [who flew to England in 1941 ONLY because he was 'blown'] and then Bormann in the Nazi government; Schrwder and the ENTIRE Reichsbank sr. officer list in German banking; most of the major merchant banking houses in London, some of the key banks in NY, Sweden, France, Switzerland & Netherlands, along with the Bank for Int'l Settlements [infamous for its crediting the Nazis with ownership of the looted Austrian, Czech, Belgian and Netherlands gold]; the monarchs of England, Italy, Spain, Portugal, Austria [the Archduke], Hungary [Regent], & Japan; and some of the key men in the Fall of France, like Viscount Gort and Admiral Forbes; and two American generals who none of you would believe. (I would suspect that one of these 'generals' might have been Dwight D. Eisenhower — whose campaign was sponsored by the Rockefellers and through whose administration many of the national socialist policies of the Rockefellers were implemented within the U.S. Intelligence Agencies — although this is only my guess. Due to Eisenhower's part in the war against the Nazi's and his warning to Americans about the dangers of the Military-Industrial Complex, it may be that Eisenhower was an ethical man, yet had opened the door for access to certain levels of government by Rockefeller interests, aware of or unaware of the Rockefeller ties to the Nazi's AND the Military-Industrial complex. He may have merely been a 'dupe' or a 'pawn', like so many other naive members of the U.S. Government. -

10. CURRENT ORGANIZATION & GOALS FOR THE NEW WORLD ORDER

Today the Group consists of international bankers [the same core of NY, London, Swiss and German merchant bankers, but now expanded to the largest banks in many other parts of the world, notably Japan and in the Middle East], kings, at least one queen, princes, industrialists [among the world's top 100 CEOs +/or Chairmen... a heavy concentration in autos], Army, Navy, Air Force, & Marine Corps generals, State department section chiefs, Mafia chiefs, drug lords, elected officials, judges at all levels, many media owners, a host of leading lawyers, and many others. The leadership of the Group comes from its EUROPEAN parent organization, consisting of many of Europe's key bankers, industrialists, & politicians. They want to impose on this planet a centralized world oligarchy — not a democracy — akin to a FASCIST state in which there will be genocide on a massive scale, total state control over all aspects of human behavior and communication and control of the human mind and spirit through manipulation of the world's major religions, genetic engineering, drugs, tightly-controlled media and by other means. There will be death camps in which 'undesirable' races, the old and infirm, and those without "social utility" will be exterminated without a trace. The institution of state-sanctioned slavery will be re-established. There will no longer be families as we know the institution. There will be a MASTER RACE in charge of all this power — the ARYAN RACE, augmented by advanced genetics, and bred for superior characteristics. Their target date is the coming second millennium, the year 2000. If you want details of their plan, with an approximate day-to-day blueprint of life under the new regime, read Brave New World. Huxley apparently knew about the plan from his brother.

11. THE GROUP'S OPERATIONS SINCE W.W.II

When their man, Hitler, went out of control they drugged him into oblivion and implemented the death camp 'model' under Bormann. Early in

The Omega Files

W.W.II there was a conference hosted by King George in the English countryside at which representatives from all walks of life from all over agreed on a plan to undermine and overthrow the US and Russian states. Representatives of all the monarchies mentioned above attended. At the end of W.W.II, GEN. GEHLEN ran two operations in Spring, 1945 for them: the assassination of FDR using a chemical that caused the cerebral hemorrhage and immediate death and the [attempted] elimination of Hitler with a bullet from Bormann's gun [without Hitler's 'consent']. FDR's offense was that he refused to approve their COVER AGENCY, the CIA. [Not the agent level generally. The liaison and intermediate levels with some key men at the top levels, particularly in Covert Ops.] GEHLEN ran the American, AS WELL AS THE European 'security' operations until his death in '79. Their 'assassination' techniques for those who get in the way begin with character assassination. When that fails, they train and finance real assassins who generally do not use bullets these days. The favored methods are carefully tailored to the victims' medical files to make death look 'natural' through barely-detectable chemicals that artificially cause heart attacks, cerebral hemorrhages, Alzheimer disease, leukemia, & brain tumors.

12. THE GROUP'S FUNDING; CONGRESSIONAL PAYOFF

During W.W.II the Group arranged through the GERMAN war machine and von Ribbentrop's 'diplomacy' to loot the treasuries of Austria, Belgium, Czechoslovakia, The Netherlands, other states and the gold and jewels once owned by murdered Jews. Gehlen oversaw the 'Odesa' operation in about 1942-45 in which most of the bullion, stolen art, and the Jews' gold was shipped by various means to ARGENTINA. The missing gold alone, in PRE-1939 DOLLARS, was worth $600 million. [Go look up what pre-'39 $ are worth. Multiply it out.] Since then the Group has used the bullion cache as credit for its operations, including ECONOMIC WARFARE against the US. It remained in ARGENTINA at least until both of the Per_ns were in power. Bormann was one of the Nazis who controlled access to it in Argentina, but I suspect the former Argentine WWII Nazi espionage chief, Johannes Siegfried Becker, played a big role. [Bullion site switched after Per_ns. I suspect to Venezuela, based on a meeting between my informant and Becker in Venezuela in the late 1970s.] In addition, a good part of the funding over the years has come from large-scale diversions of funds from all major treasuries in the western world. I believe the principal method involves diverting cash credits for funds coming into the government through the Group's control of central banks like the Federal Reserve & apparent subversion of agency accounting chiefs. My informant has also identified the names of several of the top men in IRS and Treasury FMS. The 'skim' appears to be about .5% of all incoming funds. My informant states that a significant portion of the diverted funds go to campaign funds for members of Congress as 'protection' or the like. So there is no one in the Government who has much interest in looking into this diversion. Even those in Congress who are 'clean' are typically co-opted by promises of more power or are just squelched.

13. DESTRUCTION OF THE AMERICAN SOCIETY

This has been a carefully-planned fifty-year war. The late 40s and 50s were spent putting their agents in place and rebuilding their main clients' European industrial base — with American money. The initial steps in the American overthrow occurred in the 1960's through several of the Group's most critical agents — Earl Warren and LBJ, with assists from J. Edgar Hoover and others. [Chief Justice Warren, unlike LBJ, was an unwilling agent. The Group forced Warren to participate in the JFK cover-up and the Group's plan to alter the social structure of US because they "had something on him."] One of the first things the Group did to protect its own covert operation was one of Gen. Gehlen's specialties in WWII Nazi intelligence — divert attention to the "Red menace." There is also a pattern of identifications by my informant of petitioners and/or their chief lawyers in a series of Supreme Court cases in the 1950s and 1960s that made it impossible for the Fed or state governments to conduct thorough investigations into subversive organizations.

While I applaud the civil liberties aspects, I suspect that this was only 'window dressing' for the true purpose. What the Group wanted by the time of the "incubation period" [1995-2000] was a society that was uneducated, amoral, uncommitted to democratic institutions, living in fear, with a sudden and very drastic reduction in spendable income simultaneous with societal chaos. The Group thought that this would produce the environment for 'rejection' of the democratic form of government that they seek by 2000. In the 1960s the Group's agents started the process of eliminating religious and moral ideals from American life, particularly in the schools [& in that regard go back & read the dissents in the Supreme Court cases, accurately stating that the Founding Fathers would turn over in their graves to learn that what they wrote in Philadelphia in the 1780s outlaws prayer in schools], removed as many impediments to criminality as they could get away with, dramatically increased media [TV] portrayal of violence and joblessness [role models have no jobs, bad guys live in big houses, etc.; begin your reading with 'The Early Window', by Liebert & Sprafkin], reduced the standards of education and early training for rational thought and fostered every possible dislocation in family structure they could engineer, beginning with LBJ's welfare policies...

14. THE COMING CHAOS

The plan is to unleash elemental forces of chaos that transcend government philosophy. The primitive mandate for political/social structure seems to be protection of the person from crime and disease, protection of property, a system of justice to enforce those protections, and organization for economic gain. All these refinements we've developed - democracy, fascism, communism, monarchy - come after the primitive mandates have been met. The theory is that if you remove enough of those basic protections the government will fall because it is not performing the more important, elementary functions. This subject is an enormous one which I could not begin to describe in such a short piece as this. The reader will have to fill in the blanks left by the following examples:

DISEASE: The Group developed the AIDS virus principally at Albert Ludwigs University in Freiburg im Brisgau. It seems that Dr. Strecker and the London Times [5/11/87] were correct in suspecting that the epidemic was man-made and connected with the World Health Organization's smallpox eradication program in Africa [My source identified the names of a senior member of the Global Commission in 1979, who handled at least Ethiopia and Somalia, and W.H.O. representatives for Central Africa, where the AIDS virus is taking the largest toll, and for Western Africa] and the 1978-79 hepatitis B vaccine experiments among homosexuals in the U.S. [My source identified the name of one member of the NY City team. I could not obtain the names of the team members for S.F.] They chose homosexuals because they believed that few would care what happened to them and hoped the disease would spread throughout the country before anyone realized that it would kill ANYONE — not just gays. During the "incubation period" [1995-2000] the Group plans to introduce new diseases that will be "far more aggressive, far more vicious" than AIDS. (Apparently, we must assume that if they release a disease, they will already have developed an antidote in case one of 'them' gets infected - Branton)

The Omega Files

see also: The Population Control Agenda The Timeline of Population Control

CRIME AND DRUGS: ...Crime and illegal drugs go hand-in-hand. Drug traffic has been fostered under the covert aegis of the Group's massive apparatus within the CIA since at least Vietnam. My informant states that "Mr. Halloran" as a "contract" CIA operative in Saigon was running hard drugs from Laos and Cambodia to Bien Hoa to the US aboard military aircraft for use on American streets. It went on for years and is probably still going on, but now from other points of origin. There are alliances between the Group's agents in CIA and the military and drug lords in South America. My informant identified the names of most DEA agents-in-charge of major US offices & many US Coast Guard and Navy officers ON drug interdiction duty.

ECONOMIC DEPRESSION: The plan is for there to be a disastrous [but short-lived] depression, precipitated by a stock crash. The Group's members in the financial community certainly have the muscle to do it. My informant has identified [current=1994] either the presidents or chairmen of five of the six largest banks in NYC, many of the key officials in the NY Federal Reserve, most of the major London merchant banks, four of the largest GERMAN banks, and five of the 11 largest US stock brokerage firms.

CIVIL/RACE WAR; THE MILITARY; THE ASSASSINATION LIST: The Group's plan is to covertly foster and finance a civil war on race lines through their agents in black and Hispanic ghettoes in major cities. Once they are successful in gun control legislation the Group will ARM the minority insurgents with attack weapons to be used against essentially weaponless minority and non-minority individuals. The local police departments will be out-gunned. The military will be called in, but will be unable to control the situation due to an artificial "breakdown in the chain of command." [The percentage of senior US Army, Navy and Air Force general officers — brigadier general through general, rear admiral through admiral — identified by my informant has been astoundingly high. The rate of identification among generals and admirals in the military is equaled in only two other organizations: the State Department and the Council on Foreign Relations.] In the midst of the societal chaos, after the war begins, the Group will conduct systematic assassinations of key American civilian and military leaders who have not supported the Group's policies or its key agents. That list is referred to by my main informant and by the woman I first interviewed in

The Omega Files

1983-84 as "all the king's men." The civil war fostered covertly by the Group will frighten "middle America" into adoption of the Group's government. After the year 2000 the civil war will be used by the Group as the excuse for genocide against the Black and Hispanic races. The genocide of the black races will be global. There are also large-scale genocide plans for Hispanics and Chinese. Literally hundreds of smaller races also targeted. This will take place over a much longer period than [the] German experiment in WWII. (Remember that the 'root' of the 'New World Order' agenda can be traced back to the secret occultic societies connected to Bavaria, Germany — the Illuminati, Thule, Nazis, Vril, Rosicrucian, Black Gnostics, Skull & Bones, Cult of the Serpent, Templars, Babylon Mystery Cult, O.T.O., Golden Dawn, Jesuits, and all of the many lesser-known inter-locking secret societies which grew out of the occult-military core of the early Roman Empire and the later 'Holy Roman Empire' [HO.R.E.] — a core that had its center of power not only in Rome but also in Germany. - Branton)

15. MY ACCIDENTAL DISCOVERY OF THE GROUP IN THE MID-1980s MIND CONTROL TECHNIQUES

I encountered the Group as a result of a personal investigation into a very strange series of deaths and bizarre behavior changes I observed among my acquaintances in a chemical factory that produced raw materials for plastics manufacture. All I knew at the start was that about 50 [now 100] employees had died of leukemia, aplastic anemia, various forms of cancer, and other illnesses that fit with only two possible causes: long-term exposure to benzene or to low-level radiation. The pattern included a series of sudden, unexpected heart attacks among spouses of dead or dying workers who asked questions about the cause of their husbands' deaths. Since the plant supposedly had no radioactive materials, I litigated a large-scale case on the assumption that the only possible cause was benzene. About 3 years after the case was over [I won it.], a series of employees there began exhibiting bizarre behavior changes. One of them privately confided in me, and her confidences caused me to open a very private, personal investigation. I determined that this woman and a second female employee had been subjected to some form of trauma under hypnosis by several men connected with the plant's MEDICAL staff. Both men had participated in what seemed a NAZI group called [the] ORDER OF THE FOURTH REICH.

Both of the women were interrogated under hypnosis by the experts referred to earlier, under my direction. During the first 18 months of interrogations we learned that a form of "mind control" was used on the women and MANY other plant employees, as well as on my main [male] informant to conceal the covert manufacture of an illicit product at that factory. The Group's agents used a "mind control" method that concealed their observations and memories of its production from THEMSELVES. Here is how it worked: Employees' trust was gained by the Group's agents in the plant medical department. When the employees were called in for medical exams or given 'medication' by the plant physician and some of his staff, the employees were instructed in methods they were use to, to forget events they had observed at the plant. The employees were taught to "remember to forget" incidents that the Group's agents did not want them to recall. In some cases these instructions were accompanied by physical torture under drugged hypnosis until the employee complied with the instructions. The subject is highly technical, but the end result was the concealment of a witness's memory from the witness's own consciousness, except in a hypnotic state.

TRAINING OF UNCONSCIOUS ASSASSINS ALSO KNOWN AS 'U-BOATS,' INCLUDING OSWALD, SIRHAN, possibly RAY, & MANY OTHERS LIKE THEM:

The subject cannot possibly [be] treated in the short space I have left. Bare bones: Victims are drugged into regression to early childhood. They are subjected to incredible pain, many expiring in the process. The natural response to the levels of pain DR. MENGELE had perfected was dissociation of the conscious mind. In that state they were given new, GERMAN names and trained as one would train a killer guard dog. They kill on command.

THEY ARE ARTIFICIALLY-PRODUCED 'MULTIPLE' PERSONALITIES. One of the top people in their development appears to have been Sirhan Sirhan's psychiatrist, DR. DIAMOND. There were other prominent psyche folks in on it. They have no memory of the kill, except when prompted by the proper stimuli. Mengele told my informant THAT HE personally did the training on Oswald. Location unknown, but we suspect Mexico City in Summer, 1963. [The] CIA gave John Marks [Search for Manchurian Candidate] what appears to be a real hokey, perhaps forged or fabricated, "field report" for the initial field test of an unconscious assassin in Mexico City in July, 1963 [see Marks' book, p. 190]. I suspect that if someone can get that file and bust a few balls, they'll find the memo given to Marks in his FOIA litigation was a substitute for one that named Oswald and depicted a suc-

The Omega Files

cessful 'experiment.' The likely control of the project we suspect to have been GEHLEN, but the CIA Director mentioned above may have also played a major role. Oswald was trained as a 'patsy' only. He fired no shots. Sirhan was given the full course. His back-up was a man posing as a guard. Ray [who killed Martin Luther King] had the Oswald-type training... Anonymous To find out more about the anon service, send mail to help@anon.penet.fi.

Due to the double-blind, any mail replies to this message will be anonymized, and an anonymous id will be allocated automatically. You have been warned. Please report any problems, inappropriate use etc. to admin@anon.penet.fi. (Note: According to several sources, the United Nations Organization or UNO is deeply involved in this fascist global conspiracy. Just note the controversy surrounding former U.N. Secretary General and Austrian Kurt Waldheim concerning his Nazi past and allegations that he is a war criminal, although he adamantly denies this. An interesting personal connection came from an individual whom I was in contact with some years ago, by the name of Tawani Shoush. Shoush claimed to be a full-fledged Nazi who served on a German U-Boat during World War II. In fact he served — if we are to believe his story — on one of two German U-Boats which turned up in Argentina several months after the war, and from there he moved to the North United States. He claims to maintain contact with a secret Nazi S.S.-connected Society which reputedly has retrieved the "Spear of Destiny" which so fascinated Adolph Hitler, after it had been hidden in an ice cave in Antarctica following the end of the war. Shoush claims to have seen the spear for himself, and claims that this secret S.S.-connected Society has been using it as the center-piece of occult rituals which are being carried out in an effort to loosen the spiritual forces that will lead to the establishment of a European Alliance, with Germany at the center, and especially as a means to summon a "great leader" who will rise out of Europe and finish the work that Adolph Hitler began.

He called this group "The Order". Incidentally he has also written and published information in the form of a "Lost Diary" of Admiral Richard E. Byrd telling of Byrd's supposed visit with a friendly race of 'Aryans' called the 'Aryanni' — whom Shoush also claims to be in contact with — at the North Pole. Some people, for instance Harley Byrd, claim that Shoush is a Nazi agent who is trying to conceal the existence of hostile Nazi and Alien forces at the SOUTH Pole by diverting attention to supposedly friendly 'Aryanni' UFOnauts at the NORTH Pole. It is strange that this 'Diary', which is most likely a hoax, has the 'benevolent' Aryanni telling Admiral Byrd of the evils of nuclear weapons and how we should disarm our nuclear arsenal to avoid a global holocaust. At the same time, according to this 'Diary', these supposedly benevolent people bid the Admiral farewell in GERMAN. In addition, in the 'diary' the Aryanni referred to their craft as 'FLUGELRADS', which is the German word for 'Wing-Wheel'. Harley Byrd claims that the Admiral did NOT meet with aliens at the North Pole... it was the SOUTH pole where he encountered what Harley insists was a collaboration of Nazi's, Greys, Draco, rebel Pleiadeans and a few collaborating 'Sasquatch' people as well. However in order not to divert from the flow, the United Nations Connection's of the Nazi's — via Kurt Waldheim and others — are historical fact. One source other than Shoush even reported that at one point Kurt Waldheim himself was in possession of the 'Spear', suggesting that this former U.N. Secretary General wasn't a small fry but a MAJOR player in the Nazi conspiracy. This might explain the following article which suggests that the "National Socialists" have already begun the early stages of their attempted takeover of North America. - Branton)

16. U.S. MILITARY OFFICERS — SHACKLED BY U.N. FORCES

A report from SEVENTH WEEK MAGAZINE states that U.S. Military Officers were observed gagged, cuffed, and shackled to their seats aboard a white U.N. 747 en route to the Federal Transfer Center in OKLAHOMA! Part of this report follows: "At a survival/preparation seminar in S.E. Oklahoma, on 3/25/95, an attendee interrupted one speaker, and stated that a neighbor, who apparently serves as a reserve crew member aboard one of the all white, unmarked, United Nations B-747 aircraft [which are assigned to FEMA, Black Operations, i.e. U.N. / N.W.O and hubbed at the Federal 'prisoner' Transfer Center or FTC at WILL ROGERS AIRPORT], had been dead-heading back to Oklahoma City on the flight. He descended from the flight deck to see what the "prisoner cargo" consisted of, however, not only did he see the normal armed, black uniformed guards, and a load of bound humans, but he saw several U.S. Military officers, in full uniform, gagged, and shackled to their seats! They were in the front of the cabin, and from their visages, he discerned that they were violently angry at their situation. No doubt! "At this point I guess you might think this is a joke? Nope, because in April 1993, and July 1994, an ex-Army intelligence analyst postulated THIS EXACT SCENARIO would happen! He also stated, in the 94 interview, 'they' were going to use white 747's to fly 'detained' [kidnapped] conservative, etc., etc., 'po-

The Omega Files

litical' prisoners around the U.S., via the TFC, to the NOW-existing, 130 FEMA "RESISTER/DISSIDENT" DETENTION CAMPS.

The above operation, among many others in this overall incredible takeover conspiracy, INCLUDES EARLY-ON LEADERSHIP KIDNAPPING, PERFORMED BY FOREIGN [ASIAN] CREWS NOW HIDDEN IN THE U.S. [or underneath 'closed' U.S. bases], using the 3,000 choppers provided to the U.N. under the auspices of the 1989 "Open Skies Treaty," signed by good ole New World Order Sultan George Bush; a member of the Skull and Bones Secret Society, and the Trilateral Commission. The Treaty allows for the aerial observation of the U.S. [and, yes, your house — if you have been tagged for observation, along with your phone being tapped], No Questions Asked! The majority of the recent BLACK CHOPPER sorties have nothing to do with lawful military/police department operations, but are presently locating, and SETTING UP for seizure — people/guns — who will not take the 'mark' of the coming One World Government/Order! So prepare accordingly!" There numerous suggestions that the Rockefeller empire and their secret society hosts in Bavaria Germany [the Rockefeller's native land] are the secret manipulators behind the United Nations Organization or UNO. On the outside Nazism and Communism may seem to be in conflict, however it was the Rockefellers and the German Black Nobility cults who created BOTH movements. Tyranny is tyranny, whether it be National Socialism or Global Socialism. Perhaps the Bavarians created two types of Socialism: Global Socialism — as a means to tear down the international competition; and National Socialism — as a means to build up the German empire.

We should NEVER forget that Lenin, the Communist Revolutionist, was an agent of the GERMAN government. What is not commonly known is that Stalin murdered nearly 6 million Jews during the World War II period, as did Hitler. This means 12 million or more Jews were murdered during World War II. As of the mid-1990's some 12 million known Jews remain in the world — ironically, nearly 5-6 million of them in Israel and about the same number in America, although there are still small pockets of Jews scattered throughout various other countries. The following information which appeared on the Internet was provided by an anonymous 'Insider' who identifies himself only as "One Who Knows". You must realize that although some people may possess patriotic feelings, these are not always combined with suicidal intent. In other words there may be very good reasons why some Intelligence Agency 'Insiders' choose to remain anonymous, especially when this kind of incendiary information is involved. I would suggest however that some of the best 'evidence' may not appear as a result of a person's identity or character — since some of those involved have in the past taken part in activities that they regret — but instead as a result of how the information compares with other sources. So, not willing to implicate themselves or make themselves a 'target' by one side or the other or both, they instead fight 'the evil' the only way they know how... to expose it anonymously. So read the following and compare it with the remainder of the revelations given in this section, and make your own determinations as to how the following 'fits-in' with the rest of this enigmatic 'puzzle':

17. ADMIRAL BYRD AND OPERATION HIGH-JUMP ...

In 1947, Admiral Richard E. Byrd led 4,000 military troops from the U.S., Britain and Australia in an invasion of Antarctica [Operation Highjump and follow-up], but encountered heavy resistance from Nazi "flying saucers" and had to call off the invasion. A Rear-Admiral who was in that invasion has retired in Texas, and said he was shocked when he read the "Fire From The Sky" material. He knew there were a lot of aircraft and rocket shoot-downs but did not realize the situation was so bad. (Note: Here the writer is referring to accounts given in other writings, suggesting that AS the Soviet Union was falling the Bolsheviks who were in the process of being ousted from Russia took refuge in the CIA and Pentagon, from where they attempted to provoke a nuclear war with Russia which they would ride-out in their massive underground bunkers. In response, the Tzarist Russian's sent a strong message to the Bolshevik 'elite' in the Pentagon and CIA that this would not be allowed — by shooting down satellites and aircraft in retaliation. The idea of a KGB presence in the CIA might seem to conflict with the 'Nazi' presence there, yet NOT if you consider the fact that the Rockefeller's — according to Economics expert and advisor Antony Sutton and others — had financially backed BOTH the Bolsheviks AND the Nazis in their military efforts as two Hegallian or Machievellian 'clubs' to 'beat' the planet into submission to a New World Order.

This might explain the early treaty between Hitler and Stalin, the close alliances that both Karl Marx and Adolph Hitler had with the Jesuits, and the fact that the Bolshevik revolution was actually planned in Bavaria with German Intelligence's plan to send their agent Lenin from Germany to Russia to stir up the revolution. We must remember that National Socialism [Nazism] IS 'Socialism' none-the-less. In this context the polarizing 'left-wing' - 'right-

The Omega Files

wing' political theory turns out to be FALSE. If this theory is taken to its logical conclusion then an extreme left-wing system would tend to liberalism and anarchy while an extreme right-wing system would tend to conservatism and totalitarianism. You could say that both left and right wing philosophies compliment each other in the sense that Totalitarianism cannot exist without the threat of anarchy to justify it. For instance in order to JUSTIFY a totalitarian takeover of the United States or the World the UN/NWO 'elite' would AND DO support ANARCHY in order to create for instance a national emergency and in so doing justify the implementation of certain executive orders and martial law. The Bolshevik 'Socialists' certainly were NOT anarchists but totalitarians just like the Nazi or National 'Socialists'. In reality TRUE Communism would be control of the country by a UNION of workers, with power equally distributed among all workers. Vladimir Lenin felt that the 'workers' were not worthy nor capable of running the government in a collective sense, and that a small group who were 'trained' in the precepts of 'Communism' should run the government and the Revolution instead. So in essence 'Communism' as it exists in Asia is NOT Communism but dictatorship. If anything, democracy would be closer to TRUE Communism than the FALSE Communism of Asia, with the PEOPLE having control through the electoral process. But of course that has been subverted with the rise of the 'Executive' Alien-Military-Industrial government within the United States, which is controlled by a alien-corporate ELITE rather than being equally control among the common citizens. Now are you getting the picture?

The so-called ELITE gain their power through MISREPRESENTATION and DECEPTION! They intentionally cloud the true nature of reality, lest the masses wake up and see how they are being exploited, and take back control. The 'fraternal elite' were fully aware of the fact that their brand of 'Communism' was not Communism or Socialism at all, however they used the promise of 'Communism' in order to LIE to and DECEIVE the targeted countries into accepting their 'Communist Dictatorship' — which would seem to be a contradiction in terms, like 'Military Intelligence'. But for the sake of the Machiavellian 'game' that the Rockefellers and others were running, the 'illusion' of polarity between the LEFT and the RIGHT had to be maintained. And when the Bolsheviks began to lose power, the Rockefellers did exactly what they did with the Nazis, they took their 'children' back under their wing and gave them refuge within their Military-Industrial Machine. So in essence the most powerful government on earth is a corporate empire, and this would confirm the Biblical proverb that "the love of money is the root of all evil".

The Omega Files

When the Greek Orthodox and Tsarist factions started to regain ground among the Russian Socialists during WWII, Roman fascists apparently decided that they would put pressure on the Nazi's to attack their 'Protestant' Greek Orthodox enemies in Yugoslavia... the Serbians. Since the Roman-backed Croatian-Catholic-Nazi USTACHI killer squads were determined to carry out genocide against the Russian-backed Serbian Greek Orthodox, one can easily see how the Balkan states became the tinderbox for both the first and second world wars, and in both cases Germany was at the center. Remember that the German Kaiser Wilhelm ['Kaiser' literally means 'Caesar' in German, a carry over from the Roman and Unholy Roman Empire's] as well as Adolph Hitler himself was determined to bring back the Roman Empire, which would obviously have been Rome's goal as well. This is not surprising when we consider that the blasphemously named 'Holy' Roman Empire — which rose from the decay of the earlier fallen Roman Empire — had its headquarters in Germany.

Getting back to the conflict between the Tsarist and Bolshevik Russians... In addition to attacks on American satellites, missiles or planes by 'Cosmospheres' manned by Tsarist or nationalist Russians, there is also evidence of attacks against the same by the 'Nazi' and 'Grey' space forces as well. These attacks have not come from only one source. One more thought... the political struggle is, as suggested above, not so much between the right and left 'wings', especially the extremists — at one extreme being slavery/tyranny and at the other extreme criminality/anarchy, BOTH of which are co-dependent threats to Liberty and Freedom. The actual struggle is between BALANCE and EXTREMISM. Anarchy would be symbolic of a horse roaming wild and useless with no restraints. Tyranny would be that same horse locked in a stall and never being able to see the light of day. A true democratic-republic would be symbolized by that horse being allowed to roam 'free' in a wide open pasture, however the pasture nevertheless has its fenced-in 'limits' that the horse could not pass. However in that the pasture provides plenty of freedom within its confines, the horse is satisfied. - Branton) The invasion of ANTARCTICA consisted of three battle groups from Norfolk, VA, on Dec. 2, 1946. They were led by Byrd's command ship, the ice-breaker "Northwind," and consisted of the catapult ship "Pine Island," the destroyer "Brownsen," the aircraft-carrier "Philippines Sea," the U.S. submarine "Sennet," two support vessels "Yankee" and "Merrick," and two tankers "Canisted" and "Capacan," the destroyer "Henderson" and a floatplane ship "Currituck." A British-Norwegian force and a Russian force,

The Omega Files

and I believe some Australian and Canadian forces were also involved. On March 5, 1947 the "El Mercurio" newspaper of Santiago, Chile, had a headline article "On Board the Mount Olympus on the High Seas" which quoted Byrd in an interview with Lee van Atta: "Adm. Byrd declared today that it was imperative for the United States to initiate immediate defense measures against hostile regions.

The admiral further stated that he didn't want to frighten anyone unduly but that it was a bitter reality that in case of a new war the continental United States would be attacked by flying objects which could fly from pole to pole at incredible speeds. [Earlier he had recommended defense bases AT the NORTH Pole.] Admiral Byrd repeated the above points of view, resulting from his personal knowledge gathered both at the north and south poles, before a news conference held for International News Service." When Byrd returned to the States, he was hospitalized and was not allowed to hold any more press conferences. In March 1955, he was placed in charge of Operation Deepfreeze which was part of the International Geophysical Year [1957-1958] exploration of the Antarctic. He died, some have suggested he was murdered, in 1957... UFO researchers are also aware of strange sightings of 'flying saucers' with swastikas or iron crosses on them, 'aliens' speaking German, etc. (Note: I have also heard of abductees who have been taken to underground bases with swastika emblems on the walls, or as in the case of abductee Alex Christopher, have seen Reptiloids and 'Nazis' working together aboard antigravity craft or within underground bases. See The KSEO 4/26/96 Interview with Alex Christopher So Barney Hill was not the ONLY one to describe the Nazi connection to UFO abductions. - Branton). An example is the American Reinhold Schmidt — whose father was born in Germany — who tells in his book "Incident At Kearney" [Nebraska] that he was taken on a 'flying saucer' on several occasions. He said the crew spoke German and acted like German soldiers. He said they took him to the Polar region [if someone were making up a story, why would they claim to be taken, of all places, to the pole?] (Note: Other sources have implied that an — underground? — 'Nazi' base exists somewhere in Nebraska. - Branton)

After returning he was subjected to persecution by the U.S. Government. His description [of the aerial discs] matched pictures captured from the Germans. (Note: For video's detailing an in-depth historical analysis of the Nazi cults, numerous details on the Nazi aerial disc projects, AS WELL AS actual photo-footage retrieved from classified sources of these aerial discs

The Omega Files

in operation, and also investigations into the "New Berlin" bases below Neu Schwabenland, Antarctica — contact: Vladimir Terziski, President, - American Academy of Dissident Scientists, 10970 Ashton Ave. #310, Los Angeles, CA 90024, phone and fax: USA-[310]-473-9717. - Branton) In 1959, three large newspapers in CHILE reported front page articles about UFO encounters where the crew members appeared to be German soldiers. IN the 1960s there were reports in New York and NEW JERSEY of flying saucer 'aliens' who spoke German, or English with a German accent. In the Julius and Ethel Rosenberg atomic espionage trials, they spoke of "warships of space." Since they had access to top secret information, about what were they talking?

18. HITLER ESCAPED!

I remember hearing, in the 1950s, rumors that Hitler had escaped to a secret Nazi base at the South Pole. In 1952, Dwight D. Eisenhower said: "We have been unable to unearth one bit of tangible evidence of Hitler's death. Many people believe that Hitler escaped from Berlin." When President Truman asked Joseph Stalin at the Potsdam conference in 1945 whether or not Hitler was dead, Stalin replied bluntly, 'No.' Stalin's top army officer, Marshall Gregory Zhukov, whose troops were the ones to occupy Berlin, flatly stated after a long thorough investigation in 1945: "We have found no corpse that could be Hitler's." The chief of the U.S. trial counsel at Nuremberg, Thomas J. Dodd, said: "No one can say he is dead." Major General Floyd Parks, who was commanding general of the U.S. sector in Berlin, stated for publication that he had been present when Marshall Zhukov described his entrance to Berlin, and Zhukov stated he believed Hitler might have escaped. Lt. Gen. Bedell Smith, Chief of Staff to Gen. Eisenhower in the European invasion and later Director of the CIA, stated publicly on Oct. 12, 1945, "No human being can say conclusively that Hitler is dead." Col. W.J. Heimlich, former Chief, United States Intelligence, at Berlin, stated for publication that he was in charge of determining what had happened to Hitler and after a thorough investigation his report was: "There was no evidence beyond that of HEARSAY to support the THEORY of Hitler's suicide." He also stated, "On the basis of present evidence, no insurance company in America would pay a claim on Adolph Hitler." Nuremberg judge Michael Mussmanno said in his book "Ten Days to Die," "Russia must accept much of the blame [to the extent that it still exists] that Hitler did not die in May 1945." However, Mussmanno STATED that he interviewed Hitler's personal waiter, his valet, his chauffeur, his two secretaries, pilots, top generals, etc., and they

The Omega Files

all 'agreed' perfectly that Hitler committed suicide. He said they could not have gotten together afterward and made up a story that agreed in perfect detail without one flaw anywhere, so they must be telling the truth and he was absolutely convinced that Hitler committed suicide.

The story at first sounds convincing, until you realized that they could have memorized a story BEFOREHAND and these were all people who almost WORSHIPPED Hitler. Do witnesses EVER agree "perfectly" in detail in real life? Former Secretary of State Jimmy Byrnes in his book "Frankly Speaking" [as quoted in the April 1948 "The Cross and The Flag"]: "While in Potsdam at the Conference of the Big Four, Stalin left his chair, came over and clinked his liquor glass with mine in a very friendly manner. I said to him: 'Marshal Stalin, what is your theory about the death of Hitler?' Stalin replied: "He is not dead. He escaped either to Spain or Argentina.'" I still have the September, 1948, issue of a magazine called "The Plain Truth" with the headline article: "IS HITLER ALIVE, OR DEAD?," subtitled: "Here is summarized the conclusions of an exhaustive three-year investigation — together with reasons for believing Hitler may be alive and secretly planning the biggest hoax of all history." Another article in November, 1949, says "The Nazis went underground, May 16, 1943!" and details a meeting at the residence of Krupp von Bohlen-Halbach, the head of I.G. FARBEN, etc., at which they planned "FOR WORLD WAR III." Another article in August, 1952, entitled "HITLER DID NOT DIE," subtitled "Adolph Hitler's fake suicide in his Berlin Bunker now is exposed as History's greatest hoax! Positive evidence comes to light that Hitler did not die — here's new evidence that Hitler is alive, directing [the] Nazi underground, today!" The June, 1952, issue of "The Plain Truth" is headlined: "HITLER 'May Be Alive!'" The article states: "Now, NEW FACTS, or purported facts, leak out. It's reported now that in 1940 the Nazis started to amass tractors, planes, sledges, gliders, and all sorts of machinery and materials IN THE SOUTH POLAR REGIONS — that for the next 4 years Nazi technicians built, on an almost unknown CONTINENT, Antarctica, the Fuhrer's SHANGRILA — a new Berchtesgaden." The report says they scooped out an entire mountain, built a new refuge completely camouflaged — a magic mountain hide-a-way. The recently discovered continent is larger than Europe — 5,600 miles from Africa, 1,900 miles from the southern tip of South America, 4,800 miles from Australia.

It is NOT a mere ice-covered surface, but a real continent, with plains, valleys, mountain peaks up to 15,000 feet. The temperature in the interior is

The Omega Files

around zero (?) in the summer, and never drops below 20 or 30 degrees below in the winter. In other words, it is not as cold as in parts of North Dakota or Canada." (especially underground, where the natural temperature would be in the 50's, even below snow and ice. - Branton) "Bonjour" magazine, the "Police Gazette," and the Paris newspaper "Le Monde" all had articles about Hitler's South Pole hideaway. Admiral Doenitz, in 1943, stated, "The German submarine fleet has even now established an earthly paradise, an impregnable fortress, for the Fuhrer, in whatever part of the world." Although he did not specify where the exact location was, "Bonjour" pointed out that in 1940 Nazi engineers had begun construction of buildings that were to withstand temperatures to 60 degrees below zero. There have been strong rumors, from the end of the War, that Hitler escaped to the South Pole. Yet, most people simply REFUSE to believe the evidence, the idea that Hitler survived the war is just unacceptable! It is too upsetting to too many people! There is plenty of PROOF that the Americans and Russians LIED about what happened to Hitler, and there are strong rumors that he escaped to Antarctica. There is ample proof that a major group of Nazis escaped to Argentina. What do YOU think? Why did Admiral Byrd lead an "invasion to Antarctica," and why the extreme secrecy about the whole situation? In 1981, Donald McKale wrote "Hitler: The Survival Myth" to try to lay to rest the questions about what happened to Hitler. The flyleaf says: "In this book a distinguished historian examines the postwar world's most absorbing and persistent mystery, revealing why it has endured and where the mystery leads" [emphasis mine]. The back flyleaf says "Absolute certainty about what happened still eludes us today."

Just recently on TV there are STILL programs telling "at last, the final, once and for all, this is the real story" about what happened to Hitler, yet they all do not really answer the question. A recent TV program, called "What Really Happened to Adolph Hitler," after investigating numerous stories, ends by saying that, in spite of Glasnost and the new freedom of access to Russian files, the files on Hitler are still some of the most highly classified items of the Soviets. The "Diario Illustrado" of Santiago, Chile, January 18, 1948 issue, said: "On 30th of April, 1945, Berlin was in dissolution but little of that dissolution was evident at Templehof Airfield. At 4:15 p.m. a JU52 landed and S.S. troops directly from Rechlin for the defense of Berlin disembarked, all of them young, not older than 18 years. "The gunner in the particular plane was an engineer by the name of B... whom I had known for a number of years and for whom I had endeavored to get exemption from military

The Omega Files

service. He sought to tank up and leave Berlin as quickly as possible. During this re-fueling interval Mr. B... was suddenly elbowed in the ribs by his radio operator with a nod to look in a certain direction. "At about 100-120 meters he saw a sleek Messerschmitt Jet Model 332 [an editorial comment says this should be an ARADO 234]. Mr. B.. and the radio operator saw, and WITHOUT ANY DOUBT WHATSOEVER, standing in front of the jet, their Commander in Chief, Adolf Hitler, dressed in field-grey uniform and gesticulating animatedly with some Party functionaries, who were obviously seeing him off. "For about ten minutes whilst their plane was being refueled the two men observed this scene and around 4:30 p.m. they took to the air again. They were extremely astonished to hear during the midnight military news bulletin, some seven and a half hours later, that Hitler had committed suicide." On a Canadian Broadcasting Corporation program called "As It Happens," September 17th, 1974 at 7:15 p.m., a Prof. Dr. Ryder Saguenay, oral surgeon from the Dental Faculty of the University of California at Los Angeles, said that Hitler had ordered a special plane to leave from Berlin with all medical and dental records, especially X-rays, of all top Nazis for an unknown destination. He said that the dental records used to identify Hitler's body were drawn from MEMORY by a dental assistant, WHO disappeared and was never found.

An editorial in "Zig Zag," Santiago, Chile, January 16, 1948, STATES that on April 30th, 1945, Flight Captain Peter Baumgart took Adolf Hitler, his wife Eva Braun, as well as a few loyal friends by plane from Tempelhof Airport to Tondern in Denmark [still German controlled]. From Tondern, they took another plane to Kristiansund in Norway [also German controlled]. From there they joined a SUBMARINE convoy. ["U.F.O. Letzte Geheimwaffe des III Reiches," Mattern, pp. 50-51.] The Jewish writer Michael Bar-Zohar in "The Avengers," p. 99, said: "In 1943 Admiral Doenitz had declared: 'The German U-boat fleet is proud to have made an earthly paradise, an impregnable fortress for the Fuhrer, somewhere in the world.' He did not say in what part of the world it existed, but fairly obviously it was in South America." The German writer Mattern said that Admiral Doenitz told a graduating class of naval cadets in Kiel in 1944: "The German Navy has still a great role to play in the future. The German Navy knows all hiding places for the Navy to take the Fuhrer to, should the need arise. There he can prepare his last measures in complete quiet."

The Omega Files

19. POLAR DEFENSES

One thing that Admiral Byrd stated in a press conference after his defeat at Antarctica was that the Antarctic continent should be surrounded by a "wall of defense installations since it represented the last line of defense for America." Although the U.S. and Russia had been allies during the war, suddenly the "Iron Curtain" was created and we and the Russians became 'enemies'. (Note: Some say that the animosity of the Cold War directly following WWII was only an outward smokescreen to justify the expenditure on both sides for massive nuclear armament buildups — and more importantly for massive black budget projects in space and underground — and that in reality top U.S. and U.S.S.R. officials met regularly via secret submarine meetings that took place below the North Polar ice pack. This cooperation however was not complete, as there were still many at the higher levels of U.S. government who were against the military imperialist abuses of the Communist system; and many at the highest levels of the U.S.S.R. who were against the corporate imperialist abuses of the Capitalist system. 'Inner Earth' researcher Dennis Crenshaw has written an interesting essay on the Rockefeller influence behind Admiral Byrd's missions to the Antarctic, stating that the Rockefeller's had funded many of Byrd's missions. Could we imply from this that, following the war, the Rockefellers were able to reign-in many of the lower-ranking Nazi's yet many of the higher-ranking Nazi's slipped out of their control?

The corporate elite who backed the Nazi's apparently did not want the products of their 'investments' off doing their own thing. Apparently the Antarctic bases, like the Russian invasion, were NOT part of the Rockefeller's plan. However there are suggestions that the Rockefeller-backed Nazi's in America have since made contact with their comrades in Antarctica and have agreed to work together — along with the Greys — in an effort to infiltrate America and pave the way for it's fall and assimilation into a New World Order. As we will see later, there are claims that some 1.5 million 'Nazis' are now operating in various levels of American society. Just where did they come from... Antarctica? Physicist Vladimir Terziski stated that the Nazi presence in Antarctica has passed the 2 million mark, and therefore Antarctica might conceivably be able to provide a large percentage of this infiltration force. Also remember that the American, European and Antarctican 'Nazis' — due to the very secret-society foundations of their movement — would have to maintain some level of contact with their occultist 'hosts' in Bavaria, especially with the THULE and VRIL societies. - Branton) Both the Soviets and the United States ringed the poles with defense and detection bases, and in between was the barren no-man's-land of the poles where absolutely nobody lived, or did they? Could it be that we pretended we were protecting against the Russians and they pretended they were protecting against us, while really we and they were both scared of what was in between us — the Nazi Last Battalion?...

20. RUDOLPH HESS AND SECRET GERMAN SPACE BASE

Rudolph Hess, Hitler's best friend and second in command, went to England to try to stop the war with Britain and was arrested as a "war criminal" on May 10, 1941 and was kept from having any contact with the public until he was recently murdered. He was the only prisoner in Spandau prison. Ones who paid any attention to his situation at all have wondered what was the big secret he knew that made him so dangerous to the Allies? Perhaps the answer is revealed in [Christof] Friedrich's book "Secret Nazi Polar Expeditions" on page 34: Hess "was entrusted with the all-important Antarctic file... Hess, himself, kept the Polar File..." If you look at a map of Antarctica you will see that a portion of Queen Maud Land is called New Schwabenland. This is the part of the continent nearest to South Africa. The Germans made a major expedition to this area in 1938-1939 and began the construction of a major base. For details of this expedition, see the book by Friedrich. This book has pictures of the "warmwater" [geothermal] ponds and other information that will surprise you. It has maps showing that Admiral Byrd's Operation Highjump [Naval Task Force 68] military invasion landed on the side opposite the German bases... The maps of Operation Highjump say that they left the German side of the continent 'unexplored'. A man who was very influential in modern German post-war politics was Hans-Ulrich Rudel, a frequent guest speaker in German military and political circles. Rudel was the man groomed by Hitler to become his successor. It is known that Rudel made FREQUENT trips to Tierra del Fuego at the tip of South America nearest Antarctica.

One of Martin Bormann's last messages from the bunker in Berlin to Doenitz mentioned Tierra del Fuego... A book called "America's Aircraft Year Book" tells about the U.S. using captured German scientists at Ft. Bliss and Wright Field. "Among those in the German group at Wright Field were Rudolph Hermann, Alexander Lippsisch, Heinz Schmitt, Helmut Heinrich, and Fritz Doblhoff and Ernst Kugel. Hermann was attached to the

The Omega Files

Peenemunde Research Station for Aerodynamics, where Germany's V-2 rockets were hatched and launched against England. A specialist in supersonics, he was in charge of the supersonic wind tunnel at Kochel in the Bavarian Alps. He also was a member of the group entrusted with Hitler's futuristic plans to establish a space-station rocket-refueling base revolving as a satellite about the Earth at a distance of 4,000 miles — a scheme which he and certain high-ranking AAF officers in 1947 still believed to be feasible." Later evidence shows that most or all of the [air] craft and 'flying saucer' scientists (who were not captured - Branton) disappeared. The available evidence indicates they went to South America or Antarctica. The "El Mercurio" and "Der Weg" papers told of a large submarine convoy discovered by the British Navy at the end of WW II. All available Allied units engaged the convoy and were totally destroyed except for the Captain of one destroyer, who was reported as saying, "May God help me, may I never again encounter such a force." On July 10, 1945, more than two months after the end of the War, the German submarine U-530 surrendered to Argentine authorities. The Commander was Otto Wermoutt. The sub had a crew of 54 men [the normal sub crew was 18 men] and the cargo consisted of 540 barrels of cigarettes and unusually large stocks of food. The Commander was 25 years old, the second officer was 22, and the crew was an average of 25 except for one man who was 32 years old.

This was an unusually young crew and upon questioning it was learned that they all claimed that they had no relatives. A map from a Spanish book called "Is Hitler Alive?" with the route of the Fuhrer convoy shows it passed alongside South Georgia Island, where later a secret underground base was the focus of a secret battle during the Falkland Islands War. On April 4, 1944 at 4:40 a.m. the German submarine U-859 left on a mysterious mission carrying 67 men and 33 tons of mercury sealed in glass bottles in watertight tin crates. The sub was sunk by a British submarine and most of the crew died. One survivor on his death bed about 30 years later told about the expensive cargo and some divers checked out his story and found the mercury. For what purpose was this mercury to be used? And where were they trying to take it? (apparently mercury is theoretically usable as a fuel source for certain forms of aerospace propulsion. - Branton) There are many other stories of other U-boats and German survivors, mostly in the Southern Hemisphere. The Germans and other European nations required very meticulous registration records of everybody, including their relatives, employment, addresses, children, etc., and at the end of the war the Allies, cross checking these records, taking into account casualties and deaths, determined that THERE WERE [AT LEAST] 250,000 PERSONS UNACCOUNTED FOR... (That's a quarter of a MILLION, by the way. - Branton)

21. GERMAN SUBMARINES IN THE SOUTH ATLANTIC

The newspaper "France Soir" had the following account: "Almost 1-1/2 years AFTER cessation of hostilities in Europe, the Islandic [Icelandic?] Whaler, 'Juliana' was stopped by a large German U-boat. The Juliana was in the ANTARCTIC region around Malvinas [now Falkland] Islands when a German submarine surfaced and raised the German official naval Flag of Mourning — red with a black edge. The submarine commander sent out a boarding party, which approached the Juliana in a rubber dinghy, and having boarded the whaler demanded of Capt. Hekla part of his fresh food stocks. The request was made in the definite tone of an order to which resistance would have been unwise. The German officer spoke a correct English and paid for his provisions in U.S. dollars, giving the Captain a bonus of $10 for each member of the Juliana crew. Whilst the food stuffs were being transferred to the submarine, the submarine commander informed Capt. Hekla of the exact location of a large school of whales. Later the Juliana found the school of whales where designated." The French "Agence France Press" on 25 September 1946, said: "The continuous rumors about German U-boat activity in the region of Tierra del Fuego [Feuerland, in German], between the southernmost tip OF LATIN AMERICA AND THE CONTINENT OF ANTARCTICA are based on true happenings." There have been stories and books written about Germans counterfeiting U.S. currency and otherwise obtaining American money printing plates, which may account for the German use of American money. The Guinness Book of World Records says that the "greatest unsolved robbery" was the disappearance of the entire German treasury at the end of the war.

22. RAND CORPORATION

In January 1946 industrialist Donald Douglas approached the Army Air Force with a plan for government and industry to work together on long range strategic planning. This was called Project RAND, a name coined by Arthur Raymond from Research ANd Development. Much of their first government money went to the von Braun team. [McDougall, Walter al. ..."the Heavens and the Earth, A Political History of the Space Age," Basic Books, New York, 1985, p. 89.]... (Note: RAND Corp. was also involved in expanding some of the upper levels of the Dulce, New Mexico underground biogenetics research facility, according to Thomas Castello. - Branton)

23. GERMAN FLYING DISCS

Hitler's advanced technology included intercontinental ballistic missiles, vertical takeoff aircraft, jet engines, cruise missiles, sound cannons, and many other advanced items. The Allies captured plans for what became the Boeing 747 Jumbo jet. Among the most secret items captured were plans for flying disks, that were at first called "Krautmeteors." Based on the evidence, they were built as early as around 1933 and went into mass production in 1940. Scientists involved in these projects were Bellonzo, Schriever, Miethe and Victor Schauberger. Schauberger developed the "flying hat" type disc that was later seen over the United States. The final version was the Bellonzo-Schriever-Miethe Diskus, as large as 135 feet and some up to 225 feet in diameter. They traveled over 2,000 km/hr and were planned to go over 4,000 km/hr. In 1945 they could reach a speed of 1,300 mph and an altitude of 40,000 feet in less than three minutes. The Germans developed the Delta wing craft, and were working on stealth technology, etc. Many pilots saw the strange craft over Germany. However, as soon as a craft was built, Hitler ordered it disassembled and shipped somewhere — probably Antarctica. None of the craft were captured by the Allies, although some of the scientists were captured and then mostly disappeared, but can somewhat be traced to Bell Textron and to places such as Area 51, which, surprise!, is infamous for its 'UFO' sightings. Here are some examples of news items during WW II concerning Germany's UFOs, from the "New York Times:" "NEW YORK TIMES," December 14, 1944: "Floating Mystery Ball Is New German Weapon. SUPREME HEADQUARTERS, Allied Expeditionary Force, Dec. 13 — A new German weapon has made its appearance on the western air front, it was disclosed today. "Airmen of the American Air Force report that they are encountering silver colored spheres in the air over German territory. The spheres are encountered either singly or in clusters. Sometimes they are semi-translucent." ...and, "SUPREME HEADQUARTERS Dec. 13 [Reuters] — The Germans have produced a 'secret' weapon in keeping with the Christmas season. "The new device, apparently an air defense weapon, resembles the huge glass balls that adorn Christmas trees.

There was no information available as to what holds them up like stars in the sky, what is in them or what their purpose is supposed to be." (Note: In regards to the above, Bulgarian Physicist Vladimir Terziski wrote the fol-

The Omega Files

lowing about the Nazi mystery 'spheres' and aerial disc projects: "...According to Renato Vesco... Germany was sharing a great deal of the advances in weaponry with their allies the ITALIANS during the war. At the Fiat experimental facility at lake La Garda, a facility that fittingly bore the name of air martial Hermann Goering, the Italians were experimenting with numerous advanced weapons, rockets and airplanes, created in Germany. In a similar fashion, the Germans kept a close contact with the Japanese military establishment and were supplying it with many advanced weapons. I have discovered for example a photo of a copy of the manned version of the V-1 — the Reichenberg — produced in Japan by Mitsubishi. The best fighter in the world, the push-pull twin propeller Domier-335 was duplicated at the Kawashima works. Or a photo of Japanese high ranking Imperial navy officers inspecting the latest German radar station. A Japanese friend of mine in Los Angeles related to me the story of his friend's father, who worked as technician in an aircraft research bureau in Japan during the war. In July of 1945, two and a half months after the war ended in Germany, a huge German transport submarine brought to Japan the latest of German inventions — two spherical wingless flying devices. The Japanese R&D team put the machines together, following the German instructions, and... there was something very bizarre and other-earthy standing in front of them — a ball shaped flying device without wings or propellers, that nobody knew how it flied. The fuel was added, the start button of this unmanned machine was pressed and it .... disappeared with a roar and flames without [into] the sky. The team never saw it again. The engineers were so frightened by the unexpected might of the machine, that they promptly dynamited the second prototype and choose to forget the whole incident." - Branton)

24. FALKLAND ISLANDS WAR

The Falkland Islands War had more to do with NAZI'S [Antarctica] than with Argentina... The Germans, FROM THEIR ANTARCTIC BASE, began to INFILTRATE into Argentina, Chile, etc., and bought large tracts of land and swept up corporations. They also invested in corporations in Germany and elsewhere, with plans to make a comeback. They used the German treasury, captured treasure from other nations, and counterfeit American currency printed on real U.S. currency printing plates given to the Russians and captured by the Germans. (Note: It appears as if the German elite had begun to attempt to accomplish via stealth what they failed to do by force in World Wars I and II — by infiltrating North and South America and engaging in economic warfare from their extensive underground 'black budget' empire below Antarctica and also South and North America, with the help of their allies in the CIA/NSA. We are not talking Billions of dollars here, but TRILLIONS of dollars which have been siphoned from the U.S. economy via numerous ingenious methods, and used to 'feed' the Bavarian-backed underground network which stretches throughout North America and which are inhabited by European, American and Antarctican National Socialists. The wealth that has been siphoned from the American economy could otherwise have been used to prime the economy to new heights of prosperity, and that prosperity would have in turn overflowed into the other nations of the world. Apparently the Nazis realized this, and also realized that the 'Banksters' who had backed them during World War II had the REAL power. They understood that ECONOMIC power ultimately dictated political power, even in a supposedly 'democratic' country where they could 'buy off' political power from those who were more interested in immediate physical comforts and economic status rather then the long-term fate of their own country. The 'Nazis' could not have done what they have done without the help of the 'traitors' within. The same could be said for the Greys also... not to mention the CIA/Nazi/Grey collaboration itself existent within various underground bases: Neu Schwabia, Antarctica; Pine Gap, Australia; Alsace-Lorraine Mts., Germany; Montauk, Long Island; the Denver International Airport; Dulce, New Mexico; Area 51, Nevada, etc. - Branton)

Some plates were stolen by Assistant Secretary of the U.S. Treasury Harry Dexter White [real name Weiss] under Henry Morgenthau and sent to the Soviets for use in occupied Germany. He also arranged for the mass theft of tons of our special money-paper. When J. Edgar Hoover went to President Truman with all the evidence that the Assistant Secretary of the Treasury was a Communist spy and thief, TRUMAN of course removed Weiss [White] from his job — and PROMOTED HIM to head of the International Monetary Fund. I kid you not, look it up. (This tells you whose side Truman was really on. - Branton) The story has a rather common ending — when a controversy developed in the press concerning this incident, Weiss became a "suicide."

25. GERMAN ECONOMIC "MIRACLE"

For more information on how the "economic miracle" was accomplished after the war by the Germans, you can read such books as "Martin Bormann, Nazi in Exile" by Paul Manning ["...Bormann became the guiding

The Omega Files

force in the 'economic miracle' that led to the rebirth of German industry and finance in the thirty-five years following political and military defeat. In the waning months of World War II, as the Third Reich was tottering and finally crumbling in defeat, Bormann set up 750 CORPORATIONS scattered among those nations that had remained neutral. Those corporations received the fleeing wealth of Germany and became the power base that enabled Germany to climb back to economic and political strength." From flyleaf]. This book expands on the meeting in Strasbourg on August 10, 1944, mentioned in Michael Bar-Zohar's book "The Avengers." In 1986, while researching these subjects, we received 161 pages under a Freedom of Information search concerning what happened to the German treasury at the end of WW II. Many of these documents had been SECRET until declassification to fulfill our request. One document was No. 19,489, November 27, 1944, Subject: Transmitting Intelligence Report No. EW-Pa 198 [?, barely readable] by G-2 Economic Section, the Secretary of State, from Lt. Col. John W. Easton, Economic Warfare Division. The cover letter stated "I have the honor to enclose Intelligence Report No. EW-Pa 198 by G-2 Economic Section, SHAEF ["Supreme Headquarters Allied Expeditionary Forces"], dated November 7, 1944, describing the plans of German industrialists for the post-war resurrection of Germany. Among the topics dealt with in this report are: patents, financial reserves, exportation of capital, and the strategic placing of technical personnel." It is obvious that Manning quoted from these documents in his book on Bormann. In describing the meeting of August 10,1944, in Stasbourg, some sentences in the documents stand out: "German industrialists must, it was said, through their exports increase the strength of Germany.

They must also prepare themselves TO FINANCE THE NAZI PARTY which would be forced to GO UNDERGROUND as Maquis [in Gebirgverteidigungsstellengehen]. From now on the government would allocate large sums to industrialists so that each could establish a secure postwar foundation in foreign countries. Existing financial reserves in foreign countries must be placed at the disposal of the Party so that a strong German Empire can be created AFTER the defeat. It is also immediately required that the large factories in Germany create small technical offices or research bureaus which would be absolutely independent and have no known connection with the factory. These bureaus will receive plans and drawings of 'new weapons' as well as documents which they need to continue their research and which must not be allowed to fall into the hands of the enemy"

The Omega Files

[author emphasis]. The last sentences in this document are, "After the defeat of Germany the Nazi Party recognizes that certain of its best known leaders will be condemned as war criminals. However, in cooperation with the industrialists it is arranging to place its less conspicuous but most important members in positions with various German factories as technical experts or members of its research and designing offices." Some of the documents were concerning "Looted Gold" [1945-1948]. (Note: A massive shipment of gold which disappeared from an Allied train which was dynamited in a rail tunnel, was later used to finance such Thule Society backed projects as the Montauk or Phoenix Experiments, as a means to counter the Navy's own Philadelphia or Rainbow experiments. The CIA itself delivered over into the hands of the Thulist 'Nazis' much of the Philadelphia experiment's research and technology. - Branton) Accession Number 56-75-101, Agency Container Number 169, File Number BIS/2/00." These documents concern Germany's 'looted' gold being transferred to the 'Bank for International Settlements' in Switzerland.

One important paragraph (#9) says: "It is clear both from correspondence and from testimony that the management of the B.I.S. during the war was 'in the hands of the Administration Council, in which the AXIS representatives have an authoritative influence' and that in 1942 the Germans favored the reelection of President McKittrick whose 'personal opinions' they characterized as 'safely known'." (It has been claimed by some researchers that the 7 most powerful Bankers in the world — who collectively control over 80 percent of all global financial transactions and over 60 percent of all global trade — have in the past met regularly at the Bank of International Settlements or 'B.I.S.' office in the fitly named 'Tower of Basel' in Basel, Switzerland. - Branton) Enclosed in the file is a clipping from the "New York Times," date not included but appears to be in 1945, that states: "McKITTRICK SLATED FOR POST AT CHASE. He Will Take Over Duties as Vice President of Bank Here Next Autumn. Thomas H. McKittrick, American banker who has served as president of the Bank for International Settlements [B.I.S.] since the beginning of 1940, will become a vice president of the [Rockefeller's] Chase National Bank of New York next fall, Winthrop W. Aldrich, chairman of the board of Chase, announced yesterday." The article ends by quoting McKittrick: "I realize it is my duty to perform a neutral task in wartime. It is an extremely difficult and trying thing to do, but I'll do the best I can." Another formerly Top Secret document declassified was "Subject: Conversation in Switzerland with Mr. McKittrick, President of the Bank for Interna-

The Omega Files

tional Settlements" from Orvis A. Schmidt to Secretary of the Treasury Morgenthau, dated March 23, 1945. It describes McKittrick's dealings with the real head of the Nazi banking system, a Vice President named Puhl. "Puhl was described by McKittrick as a career banker who had been with the Reichsbank for some twenty years, who does not share the Nazi point of view... the Swiss National Bank said that in order to be sure they were not obtaining looted gold they had requested a member of the Reichsbank, whom they regarded to be trustworthy, to certify that each parcel of gold which they purchased had not been looted.

The person who had done this certifying was Puhl." Puhl was Reichsbank Senior Vice President Emil Johann Rudolf Puhl. He was in charge of taking booty into the bank and was in charge of it for the Nazis. His Senior Shipping Clerk Albert Thoms said that they needed up to thirty men to help him sort and repack the valuables, which consisted of "millions in gold marks, pounds sterling, dollars and Swiss francs, 3,500 ounces of platinum, over 550,000 ounces of gold, and 4,638 carats in diamonds and other precious stones, as well as hundreds of pieces of works of art" [p. 226, "Aftermath," Ladislas Farago, Avon, 1974]. This material was shipped out of the country in Operation Fireland or Aktion Feuerland in German, which Farago explained in a footnote in his book on Bormann: "The transaction was named 'Land of Fire' after the archipelago of Tierra del Fuego at the southern extremity of Argentina and Chile, THE AREA TO WHICH SOME OF THE SHIPMENTS WERE ORIGINALLY CONSIGNED." [p. 228]. On the next page Farago said: "Only a relatively small portion of the SS treasure was impounded by Bormann and sent overseas in the course of Aktion Feuerland. Much of it is still missing." Germany had developed self-sufficiency before the end of the war, and was manufacturing their own oil, produced 'butter' from coal, invented powdered milk, developed freeze drying, learned to store flour indefinitely, were growing their food in greenhouses on chemical 'soil,' etc. These projects were also necessary for survival of the secret 'UFO' force, which Hitler called the "Last Battalion," at the Antarctic. The counterfeiting of British and American money was under Operation Bernhard. The fake British notes have been often discussed in books and articles about Bernhard, but the fake American currency is not as well known. Recently the U.S. announced that it was issuing new money to counteract the counterfeit, which was said to be coming from Saddam Hussein and Lebanon. It would be more correct to say it is coming from South America, but that money is supposed to all be drug money. Life gets complicated. When 'CONTACT' newspaper

The Omega Files

first ran the series on "Fire From The Sky," it followed with a reprint of the information about the truth about the Falkland Islands War.

In that series, it revealed that the Russians, working with Rockefeller forces, defeated the British Bolshevik forces on South Georgia Island. If you have not read that series, this information may not make sense to you. It is important to know that information, if you intend to try to understand what is happening. NAZI forces were involved in the Falkland Islands War, on the side of the Russians. This is hard to believe if you have no idea of what IS. (See "Fire From the Sky": Fire From The Sky: Battle of Harvest Moon & True Story of Space Shuttles

The Russians were NATIONALISTS, as opposed to [the] Bolsheviks who took their country away from them. The [so-called] Bolsheviks were trained in the lower East Side of New York City and financed by New York and London bankers. (Over 200 were trained to operate as the first Politburo and taught the Communist 'philosophy' IN New York by the Rockefellers. - Branton) They invaded Russia, killed the Tzar and many Nationalists and took over the government. Can you begin to see how someone like Boris Pash, with a Russian Nationalist family background, could work with Nazi Gestapo and SS agents?... In 1982, on April 20, Hitler's birthday, the Russian/Rockefeller/Nazi commando force broke through and inserted a neutron bomb into the underground naval base at South Georgia Island. (As suggested earlier, the Rockefellers had originally backed the BOLSHEVIKS and the Nazis. Later they began backing the Russian NATIONALISTS and the Nazis after the Bolsheviks were kicked out of Russia and wormed their way into the Pentagon, from where they planned a global nuclear holocaust which they would ride out in their underground bunkers. THIS is where the Rockefellers and Bolsheviks came into disagreement, as the Rockefellers resisted the apocalyptic plans of the ousted Bolsheviks because they were not financially 'profitable'. A Nuclear war would most likely result in a global economic collapse as well, something that the Rockefellers did not want. It would seem that the Rockefellers are opportunists. Now that the Russian nationalists had once again gained control of Russia, the Rockefeller-Nazi alliance embraced their nationalist 'brothers' who held the POWER.

If only the Nationalists KNEW who 'created' their Bolshevik enemies in the first place. The Rockefeller corporate empire is a chameleon, changing its colors to fit the current circumstances. - Branton)... Alexander Haig was the General representing the Rockefellers. In his book 'Caveat,' the chap-

The Omega Files

ter on the Falklands starts: "On March 28, 1982, a Sunday, the British Ambassador, Nicholas ['Niko'] Henderson, brought me a letter from Lord Carrington. A party of Argentineans (Argentina — where the Nazi's had a major presence in addition to Antarctica. - Branton), wrote the foreign secretary, had landed nine days earlier on the island of South Georgia, a British [Navy] possession lying in the South Atlantic a few degrees above the ANTARCTIC Circle and some 600 miles to the east of the Falkland Islands, a British Crown colony." I'll bet you thought the Falkland Islands War was about the Falkland Islands! Much ado was made in the media about the conflict between Jeane Kirkpatrick and Alexander Haig. Kirkpatrick is a Zionist and was the U.S. Ambassador to the United Nations. She has a regular feature column in "The Jewish Press" newspaper, "The Largest Independent Anglo-Jewish Weekly Newspaper." Haig has had a long relationship with Henry Kissinger, to whom Haig became senior military advisor in 1969. Remember that Kissinger came out of the [pro-Nazi] PAPERCLIP Operation personnel.

In January 1982, Reagan replaced his national security advisor, Richard Allen, with William P. Clark, another PAPERCLIP person, and who was Haig's deputy. Nixon said, "When you see the lights burning late in Henry's [Kissinger] office, it's usually Al Haig." ["War In The Falklands, the Full Story" by the "Sunday Times" of London Insight Team, Harper & Row, New York, 1982, p. 123.] If you doubt the fact that the Nazis never gave up and that they planned to continue the war after their defeat in Germany, and planned to make a come-back to finally achieve their goal, then perhaps you should read the following books: — Connell, Brian, "A Watcher On The Rhine," William Morrow & Co., New York, 1957. "Old wine in new bottles," how the Nazis have come back into power. — Horne, Alistair, "Return To Power," Fredrick A. Praeger, Inc., New York, 1956. "The struggle for unification, rather than any revival of Nazism, may one day force Germany out of the Western camp." — Tetens, T.H., "The New Germany And The Old Nazis," Random House, New York, 1961. "A frank and often shocking account which details how 'Hitler's own' have managed to return to power in almost every walk of German life..." — Winkler, Paul, "The Thousand-Year Conspiracy," Charles Scribner's Sons, 1943. "Secret Germany behind the mask." — White, Theodore H., "Fire In The Ashes," William Sloane Associates, New York, 1953. The fire of Nazism in the ashes of Europe. — Sayers, Michael and Kahn, Albert E., "The Plot Against The Peace," Book Find Club, New York, 1945. "...uncovers Nazi Germany's secret plans for a THIRD WORLD WAR." (After all, they more-or-less got the first two world wars going, didn't they? - Branton) — Schultz, Sigrid, "GERMANY WILL TRY IT AGAIN," Reynal & Hitchcock, New York, 1944. Does the title give you a clue? — Dornberg, John, "Schizophrenic Germany," MacMillan Company, New York, 1961. "Is the new West Germany of the postwar years as democratic as we have been led to believe, or does Nazism still smolder?" — Lord Russell, Brigadier, of Liverpool, C.B.E., M.C., "Return of the Swastika?" David McKay Co., New York, 1969. Russell was part of the Nuremberg prosecution team. — Sutton, Anthony C., "Wall Street And The Rise Of Hitler, '76 Press, Seal Beach, Calif., 1976. There are more, these just happen to be the ones in my personal library. I read them, mostly about 20 or 30 years ago. I do not mean to give the impression that Germany is the source of the world's problems; Germany has simply been a part of a much bigger picture...

26. Sam Russell's 'OPEN MIND FORUM' program

More information on the Nazi Antarctic efforts and their attempts to impose a global dictatorship comes from Bulgarian physicist Vladimir Terziski. The following interview between Talk Show host Sam Russell and Terziski took place between 8-10 P.M., June 5th, 1993 on Sam Russell's 'OPEN MIND FORUM' program, KTKK [K-TALK] Radio in Salt Lake City, Utah. We will quote only those portions of the extensive conversation which tie-in directly with the subject at hand (Note: Some of the spellings of the names mentioned in the interview were transcribed phonetically from the tape. Actual spellings of these names which are identified as such may be different than they appear in the transcript, due perhaps in part to Mr. Terziski's Bulgarian accent):

SAM RUSSELL - ...I guess a place to start here, the Germans during World War II evidently had what was called the 'Foo Fighter', and this I guess is the name that the allied pilots gave to this curious-looking thing that would bob and weave and run around through the squadrons as they were flying over Germany to bomb and so on.

VLADIMIR TERZISKI - Exactly, the Foo Fighter, the 'fiery' ball. 'Foo' is 'fire' in French, it's also wind in Japanese... By the way Renato Vesco, who was the Italian [counterpart of] Wernher von Braun, the research scientist in charge of the ITALIAN Air Force and Space Research and Development program during the war, in his highly suppressed book in this country — which is also available through our Academy — 'INTERCEPT BUT DON'T SHOOT',

The Omega Files

talks about the whole family of turbojet saucers that were built by the Germans, all the way up to the Foo Fighter, the KUGELBLITZ and the FEUERBALL, two different models of basically the same device. And he also mentions a lot of ATTACKS of these machines on enemy bomber formations with DEVASTATING results for the bombers. Some of the Foo Fighters were doing 2900 kilometers an hour and up... a bomber would do maybe 300, 400, 500 at the most... so we're talking about 6, 7, 8 times the bomber speed. The most interesting thing that has not come up into, let's say, the work of Renato Vesco [because he talks only about the turbo-jet family of saucers... basically very simple saucers made with piston engines with propellers, spinning the lenticular airframe, the lens-shaped air frame of the craft thus creating gyroscopic antigravity — and some of them were hybrids between helicopters with spinning rotor, basically aerodynamic lift and the gyroscopic lift of the spinning heavy mass of rotary engines.

I wouldn't be amazed [if] the rotary engine itself were created to power a gyroscopically spinning saucer that had a big helicopter propeller on top, so it's kind of a hybrid between a helicopter and a saucer]... I even discovered...extremely rare drawings by the genius of German aviation, Lipish, the guy who built the first supersonic glider in the '30s and it is not Chuck Yeager who broke the sound barrier, but probably the Germans 10 years earlier with their... supersonic gliders that Lipish built. Anyway, Lipish was designing at the end of the war a supersonic ram-jet propulsion craft with anti-gravity assists. They had the fuel tanks spinning inside the jets...going through the engine part of the object to the engine duct, spinning the fuel around thus creating additional anti-gravity lift and greatly improving the lift capabilities and the inertial responses of the craft. So to sum it up in a nutshell, I have...several very brilliant videos with dozens of photographs and engineering drawings, sketches and so on. The Germans had PROBABLY 50 MODELS of flying saucers powered by every existing engine in their arsenal... piston engines with propellers, rotary...engines with propellers, inboard and outboard turbo-jets, pulse (?) jets, ram-jets and rocket engines. The rocket-engined craft... could go into orbit, the bigger models could go to the moon and back with literally a truckload of kerosene and oxygen. On top of the saucer space flights the Germans had [an] extensive space program with rocketry. I discovered just several days ago the man-made winged version of the V-2 rocket... was doing sub-orbital flights with an altitude higher than the altitude of the Mercury, the Vostock, space capsules. They had space programs with their Zanger-Brent strato-

The Omega Files

spheric ram-jet...bomber... antipodal, basically circling three quarters of the globe trajectory... That was the grandfather of the Aurora craft that is rumored so much these days in Area 51. (Take note that both the American and Russian space programs depended on the German scientists they had both acquired following World War II. It is possible that these researchers were intentionally made-out to be the 'cream' of German aerospace science, when in fact the most intelligent scientists may have found their way to the Antarctic base following World War II - Branton). The aircraft industries of the Allies after the war had a difficult time duplicating and regurgitating the German designs that the Germans came up with...

S.R. - Wow! That's amazing...

V.T. - Many of these things have not been duplicated yet, but the most astonishing photographs came — and I have copies of these and they are available — from the GERMAN SECRET SOCIETY 'Tuligezelshaft' and the 'Templehofgezelshaft', the German branch of the KNIGHTS TEMPLARS which are also the INTERNATIONAL BANKERS so they have absolutely no problems financing these projects. Few of the (—indistinguishable— lower-ranking German scientists...? - Branton) even knew that these projects were running. Many of them privately had been complaining that they were the dumbest fools because all the smart guys disappeared after the war into the German South Polar underground colony, and only basically the intelligent weaklings [remained in Germany]... We made a brilliant audio-tape, by the way all of these things that we will be talking about are available in two dozen very good video tapes and about as many audio tapes.

S.R. - We will have to be sure and tell the folks how they can find out how to get a hold of those, O.K.?

V.T. - It's very simple, they can call us here in Los Angeles at area code [310]-473-9717...

S.R. - ...I'd like to ask a question about your knowledge of the Russian technologies. It is said that the Russians are really a lot farther ahead than we are...

V.T. - Not at all...

S.R. - Technologically.

V.T. - My feeling is that not only the French Revolution and the Paris Commune and the Communism of Marx and Engels was financed and mas-

The Omega Files

terminded and orchestrated by the [Bavarian] Illuminati, but so was the Bolshevik Revolution, the Nazi uprising in Italy, or the National Socialist and Nazi movement in Germany. And along that line, Wall Street has secretly been going to painstaking efforts to help behind-the-scenes the Russians in order for them to become a real strong external enemy and not to be just a 'paper bear', a flimsy paper bear. I have numerous accounts of how the Germans built all the munitions plants, 14 out of 15 munitions plants BEFORE the war started, the Second World War started. They were all built by Germans... Rolls Royce built the turbo-jet factory for the MIG fighter plane engines, just in time for the beginning of the Korean war. I have a photograph in my possession of the best (at the time? - Branton) American strategic bomber, the B-29, the one that dropped the bomb over Hiroshima and Nagasaki. Under it's wing there is hanging the best German twin-engine rocket interceptor, supersonic swept-wing rocket interceptor the DFS-346, and all of this under the red star markings of the Russian Air Force. How can somebody claim that there is not a secret siphoning of the most advanced technology behind-the-scenes... of the Cold War in order to make Russia the real enemy. I've heard rumors that the Russians were given enriched uranium to build their first nuclear bomb, and when they couldn't do even that they were given a whole nuclear bomb that was smuggled out in the luggage of the Russian ambassador straight on a flight from Washington to Moscow according to the words of Victor Suvaro, the genius of the Russian Intelligence novels. And basically those are documentary books that he has written. The best of them is 'AQUARIUM', for any one of our listeners who would like to acquaint himself with the workings of a secret society. Later on the Russians were sold a nuclear submarine in order to make their sagging strategic fleet a more real, threatening menace. Why would the [Bavarian] Illuminati need a strong enemy in the Russias? Very simple, because otherwise they cannot keep the secrecy around these giant underground projects going on. Now the best reason they use is 'Oh well, we cannot tell you about that, we cannot discuss this even in Congress because the Russians would know.' It was cleverly used on both sides of the 'curtain' in order for the [Bavarian] secret societies in both Russia and the United States to quietly engage in — and justify the massive financing of — these projects.

Back to the Germans, the most interesting claim that they are [making] in another documentary film... available from us, is that they landed on Mars in mid-January 1946 after 8 months of heavy flight with a basically volunteer suicide crew of Germans and Japanese in a giant 230 foot diameter

The Omega Files

dreadnaught... again running on free energy, basically the Hanz-Kohler converters of gravity energy into electromagnetic energy of the flight. Another interesting thing that I found is a whole range of mind control experiments in Germany that were repeated verbatim by the super powers after the war. Mind control with ultrasound, when they were inducing and indoctrinating their crack S.S. troops, mind control with all kinds of synthetic hallucinogenic drugs, or all kinds of the 'proper' mushrooms, mind control that was developed using the Wilhelm Reichian technology. In the initial states this [involved] types of sodomic mind control that was practiced by certain of the Ahrimanic and Luciferian orders of Tibetan monks that were visited by these numerous German ethnographic expeditions in the '20s and '30s, and all of this secret knowledge was later brought to Germany.

We produce a fascinating tape here with Al Bielek and T. Johnson from Las Vegas on the magical-occult connections of the Third Reich, and we called the tape 'OCCULT NATIONAL SHAMANISM' in analogy to 'National Socialism', a fascinating tape that basically brings together about a dozen extremely rare books on the occult connections of the Third Reich, the dabblings with satanism, with witchcraft, with all kinds of unspeakable aberrations, including sexual aberrations... the Germans were in contact with half a dozen [malevolent] alien races in these big underground establishments, some of these underground bases were 2 kilometers long, one kilometer wide. I have found the drawings of the tunnel systems with these bases from incredible places including...the American Bombing Survey reports of underground — huge industrial establishments under the German mountains... the bottom line is that by the time the war ended the Germans were VERY HEAVILY doing all these major parts of the ILLUMINATI secret technologies on the planet... (Were the Nazi's the Military Research & Development arm of the Bavarian Illuminati? - Branton) Mind Control technologies, a whole dozen of mind-control... I mean we have a tape here on mind control that was going on in the German bases. But the most important thing about their research was GENETIC ENGINEERING... Quite a well-known movie producer in southern California that produced one of the best known UFO documentaries that won a big award has mentioned to me in a private conversation that while researching for that film he saw in a military-government archive a documentary, a silent documentary film about horrific genetic experiments on live human beings, I mean cutting off heads, dismembering, re-assembling, human bodies from parts — all these frankensteinian experiments in the German genetic program... and finally

The Omega Files

the film culminated with footage of living, walking, breathing HYBRIDS between HUMANS and ANIMALS that were produced in German concentration camps half a century earlier.

The Reife [spl?] microscope, the Royal Reife microscope which is rumored to be a Tesla scalar-wave microscope that has an extremely...high resolution power and can see many levels of complexity beyond the hierarchical level of the cell, was probably the magical key to the human genome kingdom, the microscope was discovered in the '20s in Berlin and probably gave the key to the Germans to the human genome. The big 10 billion dollar human genome project that is right now beginning to drain budget dollars run through the Dept. of Energy here, is nothing but a smokescreen for the REAL mastery of the human genome half a century earlier by the Illuminati that are running computerized designs of clones and human beings and all that stuff in the underground labs. (Note: Bavarian cultists and Grey aliens are reportedly working together in the production of so-called 'hybrids' within the underground joint-operational facilities. Most of the hu-brids [human-hybrids] who are born with imputed reptilian DNA or DNA from other animals are the unwilling servants of the draconian collectivists from birth. Some of these 'people' have escaped from the domination of the Collective and have joined with more friendly 'Federation' forces, or have been rescued by the same from captured bases or ships, according to contactee Alex Collier, and others. - Branton)

S.R. - Hmm.

V.T. - I take very seriously films, not only films like 'BOYS FROM BRAZIL' about the secret experiments in 'education' of abducted children... the [secret] government has been the biggest consumer of abducted children in this country, and I called just on a hunch this Milk Carton 1-800 number, chasing a rumor that 400,000 CHILDREN were missing from this country each year, [close to] half a million each year. I thought 'Nah, maybe 20, 30 thousand, it's not possible.' And the lady there said... 'No, we don't have ANY statistics.' 'Well, any newspaper articles, anything?' 'No, no, we DON'T have anything.' And I was beginning to get more and more suspicious. Finally she made an 'educated' guess, having worked for 5 years in the system. She said, 'About maybe 200,000 children a year or so.' Within only 5 minutes...research I did, I got half of the wildest rumor that I've heard of, half a million missing every year. Most of them disappear in the underground...of the New World Order...

The Omega Files

S.R. - Vladimir Terziski. He is a UFO researcher. He is a co-founder with Al Bielek of the 'American Academy of Dissident Scientists'. [Sam Russell takes a call at this point. The question is in regards to Vladimir's professional background]

V.T. - Well, I studied Physics and Engineering at Tokai University in Tokyo, I have a Bachelor Degree in Physics, and a Master Degree in Electronics Engineering. I worked for four years at the Solar Energy Research Institute for the Bulgarian Academy of Science before immigrating to the United States. I studied for 3 and a half, 4 years, Sociology at Arizona State University, and at UCLA, and I'm slowly dragging this additional Degree of mine to a completion these days...

S.R. - ...Well, O.K., let us move along and pick up on what you were talking about as we broke right there. This having to do with the genetic cloning and so on.

V.T. - I have two more items, basically very important items to finish and then we can go into the general discussions. To cap off the whole genetic research effort on the planet, it is not an idea of a few crazy frankensteinian scientists here and there in the secret underground bases, it is not a crazy idea by the secret government or even by some high levels of alien races that are using us as convenient guinea pigs... It is a much higher level of 'party line' agenda coming, my feeling is, from the... basically the fallen angelic presence on our planet that has been masterminding [the conspiracy]... probably 90% of the alien races that have visited our planet...most of them have been coming here on the planet sub-contracting for that particular branch of the 'celestial management' and the biggest point on their agenda is... on top of advanced interstellar TRANSPORTATION and COMMUNICATION have been — the creation of life (or rather the RE-CREATION or re-arrangement of existing biological matter, since created beings whether standing or fallen can only RE-STRUCTURE that what has already been created. - Branton), and MIND CONTROL of course.

[These] have been the four extremely important points, the highest points on their agenda. So the 'creation' of all of these frankensteinian monsters is not an aberration of a sick mind or probably a latent satanist movie producer. It is not a whim by some Financier that is financing these projects... it is really an incredible saga on a Universal or Galactic level... these hierarchies that are trying to outdo and outbid each other and trying to prove to probably higher levels of celestial overseeing bodies that they can do a better management and a better 'creation' of this and that including living beings. So I put the whole creation of artificial life from the crude mechanical robots created by the Illuminatial chemists [alchemists] in the medieval centuries to the frankensteinian conglomeration of human beings from...body parts in the late 19th century, and the first creation of primitive clones in the early 20th century through the limited experiments of hybridization between humans and animals that were going [on] in German concentration camps during the war. And... the biggest effort that was in front of the German hierarchy was the creation of the 'Master Race', the 'super men'.

And what they did on a small scale in the concentration camps, later on in the late '40s and early '50s they did on A TEN TIMES BIGGER SCALE IN THEIR SOUTH POLAR COLONY. The rumor is that these days there is a city called the NEW BERLIN, a big underground city under the South Pole, south of South Africa in the Queen Maud land... under the GERMAN jurisdiction, under the German nomenclature. A 2,000,000 strong colony that engages primarily in space travel and human genetic engineering. And basically, a very careful analysis of the German technology — and I repeat I am not a religious freak, I entered into conspiracy theories only because of necessity, to figure out the anti-gravity stuff that I was interested in. I'm primarily a physicist and an engineer, and I'm fascinated a lot more by an explanation of the physics of the local universe or of the energy management system in our Grand Universe than of, should we say, standing or fallen angelic management structures around our planet — but tracing the technologies, I have come to piece the big puzzle, this big galactic and universal puzzle together...

S.R. - ...We are just virtually out of time. Vladimir, we've had some questions off the air regarding what you might have available to send people in the written format or in electronic.

V.T. - I have a video list of probably 50 publications, videos, audios, booklets, articles and so on. Anyone who is interested can give us a call at area code [310] 473-9717. And I will be soon in one of the bookstores in Salt Lake City, I actually sent a lot of material that was exhibited at the Preparedness [Expo] Show.

S.R. - We have to leave it there, Vladimir I appreciate very much your coming on, I know the notice was very short and I appreciate it. It's been a fascinating hour for me, I hope for our listeners as well, and I'll hope to do it again some time.

V.T. - Sam, with the greatest of pleasure. I repeat again, this was only a 'little revelation' of the working of the dark side... one should not be pessimistic, on the contrary just by shining the light on these ugly deeds of the Illuminati, that's all there needs to be done in order for them to start melting like an old snow under the hot summer rays...

S.R. - Thank you very much Vladimir, a terrific way to end it... (Note: Vladimir Terziski is "...a Bulgarian born engineer and physicist, graduated Cum Laude from the Master of Science program of Tokai University in Tokyo in 1980. Served as a solar energy researcher, Bulgarian Academy of Sciences, before immigrating to the U.S. in 1984. [He is also an] International UFO researcher with command of English, Japanese, Russian, German, and Bulgarian [and] Creator/lecturer of UFOLOGY-101 course for University level attendance. - Branton)

With the previous foundation laid, I feel that this would be an appropriate place to include the following information which has made the rounds of the electronic newsgroups: From: dona@bilver.uucp (Don Allen) Newsgroups: alt.alien.visitors,alt.conspiracy,alt.activism,sci.skeptic,misc.headlines, alt.politics.bush Subject: UFO "October Surprise" and USA TAKEOVER?! Message-ID: <1992Jul31.011541.6582@bilver.uucp> Date: 31 Jul 92 01:15:41 GMT Organization: W. J. Vermillion - Winter Park, FL Lines: 285

27. ATTENTION: CIVIL WAR IS ABOUT TO BEGIN IN THE UNITED STATES!

YOU AND YOUR LOVED ONES ARE IN ACUTE DANGER! RACE RIOTS AND SLAUGHTER OF AMERICANS WILL BE THE FIRST SIGN! THIS IS NO JOKE!

On July 4, 1992, at a UFO convention in Arcadia, CA, Mr. Michael Younger, a member of the super-secret COM-12 group and a scientist who worked at Groom Lake, Area 51 in Nevada, stunned the audience of over 200 people with the following incredible information, which, if true, endangers the lives and freedoms of every American. Here is the amazing scenario of the planned events:

Beginning in August of this year, 1992, a conspiracy long at work behind the scenes of our government, will make its first overt move. These conspirators plan to create a dictatorship in the United States, suspend our

The Omega Files

Constitution and attempt to confiscate all guns and firearms in American homes.

Stage 1 being to create "race riots" in major U.S. cities such as New York, Chicago, Detroit, etc.; these to begin in August. This will be preceded by a month of subliminal programming via TV and other media to condition the people for civil war in the United States. The accent will be on rap records such as "Body Count" released by Time-Warner [a ROCKEFELLER corporation] by musicians "Ice Tea" and "Sister Solj" whose lyrics in such songs as "Cop Killers" are designed to inflame and polarize its listeners. These rap songs contain such lines as "kill white policemen," "kill the pigs", "kill whitey", and "Why not kill whitey, if he can kill us?" etc.

In August Stage 2, code-named "Operation Hot August Nights" will take effect. Special agents of the conspiracy, masquerading as police, will open fire on minorities, namely Black Americans and Hispanics and Orientals. Other agents will set off incendiary bombs as they did recently in the Los Angeles riots, which essentially was a "test case" that surpassed the expectations of the conspirators. These special agents, masquerading as police, massacre these Blacks and minorities and fire at the real policemen. This brings in more police and the riots escalate. "Skin heads" and other gangs, already fully armed, join in the fray. The real police, vastly outnumbered, cannot handle the rioting. The National Guard is called in and fired upon by [other] special agents masquerading as gang members, who also enlist other gang members to fight the police and national guardsmen.

These riots continue through August, with many minority Americans slaughtered in major cities. (Note: Although this did not come off as planned in August — possibly because the project had been compromised — the Globalist plans are still in effect, even if they have experienced temporary postponement or set-back. Also, a growing number of reports of United Nations military equipment being seen passing through U.S. communities on trains, trucks, etc., have been surfacing in recent years. I personally have learned of a few related incidents. I have come across reports of National Guardsmen undergoing specialized house-to-house search and seizure training and urban warfare tactics. I was also told that two men who managed to sneak into a Federal military plane 'graveyard' outside of Phoenix, Arizona had came across several freight train box-cars in which they discovered what they estimated to be from 2 to 3 million brand-new SHACKLES that were apparently being stored there, just waiting to be used!

The Omega Files

Keep THIS in mind while reading the following references to potential U.N. involvement in the attempted takeover. Compare this with various implications concerning National AND Communist 'Socialist' control of the U.N. Could the reason why the 'Commies' and 'Nazis' get along together within the U.N. be due to the fact that they are both backed by the Bavarian-Rockefeller alliance? Could it be that the L.A. RIOTS which began on April 29 1992 were a test-run for a plan to incite race riots and a civil race war in the United States? This is suggested by the following quotes from researcher Val Valerian: "During the UFO EXPO West 92 in Los Angeles, which took place a week after the riots in Los Angeles, I chanced to run into some fellow investigators who had observed several ships loaded with electronic antennae off the coast of Los Angeles two days before the riots took place. There are groups in Southern California that regularly conduct frequency analysis of various metropolitan areas, and they reported that the Los Angeles area was HEAVILY DOSED WITH BETA FREQUENCIES shortly before the riots occurred. Beta frequencies can produce anxiety states, and this most certainly exacerbated another scenario, which was a controlled exercise in population manipulation... On April 30th, the Compton Police Dept. revealed that it had arrested six people for arson, and that when questioned about their activities, the youths said they 'were on a mission to burn down 10 buildings an hour'. Their car contained 10 gallons of gasoline for use in these firebombing operations. Law enforcement sources also report that many of those arrested during the disturbance had identical cover stories, indicating that there were many such groups under the coordination and control of someone. The Los Angeles riots were in fact intelligence agency operations that were used to invoke the application of military troops; they were an attempt to start nationwide riots that would require the invocation of martial law and FEMA plans. Another indicator that the 'riots' were probably an intelligence operation is that the day before the Rodney King verdicts were released, a mass leaflet was distributed in South Central Los Angeles by a group calling itself the 'Revolutionary Communist Party'.

If you are at all familiar with 'U.S.' intelligence agency practices, it can immediately be seen that RCP is a front for CIA activities. Most 'revolutionary' and 'terrorist' activities are in fact performed by the very intelligence agencies which claim to exist for the prevention of such activities. The leaflet said, 'There's No Justice in the Courtroom — It's Right to Rebel.' Within days of the incident, Los Angeles Mayor Tom Bradley [who is also a MEMBER of the Tri-Lateral Commission, folks] used the press-orchestrated clamor

The Omega Files

for 'police reform' to put TLC counter-insurgency apparatus in place which launched a virtual war on local law enforcement, effectively paralyzing, if not destroying, those functions. TLC member Tom Bradley, as it turns out, appointed fellow TLC member Warren Christopher to form the 'Independent Commission to Investigate the LAPD.' Christopher, whose 'specialty' is riots and urban insurgency, is a partner in the law firm of O'Melveny and Myers. In the early 1960's, he and fellow TLC member Cyrus Vance, then at the Pentagon, drafted 'Operation Garden Plot', a plan for military martial law in American cities in the event of 'domestic civil disorder'. Of course, there is no distinction made of the 'cause' of domestic disorder, if you get my point. Warren Christopher, in fact, was one of the creators of the Law Enforcement Assistance Administration [LEAA], during the Johnson administration, when he was Deputy Attorney General. LEAA was one of the early attempts to implement a top-down federal takeover of local police departments in the U.S. It is apparently a long-standing policy of the Trilateral Commission to foment civil disturbance and unrest, not just in the U.S. but worldwide, in order to foster the imposition of world dictatorship.

Don't stop now — it gets more interesting. Also appointed to the Christopher Commission by TLC member Tom Bradley, Mayor of Los Angeles, is a man by the name of Mickey Kantor, who just happens to be the national campaign manager for the Democratic Presidential candidate and TLC member William Clinton, who is himself at the heart of the drug-smuggling operation that was detailed on April 21, 1992 on NBC televisions 'A Current Affair'; drugs have been flown in and out of the airport in Mena, Arkansas since the early Reagan days, and according to the television broadcast, both BUSH and CLINTON are aware of it; every time there is an effort to look into it, THE INVESTIGATION GETS STONE-WALLED BY THE FEDERAL GOVERNMENT. Check it out for yourself..." - Branton)

Stage 3: In September, President Bush calls in United Nations troops to quash the riots and restore law and order. American troops had indicated they did not wish to fight against American civilians. Bush executes Executive Orders, already in effect, which now give the UN FORCES complete rights and freedom to enter American homes, to confiscate all devices that are capable of communicating information, which includes video cameras, VCRs, computers, mimeographs, anything that can print, copy machines, etc. These troops are furnished certain lists of names, particularly those known as 'Patriots' and these patriots and their families are rounded up first,

The Omega Files

and if not executed on the spot, are sent to any of the 13 [major] concentration camps now fully activated in the United States. There is nobody left to tell what really happened. Curious neighbors will be told it was a justified "drug raid." Those who escape to the hills and mountains are hunted down by "search and destroy" troops, specially trained for mountain warfare. During September all borders will be closed down, as well as airports. No one is allowed to leave the United States.

Stage 4: In October an 'official' announcement will be carried live on TV, that extraterrestrial aliens, probably Zeta Reticuli 'Greys' have invaded the Earth, with some actual aliens [revealed] on the show. This is actually a fake invasion. The aliens have BEEN on Earth for many years, [and] made treaties and agreements with our governments; there are millions of them in secret underground complexes such as DULCE, New Mexico, which are responsible for the abduction of American children and citizens and the cattle mutilations documented in books and on TV, such as the recent special 'Intruders'. This announcement will cause the entire world to mobilize under UN supervision to fight the 'invaders'. (Note: ...just as we 'mobilized' under the U.N. to fight the 'Communists' in the pre-planned Korean war, when in fact the pro-Socialist U.N. officials were already in league with the Communists and were betraying our troop movements and plans to the Reds at every turn, according to General Douglas McCarthur. Incidentally the General's comments regarding this betrayal have mysteriously remained out of the 'official' mainstream historical texts. McCarthur, by the way, was an advocate of the belief that the Third World War would involve a space war with aliens in our skies. Could an interplanetary version of this Machievellian scenario be in the works, with the New World Order taking the place of the United Nations, and the 'Alien Grays' taking the place of the 'Communists'? An interesting thing about Michael Younger himself is that others have confirmed the existence of COM-12 and a similar agency called the CABAL. These two NAVY INTELLIGENCE agencies are aware of the presence of the Greys and are OPPOSED to any further dealings with them based on known betrayals of established treaties. COM-12 and the CABAL are involved in an 'Intelligence War' with two fascist agencies connected to the NSA-CIA known as MAJI and AQUARIUS. These two agencies maintain ACTIVE interactions with the 'Grey aliens' and according to some these agencies are actually CONTROLLED by these entities via mind-control implants. Take careful note of the fascist or 'Nazi' origins of both the CIA and NSA as Trojan horse or fifth-column agencies in American Intelligence. COM-12 and

The Omega Files

the CABAL are working with humanoid ET's who are determined to prevent the reptiloid ET's working through MAJI and AQUARIUS from interfering with the affairs of this planet.

The conflict between these two ET groups has apparently led to planet earth being the center of an ancient dispute between these two galactic superpowers, the humanoid non-interventionists of the Pleiades-Andromeda constellations and the reptiloid interventionists of the Orion-Draconis constellations. COM-12 and the CABAL are determined to maintain American independence under the U.S. Constitution, whereas MAJI and AQUARIUS are determined to betray America to the New World Order. COM-12 and the CABAL are intentionally 'leaking' information damaging to MAJI and AQUARIUS to the public, and it 'may' have been due to their efforts that the L.A. Riots take-over scenario failed to materialize into a National Emergency and a New World Order takeover at THAT time. The New World Order advocates have tried several times in the past and will continue to do so in the future. For some reason they are desperate to bring about the New World Order takeover of the United States of America by the year 2000. That is definitely their goal. If all else fails they may attempt an all-out United Nations invasion of the U.S., using whatever possible means they can to "justify" such a "U.N. Operation." - Branton) During November the chaos continues and more 'UN' troops pour into the United States, mostly mercenaries who have fought in African nations and other 'hot spots' previously. [The butchery of these troops is well documented].

Stage 5: In December a well-planned 'crash' of the stock market will occur, a dramatic drop to at least 1500 on the DJ Industrial Average. This event [is] planned to further weaken, panic and confuse the population.

Stage 6: ...The Constitution of the United States is suspended and the people are now living under martial law in a totally FASCIST state. Who are these conspirators? According to Mike Younger, at the end of World War II, Nelson Rockefeller brought 3000 high Nazi party officials from Germany illegally into the U.S., without permission. As of today it is believed there are now 1.6 million Nazis in the U.S., many high in government and major corporations, such as ATLANTIC RICHFIELD in New Jersey. Incredibly, these Nazi fascists are attempting to set up a "4th Reich" to continue the thousand-year plan of Adolph Hitler, [with its intent] to eventually eliminate "non Aryan" people such as Jews, Blacks and other 'dissidents'. In January, 2000, when the 'real' alien invasion occurs, the planet will be officially turned over to the alien invaders, the Nazi rulers expecting to get 25% of the Earth for themselves. The writers of this document did not originate the above material, but are simply passing this information along to you to do with what you feel is necessary. We have no way of knowing that these things will happen [we hope and pray they do not], but if any of the above should occur, you can rest assured the balance of this evil scenario will follow. Their two main immediate goals are to DISARM American citizens and SUSPEND our Constitution.

28. Mind Control Projects Out of Atlantic

URGENT: MAKE 30 COPIES AND MAIL TO MEDIA, POLITICIANS, CHURCHES, ORGANIZATIONS. POST ON BULLETIN BOARDS, PASS OUT TO CITIZENS IN THE STREETS! TIME IS RUNNING OUT! ACT NOW!

Don —-" Don Allen "- // Only | Tavistock + Esalen = "New Age" Internet: dona@bilver.uucp \X/ Amiga | Rothschild + Rockefeller = FED UUCP: .uunet!peora!bilver!vicstoy!dona | UN + Maitreya = "Twilight Zone" "A democracy cannot be both ignorant and free" - Thomas Jefferson From: dona@bilver.uucp (Don Allen) Newsgroups:

alt.conspiracy,alt.alien.visitors,talk.politics.guns Subject:

FILE: UFO OCTOBER SURPRISE - C.A.C. part 2/2 Keywords: NAZI WORLD TAKEOVER PLAN - NEW WORLD ORDER Message-ID: <1992Aug29.193917.15933@bilver.uucp> Date: 29 Aug 92 19:39:17 GMT Organization: W. J. Vermillion - Winter Park, FL Lines: 515 UFO NAZI OCTOBER SURPRISE (...more information from the Arcadia, California conference which featured Michael Younger, a member of the secret Navy Intelligence unit COM-12, which is attempting to maintain a rear-guard defense of the U.S. Constitution, Bill of Rights and Declaration of Independence. - Branton)

Many of these [Nazis] became agents of the Central intelligence Agency [CIA], NASA, also NSA, and in the FBI and other government agencies, so that the Nazis had more or less totally infiltrated the United States government in many of the most key and sensitive positions... They also were used in and given jobs within many of the corporations owned by the ROCKEFELLERS, including ATLANTIC RICHFIELD. It was through Atlantic Richfield that much of the mind control programs were implemented and used... One of the Nazi's [Doctor's], working with 300 elite scientists on these projects, developed a certain drug that could be used on children [inducing] severe pain and torture, where the child would normally black out, and

The Omega Files

become unconscious. The doctor could administer or inject the drug and it would keep the child from blacking out, and thus the doctor could then inflict greater pain, going far beyond the threshold of human endurance, which in turn would allow the mind of the child to become totally wiped out, a total blank so that the child forgot identity, forgot personal identity, forgot even how to add or subtract or carry on conversation.

Mind-Controlled Children Used as Sex Slaves The child would need to be totally programmed from the beginning, starting from a blank consciousness. This technique of brainwashing or mind control allowed them to create whatever kind of person they wanted. They created many of these children to become sex slaves for their own kind, and those children then became used by others for as long as they were wanted, to be disposed of when the [person] was tired of them or finished with them. According to this [Michael Younger's] tape, the man responsible for distributing the children among various Nazis for sex use was named Larry King, not the Larry King of the television and talk-show host, but a younger man, a different person, who would barter in human souls and sell these children to men for sex purposes, for parties or for whatever, allowing them total ownership of the child as though the child were simply an object. The [Nazis] were free to destroy the child or to keep the child... Some of the children were used for satanic purposes according to the tape. They were used for satanic rituals which, in some of the rituals, included being skinned alive and having the heart pulled out of the child while the child is still living...

[This] Larry King would sell these children, making huge amounts of money for these various purposes, and if the children did not work out, they were simply disposed of. In many cases, if they were brought back to be disposed of, they would be sent to the Atlantic Richfield complex in New Jersey and the complex would work with the children to try to 'salvage' them. [re-enforce a state of mindless automatic obedience] Atlantic Richfield Complex Scene of Mass Child Murders & Burials If this did not work they were simply taken out into the back area and shot and put into a trench which had been dug by a bulldozer and the bulldozer would then move dirt over them... "The Milk Carton Kids and What the Nazis are Doing to them" (Joseph Mengele, Hitler's Evil Doctor is Alive and Well) Mike Younger discussed...what is termed the "Milk Carton Kids," the disappearing children of this nation whose faces appear on milk cartons... many of these children have been abducted by Nazis and [the tape] speaks in particular of a

The Omega Files

program...which is directed toward mind control. Joseph Mengele, the Nazi doctor that worked most closely with Adolf Hitler, was not yet dead as reports have indicated... Dr. Mengele was still operating a mind control center in Florida, which specialized in manipulating the minds of children. The idea of dealing with children fascinated the Nazis because their minds were already easily controlled and easier to alter than were adults. Plus, they had the ability to control them with greater ease because of size, and also they had the ability to use a mind-controlled child according to the way they wished. Mike Younger, speaking of this, told of how he and his lawyer had infiltrated the Nazi groups and had gone to the New Jersey Atlantic Richfield [ARCO] complex to a meeting of Nazis and throughout the day they kept hearing intermittent shots. (Note: The Brookhaven National Laboratories which assisted in the Montauk Projects is also located in New Jersey, and there is also a strong neo-Nazi or white-supremacist political movement active in this area as well.

In addition to this, the Standard-Exxon Oil Company which during WWII established a merger with the Nazi Company I. G. Farben — which utilized slave labor — is also based in New Jersey. Not to mention the I.T.T. complex in New Jersey as well, which is owned and controlled largely by the German KRUPP family. Those Patriots who are native to that area should keep on the lookout for any leads on Nazi activity there and, once they have discovered signs of such activity they should cautiously investigate, document, and expose it for all to see. - Branton) They did not know what those shots were until they were taken to another place over-looking the site of the complex and they saw the children being taken out, forced to kneel down by the trench and shot in the back of the head with .22 pistols. After three or four would be shot, the bulldozer would move forward a few feet, covering them, and then the process would begin again. Each time a few would be shot and fall into the trench, and the bulldozer would move dirt over them. [Michael Younger], speaking to a group of approximately 200 or so people in Arcadia, explained all of this; the lawyer who had accompanied him became so frightened of the story and of the events that he decided himself not to talk in person, the next day when he was scheduled to speak [he did not], but instead to present a video tape. He was convinced that if he showed up there, he would be killed.

This man, being Jewish; the Jewish attorney decided that he would be killed if he showed up there and thus, left instead a video-tape describing

The Omega Files

this incident and the treatment of the children who had disappeared. The term "milk carton kids" was a derogative term used as a joke by these Nazis because they never returned and they thought this was a rather funny way of describing the kids. The fact that their pictures were put on milk cartons did not help the children, but the Nazis did believe it showed some kind of effort by the society, which had been lacking previously. They did not admire the fact that an effort was being made to locate the children, but they thought it was a joke to have their faces plastered on milk cartons, when they would never be seen again... During the presentation in Arcadia, a film was shown in which the United Nations armies were brought into a West African nation to bring 'peace'. They encountered several hundred civilians, and thus opened fire on them with machine guns and rifles. Vividly shown in the film was one lady carrying her child. The head of the child suddenly exploded as a .30 caliber machine gun bullet blew it open like it was a watermelon, and then another bullet struck the mother and she fell down. The masses, the several hundred women and children eventually were all slaughtered by the United Nations troops who had come to bring 'peace', and they joked and laughed about their job and how they had completed that and now must get on and find others.

The film itself had been brought back to be put on television to alert the masses but no station would allow it to be shown, and thus, the film was presented at this meeting and was made available for individuals to purchase, but such does not allow the masses to know what really occurs with these mercenary United Nations troops... There were several hundred people present. When someone asked: "Does George Bush know he's a target for assassination in March?" [the answer was...] "He does now! He knows that his Vice President is behind it..." (Note: One source has stated that George Bush was the former director of a 'secret government' group which wields even more power than the CIA, that is the MJ-12 or PI-40 organization which is an extension of MAJI. When Bush left the position, Dan Quayle reportedly took over, in which case Quayle would have been at the time one of the most powerful individuals in the 'secret' government power structure, IF this source was accurate. There are incidentally reports that MJ-12 itself is currently fragmented between the pro-Grey advocates in MAJI/AQUARIUS agencies and the anti-Grey activists in the CABAL/COM12 agencies. - Branton) Mike Younger also indicated that there were further efforts on their part to prevent this plan from being carried out. The people whom he works with have been working to expose George Bush in his Iran/Contra

The Omega Files

connections and his dealings with his brother in illegal operations in Japan, in hopes that these things will eventually cause enough people to question him and not vote for him... there are quite a number of these (agents, like Michael Younger and others connected to COM-12 - Branton) working to try to bring intelligence agents over to the good side and trying to bring military leaders over to the good side, and that there are quite a few people within the intelligence and military groups who know what is going on, and who simply don't like it, and that [they] are preparing their own plans to counter this plan if it is indeed carried off... (Note: Apparently these campaigns were successful, as George Bush failed in his bid for re-election.

If he would have been re-elected, could it be that we would now be living in a fascist dictatorship? It should also be realized that George Bush is NOT the 'center' of the conspiracy, the NWO agenda would go on with or without him. He was actually at the time a "front man" for a force that is far more evil and more powerful than any one man alone. Neither am I implying that the nations of Germany, Austria nor Italy where the Bavarian-Roman secret societies have their roots are the ultimate 'enemy'. The enemy is the secret society power STRUCTURE itself, which controls the governments of these countries, and the means of counter-attack should be a BLATANT, FOCUSED AND UNRELENTING EXPOSURE of the deepest and darkest secrets, atrocities and 'war crimes' of these death merchants!!! - Branton)

Today, another opportunity has been presented and since these forces can no longer polarize the West against Russia, trigger a devastating nuclear war [at least not with Russia, unless it becomes a super-power once again], it has seized upon the present opportunity wherein economic depression and a growing polarizing in America against minorities, can create such dire conditions in America that the public will actually allow the President to call in UN troops to restore law and order... —" Don Allen "- // Only | Tavistock + Esalen = "New Age" Internet: dona@bilver.uucp \X/ Amiga | Rothschild + Rockefeller = FED UUCP: .uunet!peora!bilver!vicstoy!dona | UN + Maitreya = "Twilight Zone" "A democracy cannot be both ignorant and free" - Thomas Jefferson An interesting confirmation of some of the above appears in Webster Griffin Tarpley and Anton Chaitkin book: GEORGE BUSH: THE UNAUTHORIZED BIOGRAPHY, which was first serialized in THE NEW FEDERALIST, beginning with Vol.V, No. 39., and later published by "Executive Intelligence Review". Some of the claims in this massively documented volume include: — A black Republican, a good friend of George Bush who was

The Omega Files

responsible for rallying black support for the Bush presidency, became the center of a sex scandal in Nebraska following the collapse of the minority-oriented Franklin Community Credit Union in Omaha which he directed.

This man was Lawrence [LARRY] E. KING, Jr. King sang the national anthem at both the 1984 and 1988 Republican conventions. — The "Franklin Committee" made a probe into charges of embezzlement and in November 1988, King's offices were raided by the FBI and $40 million was discovered missing. Within weeks however, the Nebraska Senate, which initially opened the inquiry to find out where the money had gone, instead found itself questioning young adults and teenagers who claimed that they had been child prostitutes. Several social workers and state child-care administrators accused King of running a child prostitution ring. The charges grew, as the former police chief of Omaha, the publisher of the state's largest daily newspaper, and SEVERAL OTHER POLITICAL ASSOCIATES of King found themselves being accused of patronizing the child prostitution ring. (Could this help to confirm rumors of a large 'Nazi' infiltration force in Nebraska, similar to claims of similar Nazi presence in Dulce, New Mexico; Reno, Nevada; Montauk, New York; and New Jersey, etc? — Interestingly all of these states begin with the letter 'N', just like 'Nazi' and 'NeuSchwabenland' do, which may OR MAY NOT have any significance whatsoever, other than mere coincidence. - Branton). — Although King was given a 15-year federal prison sentence for defrauding the Omaha-based credit union, the magazines 'Avvenimenti' of Italy and 'Pronto' of Spain, among others, have charged that King's crimes were more serious: that he ran a national child prostitution ring that serviced THE POLITICAL AND BUSINESS ELITE OF BOTH THE REPUBLICAN AND DEMOCRATIC PARTIES.

Several child victims of King's operations charged him with participation in at least one SATANIC RITUAL MURDER of a child several years ago. Also the "Washington Post", "New York Times", "Village Voice" and "National Law Journal" covered the full range of accusations after the story broke in November of 1988. In fact, according to the book, King's money machinations were also linked to the Iran-Contra affair, and some say that King provided the CIA with information garnered from his alleged activities as a 'pimp' for the high and mighty. — 'Pronto', the Barcelona-based, largest circulation weekly in Spain with over 4.5 million readers stated that Roy Stephens, a private investigator who has worked on the case and who heads the MISSING YOUTH FOUNDATION, "says there is reason to believe THAT

The Omega Files

THE CIA IS DIRECTLY IMPLICATED," and that the "FBI refuses to help in the investigation and has SABOTAGED any efforts" to get to the bottom of the story. — According to this volume, several of the Omaha child prostitutes testified that they had traveled to Washington, D.C. with King in private planes to attend political events which were followed by [CHILD] SEX PARTIES. — George Bush's name had repeatedly surfaced in the Nebraska scandal. However his name was first put into print in July 1989, a little less than a month after the Washington call boy affair had first made headlines. Omaha's leading daily newspaper reported, "One child, who has been under psychiatric care, is said to believe she saw George Bush at one of King's parties." — Gary Caradori was a retired state police investigator who had been hired by the Nebraska Senate to investigate the case, and who HAD DIED MYSTERIOUSLY DURING THE COURSE OF HIS INVESTIGATIONS.

On July 11, 1990, during the course of his investigations, Gary Caradori, 41, died in the crash of his small plane, together with his 8-year-old son, after a mid-air EXPLOSION whose cause has not yet been discovered. A skilled and cautious pilot, Caradori told friends repeatedly in the weeks before his death that he feared his plane would be sabotaged. — Steve Bowman, an Omaha businessman who is compiling a book on the Franklin money and sex scandal, has stated: "We do have some credible witnesses who say that 'Yes, George Bush does have a problem.'... Child abuse has become one of the epidemics of the 1990s," Bowman told 'GQ' [GENTLEMAN'S QUARTERLY magazine]. One of Bowman's sources is a retired psychiatrist who worked for the CIA. He added that cocaine trafficking and political corruption were the other principal themes. — Peter Sawyer, an Australian conservative activist who publishes a controversial newsletter, "Inside News" with a circulation of 200,000, dedicated his November 1991 issue exclusively to the Nebraska scandal, wherein he focused on President Bush's links to the affair. In a section captioned, "The Original Allegations: Bush First Named in 1985," Sawyer writes, "...If the first allegations about a massive child exploitation ring, centered around LARRY KING and leading all the way to the White House, had been made in 1989, and had all come from the same source, some shenanigans and mischievous collusion could be suspected. However, the allegations arising out of the Franklin Credit Union collapse were not the first. "Way back in 1985, a young girl, Eulice [Lisa] Washington, was the center of an investigation by Andrea L. Carener, of the Nebraska Department of Social Services. The investigation was instigated because Lisa and her sister Tracey continually ran away from their foster parents, Jarrett and

The Omega Files

Barbara Webb. Initially reluctant to disclose information for fear of being further punished, the two girls eventually recounted a remarkable story, later backed up by OTHER children who had been fostered out to the Webb's [sic].

"These debriefings were conducted by Mrs. Julie Walters, another welfare officer, who worked for Boys Town at the time, and who had been called in because of the constant reference by the Webb children and others, to that institution. "Lisa, supported by her sister, detailed a massive child sex, homosexual, and pornography industry, run in Nebraska by LARRY KING. She described how she was regularly taken to Washington by plane, with other youths, to attend parties hosted by King and involving many prominent people, including businessmen and politicians. Lisa specifically named GEORGE BUSH as being in attendance on at least two separate occasions. "Remember, this was in 1985," the Australian newsletter emphasized. Mrs. Julie Walters in 1986 interviewed the alleged child prostitute, Lisa, who told her about Mr. BUSH. Lisa and her sister Tracey were temporarily living at the time in the home of Kathleen Sorenson, another foster parent. Mrs. Walters explained that at first she was very surprised by her revelations, but Lisa — who come from a very underprivileged background with no knowledge of political affairs — gave minute details of her attendance at political meetings around the country. Julie Walters' 50-page handwritten report states: "3/25/86. Met with Kathleen [Sorenson] and Lisa for about 2 hours in Blair [Neb.] questioning Lisa for more details about sexual abuse.... Lisa admitted to being used as a prostitute by Larry King when she was on trips with his family. She started going on trips when she was in 10th grade. Besides herself and Larry there was also Mrs. King, their son, Prince, and 2-3 other couples. They traveled in Larry's private plane, Lisa said that at these trip parties, which Larry hosted, she sat naked 'looking pretty and innocent' and guests could engage in ANY sexual activity they wanted [but penetration was not allowed] with her.... Lisa said she first met V.P. George Bush at the Republican Convention [that Larry King sang the national anthem at] and saw him again at a Washington, D.C. party that Larry hosted.

At that party, Lisa saw no women... "The polygraph test which Lisa took only centered around sexual abuse committed by Jarrett Webb. At that time, she had said only general things about Larry's trips [i.e. where they went, etc.]. She only began talking about her involvement in prostitution during those trips on 3/25/86.... "Lisa also accompanied Mr. and Mrs. King

The Omega Files

and Prince on trips to Chicago, N.Y. and Washington, D.C. beginning when she was 15 years old. She missed twenty-two days of school almost totally due to these trips. Lisa was taken along on the pretense of being Prince's babysitter. Last year she met V.P. George Bush and saw him again at one of the parties Larry gave while on a Washington, D.C. trip. At some of the parties there are just men [as was the case at the party George Bush attended] — older men and younger men in their early twenties. Lisa said she has seen sodomy committed at those parties.... "At these parties, Lisa said every guest had a bodyguard and she saw some of the men wearing guns. All guests had to produce a card which was run through a machine to verify who the guest was, in fact, who they said they were. And then each guest was frisked down before entering the party." — A Franklin Committee report stated: "Apparently she [Lisa] was contacted on December 19 [1988] and voluntarily came to the FBI offices on December 30, 1988. She was interviewed by Brady, Tucker and Phillips. "She indicates that in September or October 1984, when [Lisa] Washington was fourteen or fifteen years of age, she went on a trip to Chicago with Larry King and fifteen to twenty boys from Omaha. She flew to Chicago on a private plane. "The plane was large and had rows of two seats apiece on either side of the interior middle aisle. "She indicates that King got the boys from Boys Town and the boys worked for him. She stated that Rod Evans and two other boys with the last name of Evans were on the plane. Could not recall the names of the other boys. "The boys who flew to Chicago with Washington and King were between the ages of fifteen and eighteen.

Most of the boys were black but some were white. She was shown a color photograph of a boy and identified that boy as being one of the boys on the plane. She could not recall his name. "She indicates that she was coerced to going on the trip by Barbara Webb. "She indicates that she attended a party in Chicago with King and the male youths. She indicated GEORGE BUSH was present. "She indicates that she set [sic] at a table at the party while wearing nothing but a negligee. She stated that George Bush saw her on the table. She stated she saw George Bush pay King money, and that Bush left the party with a nineteen year old black BOY named Brent." Lisa stated that the party George Bush attended was in Chicago in September or October 1984. According to the "Chicago Tribune" of October 31, 1984, Bush WAS IN FACT in Illinois campaigning for congressional candidates at the end of October. "Eulice [Lisa] indicated that she recognized George Bush as coming to the party and that Bush had two large white males with him.

The Omega Files

Eulice indicated Bush came to the party approximately 45 minutes after it started and that he was greeted by Larry King. Eulice indicated that she knew George Bush due to the fact that he had been in political campaigns and also she had observed a picture of Bush with Larry King at Larry King's house in Omaha." The report stated: "Lisa was given four polygraph tests administered by a state trooper at the State Patrol office on Center Street in Omaha. The state trooper, after Lisa's testing was completed, told [another foster parent] he tried to 'break Lisa down,' but he was convinced SHE WAS TELLING THE TRUTH." If the deviant machinations of George Herbert [the pervert] Bush and his fellow Nazi conspirators isn't enough to fan the flames of your patriotic indignation to the melting point... then just read the following regarding their ring-leaders, the German immigrant billionaire family, the Rockefellons — er, I mean the Rockefellers:

POPULATION CONTROL, NAZIS, AND THE U.N.! —

by Anton Chaitkin

ROCKFELLER AND MASS MURDER

The ROCKEFELLER Foundation is the PRIME SPONSOR of public relations for the UNITED NATION'S drastic depopulation program, which the world is invited to accept at the UN's scheduled September conference in Cairo, Egypt. Evidence in the possession of a growing number of researchers in America, England, and Germany demonstrates that the Foundation and its CORPORATE, MEDICAL, and POLITICAL associates organized the racial MASS MURDER program of NAZI GERMANY.

These globalists, who function as a conduit for British Empire geopolitics, were NOT stopped after World War II. The UNITED NATIONS alliance of the old NAZI rightwing with the NEW AGE leftwing poses an even graver danger to the world today than the same grouping did in 1941. Oil monopolist John D. Rockefeller created the family-run Rockefeller Foundation in 1909. By 1929 he had placed $300 million worth of the family's controlling interest in the Standard Oil Company of NEW JERSEY [later called 'EXXON'] to the account of the Foundation. The Foundation's money created the medical specialty known as PSYCHIATRIC GENETICS. For the new experimental field, the Foundation reorganized medical teaching in Germany, creating and thenceforth continuously directing the "Kaiser Wilhelm Institute for Psychiatry" and the "`Kaiser Wilhelm Institute for Anthropology, Eugenics and Human Heredity." The Rockefellers' chief executive of these institutions was

The Omega Files

the fascist Swiss psychiatrist Ernst Rudin, assisted by his proteges Otmar Verschuer and Franz J. Kallmann. In 1932, the British-led "Eugenics" movement designated the Rockefellers' Dr. Rudin as the president of the worldwide Eugenics Federation. The movement called for the killing or sterilization of people whose HEREDITY made them a public burden. THE RACIAL LAWS... A few months later, Hitler took over Germany and the Rockefeller-Rudin apparatus became a section of the Nazi state. The regime appointed Rudin head of the Racial Hygiene Society. Rudin and his staff, as part of the Task Force of Heredity Experts chaired by SS chief Heinrich Himmler, drew up the sterilization law.

Described as an American Model law, it was adopted in July 1933 and proudly printed in the September 1933 Eugenical News [USA] with Hitler's signature. The Rockefeller group drew up other race laws, also based on existing Virginia statutes. The 'T4" unit of the Hitler Chancery, based on psychiatrists led by Rudin and his staff, cooperated in creating propaganda films to sell mercy killing [euthanasia] to German citizens. The public reacted antagonistically: Hitler had to withdraw a tear-jerker right-to-die film from the movie theaters. The proper groundwork had not yet been laid. Under the Nazis, the German chemical company I.G. FARBEN and Rockefeller's STANDARD [EXXON] OIL of New Jersey were effectively a SINGLE FIRM, merged in hundreds of cartel arrangements. I.G. FARBEN was led up until 1937 by the Warburg family, Rockefeller's partner in banking and in the design of Nazi German eugenics. Following the German invasion of Poland in 1939, Standard Oil pledged to keep the merger with I.G. Farben going even if the U.S. entered the war. This was exposed in 1942 by Sen. Harry Truman's investigating committee, and President Roosevelt took hundreds of legal measures during the war to stop the Standard - I.G. Farben cartel from supplying the enemy war machine. In 1940-41, I.G. Farben built a gigantic factory at Auschwitz in Poland, to utilize the Standard Oil / I.G. Farben patents with concentration camp slave labor to make gasoline from coal. The SS was assigned to guard the Jewish and other inmates and select for killing those who were unfit for I.G. Farben slave labor.

Standard-Germany president Emil Helfferich testified after the war that Standard Oil funds helped pay for SS guards at Auschwitz. In 1940, six months after the notorious Standard-I.G. meeting, European Rockefeller Foundation official Daniel O'Brian wrote to the Foundation's chief medical officer Alan Gregg that "it would be unfortunate if it was chosen to stop research

The Omega Files

which has no relation to war issues" — so the Foundation continued financing Nazi "psychiatric research" (which translates into "mind control" research. - Branton) during the war. In 1936, Rockefeller's Dr. Franz Kallmann interrupted his study of hereditary degeneracy and emigrated to America because he was half-Jewish. Kallmann went to New York and established the Medical Genetics Department of the New York State Psychiatric Institute. The SCOTTISH RITE of Freemasonry published Kallman's study of over 1,000 cases of schizophrenia, which tried to prove its hereditary basis. In the book, Kallmann thanked his long-time boss and mentor Rudin. Kallmann's book, published in 1938 in the USA and Nazi Germany, was used by the T4 unit as a rationalization to begin in 1939 the murder of mental patients and various "defective" people, perhaps most of them CHILDREN. Gas and lethal injections were used to kill 250,000 under this program, in which the staffs for a BROADER murder program were de-sensitized and trained. DR. MENGELE...

In 1943, Otmar Verschuer's assistant Josef Mengele was made medical commandant of Auschwitz. As wartime director of Rockefeller's Kaiser Wilhelm Institute for Anthropology, Eugenics and Human Heredity in Berlin, Verschuer secured funds for Mengele's experiments at Auschwitz from the German Research Council. Verschuer wrote a progress report to the Council: "My co-researcher in this research is my assistant the anthropologist and physician Mengele. He is serving as Hauptstuermfuehrer and camp doctor in the concentration camp Auschwitz.... With the permission of the Reichsfuehrer SS Himmler, anthropological research is being undertaken on the various racial groups in the concentration camps and blood samples will be sent to my laboratory for investigation." Mengele prowled the railroad lines leading into Auschwitz, looking for twins — a favorite subject of psychiatric geneticists. On arrival at Mengele's experimental station, twins filled out "a detailed questionnaire from the Kaiser Wilhelm Institute." There were daily drawings of blood for Verschuer's "specific protein" research. Needles were injected into eyes for work on eye color. There were experimental blood transfusions and infections. Organs and limbs were removed, sometimes without anesthetics. Sex changes were attempted. Females were sterilized, males were castrated. Thousands were murdered and their organs, eyeballs, heads, and limbs were sent to Verschuer and the Rockefeller group at the Kaiser Wilhelm Institute. (Remember, the Rockefellers were originally German immigrants to America. - Branton)

The Omega Files

In 1946, Verschuer wrote to the Bureau of Human Heredity in London, asking for help in continuing his "scientific research." FACELIFT... In 1947, the Bureau of Human Heredity moved from London to Copenhagen. The new Danish building for this was built with Rockefeller money. The first International Congress in Human Genetics following World War II was held at this Danish institute in 1956. By that time, Verschuer was a member of the American Eugenics Society, then indistinguishable from Rockefeller's Population Council. Dr. Kallmann helped save Verschuer by testifying in his denazification proceedings. Dr. Kallmann created the American Society of Human Genetics, which organized the "Human Genome Project" — (based at Los Alamos Labs and in turn the more covert research-and-development projects within the Dulce, New Mexico base — which is also involved in researching any and every form of sophisticated occult-technology imaginable. - Branton) a current $3 billion physical multiculturalism effort. Kallmann was a director of the American Eugenics Society in 1952 and from 1954 to 1965. In the 1950s, the Rockefellers reorganized the U.S. eugenics movement in their own family offices, with spinoff population-control AND abortion groups The Eugenics Society changed its name to the "Society for the Study of Social Biology", its current name. The Rockefeller Foundation had long financed the eugenics movement in England, apparently repaying Britain for the fact that British capital and an Englishman-partner had started old John D. Rockefeller out in his Oil Trust. In the 1960s, the Eugenics Society of England adopted what they called Crypto-eugenics, stating in their official reports that they would do eugenics through means and instruments not labeled as eugenics.

With support from the Rockefellers, the Eugenics Society [England] set up a sub-committee called the INTERNATIONAL PLANNED PARENTHOOD FEDERATION, which for 12 years had no other address than the Eugenics Society. (Note: Margaret Sanger plays a central role in this PLANNED PARENTHOOD network. And people blast Rush Limbaugh for calling Sanger a "Femi-Nazi" when in fact that's exactly and literally what it comes down to, when one considers her full support of the Nazi's 'Aryan' racial supremacy philosophies. In the 1980's there were an estimated 50 MILLION or more abortions worldwide, many of which can be attributed to the genocidal agendas of PLANNED PARENTHOOD. In her book 'PIVOT OF CIVILIZATION', in reference to free MATERNITY care for the poor, Sanger states: "Instead of DECREASING and aiming to ELIMINATE THE STOCKS that are most detrimental to the future of the race and the world it tends to render them to a

The Omega Files

menacing degree dominant." And in reference to her 'Negro Project' of the late 1930's, which aimed at recruiting black ministers, physicians and political leaders for the purpose of encouraging birth control and sterilization in the black community, Sanger wrote: "...We do not want word to go out that WE WANT TO EXTERMINATE THE NEGRO POPULATION, and the minister is the man who can straighten out that idea if it ever occurs to any of their more rebellious members." Since Sanger is part of the 'ARYAN' SUPREMACY agenda, it is remarkable that she would allow information about Planned Parenthood's REAL genocidal agenda to slip out through her writings. The core issue of most of the incendiary pro-abortion / anti-abortion arguments should not be whether a Mother's right to KILL a human being with a beating heart supersedes a child's right to LIVE. That's merely a means that Planned Parenthood has used to conceal their Fascist genocidal agendas — that is to hide them behind divisive arguments about 'Constitutional Rights' of Mothers vs. those of children.

The CORE issue should be whether or not fascist white supremacists should commit genocide against targeted 'non-Aryan' races through abortion, sterilization, infanticide, and other methods. - Branton), This, then, is the private, international apparatus which has set the world up for a global holocaust, UNDER THE 'U.N.' FLAG.

Earth Island Journal, Fall 94: ARCO, Eastlund and the Roots of HAARP — by Gary Smith: (Note: Following is an interesting by-product of ARCO [the Atlantic Richfield Co.,] which has been getting a good deal of attention throughout Internet discussion groups.

Could such a powerful project be used 'against' American citizens by ARCO or other proponents of the 'New World Order'? - Branton) All atomic and electronic technologies — from household appliances to nuclear weapons — radiate energetic particles. While the immediate impacts of human-caused electromagnetic pollution are generally imperceptible, the long-term consequences for the biosphere can be profound. In 1988, OMNI magazine raised concerns about the environmental consequences of a bizarre electromagnetic invention. According to OMNI, ARCO, the US oil giant, found itself wondering what to do with the estimated 30 trillion cubic feet of natural gas that it hoped to extract from Alaska's North Slope. While this was enough energy to supply the US for a year, the gas fields were too far from any potential customers. ARCO concluded that it would be too expensive to liquefy the gas and ship it thousands of miles to urban centers. What was

The Omega Files

needed was a client that wanted access to vast amounts of energy on-site — in the wilds of Alaska. Bernard Eastland, an MIT and Columbia University physicist with eight years experience with the Atomic Energy Commission, came to the rescue with an extraordinary plan to use the energy "at the point of production." Eastland, who soon became president of ARCO's Production Technologies International Company in Houston, proposed burning the vast Alaskan gas fields to power a huge electric generator. The resulting power would be directed into a huge antenna complex, 40 miles on a side. The antennae would be used to focus an intense beam of electromagnetic energy into the upper atmosphere where it would collide with the ionosphere to create a phenomenon called the "mirror force." Eastland was granted a US Patent (# 4,686,605) for this invention on August 11, 1987.

"You can virtually lift part of the upper atmosphere," Eastland told OMNI, "You can make it move, do things to it." One of the tricks Eastland envisioned involved 'surgically' distorting the ionosphere to disrupt global communications. Pushing the upper atmosphere around might also generate high-altitude 'drag' that could heat and deflect enemy missiles or surround them with "high-energy electrons" that might cause the missiles to detonate in mid-trajectory. The proposal appealed to the Pentagon, which invested several hundred thousand dollars 'evaluating' Eastland's work. Eastland maintained that there were 'peaceful' uses for his technology. In one scenario, he explained how beams of electromagnetic power could lift portions of the upper atmosphere and redirect the jetstream to alter global weather patterns. Using "plumes of atmospheric particles to act as a lens or focusing device," Eastland proposed redirecting sunlight and heat to different parts of the Earth's surface, making it possible to manipulate wind patterns, cause rainstorms in Ethiopia, drive hurricanes out of the Caribbean, incinerate airborne industrial pollution and sew up the hole in the Antarctic ozone layer. "Because the upper atmosphere is extremely sensitive to small changes in its composition," OMNI cautioned, "merely TESTING an Eastland Device could cause irreversible damage."

And also we have the following article, titled "DOOMSDAY DEATH RAY". Subtitle: "Is the U.S. Government Testing a Secret Mega-Weapon?" — by "Agent X"., The Nose Magazine, issue #26 [March 1995]. We have to ask ourselves, just WHO will have control of this 'weapon', especially if ARCO is deeply involved with the HAARP project? Beginning some ways into the article: In marked contrast to other advanced weapons-related programs,

The Omega Files

HAARP is not part of the officially denied 'Blackworld' budget. Rather, the military insists that HAARP is a strictly scientific program to study the aurora borealis [or Northern Lights], when in fact it is a device intended to seriously tweak the ionosphere for purposes that are less than benign. ...BUILT by ARCO Power Technologies, HAARP is due to begin initial testing as this story goes to press. During 1996, a planned $75 million increase to the already multi megabuck project will increase the output of the system to over 1.7 gigawatts, making HAARP the most powerful emitter in the world. Several smaller sites exist around the world, most notably in Russia. Though these installations cannot match the ionosphere heating capabilities of HAARP, some experts in the field who wish not to be quoted suggest that some aberrant weather conditions MAY HAVE been caused by their operation.

The weapon-development whiz kids have been interested in this sort of gizmo for quite some time. Just what in hell does the military want with the world's largest weenie roaster? Here are some possible applications I've discovered: EARTH-PENETRATING TOPOGRAPHY: Sort of a CAT scan for the planet. By heating the ionosphere to create a resonant mirror, electronic-beam steering directs an energy stream to specific coordinates on the planet. This energy penetrates the ground to a depth of a kilometer or more, and the signal return is received by satellite or aircraft. After computer processing, A RELATIVELY CLEAR PICTURE OF WHAT IS UNDERGROUND emerges. Damn handy when trying to figure out where those wily North Koreans hide their nukes — or where YOU keep your stash.

HARD-KILL WEAPON SYSTEM: The output of HAARP would have to be boosted a thousand-fold, but if that is accomplished, a shell of high-speed electrons can be constructed that encompasses the earth. Any ballistic missile or warhead passing through the shell would explode.

SOFT-KILL WEAPON SYSTEM: By directing enormous amounts of radio-frequency energy at a specific area, HAARP could overload electrical power distribution grids, fry sensitive microelectronics, detonate weapons that use electronic fuses, scramble missile guidance systems and probably upset brain chemistry.

WEATHER MODIFICATION: Heating the upper atmosphere over specific areas could change weather patterns, creating torrential floods, destroying an enemy's infrastructure or denying an enemy's harvest by

The Omega Files

drought... Weather as a weapon.

IDENTIFICATION OF SATELLITES: By illuminating orbiting spacecraft with HAARP, the constituent materials and the mission of a satellite can be assessed.

COMMUNICATIONS: Possible uses include satellite jamming, satellite communications with submarines and detection of stealth aircraft. Physicist Bernard Eastlund, president of Production Technologies Company AND FORMER 'ARCO' BIGWIG, was granted three patents over the past seven years for a system that looks suspiciously like HAARP - though much larger. His plan, using a transmitter encompassing 160 square miles and powered by massive amounts of electricity generated using vast Alaskan natural gas reserves [to which ARCO has access], was to shoot down missiles and alter the weather. ARCO initially owned Eastlund's patents, but was soon paid a visit by Edward Teller (the "father of the H-Bomb", Nevada Test Site coordinator for the "Star Wars" or SDI defense program, and major MJ-12 member. - Branton.), and development grew secretive. Eastlund declined further involvement, and the patents were quietly sold in June 1994 to E-Systems, a high-tech corporation famous for ultra-secret defense projects such as the president's customized Boeing 747 doomsday plane. "HAARP is the perfect first step towards a plan like mine," Eastlund says. "Advances in phased-array transmitter technology and power generation can produce the field strength required. The government will say it isn't so, but if it quacks like a duck and it looks like a duck, there's a good chance it is duck." "Eastlund is nuts," says an Air Force official speaking on condition of anonymity. "HAARP is much smaller and less powerful than his instrument. We are not doing anything except good science and pure research. "The real beauty of HAARP," he then adds cryptically, "is that nothing you can see on the outside is sensitive. The secret is the beam steering agility and pulsing of the transmissions... When covert operations occur, the science team, the operating funds and the mission will be black." Whatever is going on, Alaskans are mad as hell.

The federal government enjoys a long tradition of screwing over the inhabitants of the Last Frontier. Generally speaking, the feds are as welcome as a case of herpes. And studies done by the EPA, the Swedish government and others indicate that HAARP could interfere with communications, navigation systems, wildlife migration and possibly human health. "There has never been a transmitter of this power in this frequency," Eastlund

The Omega Files

says. "It would be wise to assess its impact." Though there are many questions, the military insists that all is well and there is nothing to worry about. "We are not doing anything to the ionosphere — we are just looking at it," insists Air Force Phillips Laboratory spokesman Roy Heitman. Although an ad-hoc grassroots organization called NO HAARP is trying to stop the project, founder Clare Zickuhr admits, "It's all a whitewash, [HAARP] is going to happen." An ARCO retiree, Zickuhr is convinced HAARP is a secret weapons project. "It has all the appearances of a secret program. This is not good science — they have no idea what this thing could do to the ionosphere. To put this in the hands of the military scares the hell out of me." (Remember however that, although this particular ex-ARCO employee - Zickuhr — is against the project, the HAARP facility in Alaska was never-the-less CONSTRUCTED by ARCO POWER TECHNOLOGIES.

So Zickuhr's views apparently do not reflect the views of ARCO in general in regards to the project. - Branton) And if you're not yet convinced that ARCO — The ATLANTIC RICHFIELD COMPANY — is a front for the fascist "Nazifeller" New World Order infiltration of, if not invasion of, North America, then try this one on for size: ARCO-ALYESKA, WACKINHUT, ILLEGAL SPYING, ORGANIZED CRIME... ("Oh what a tangled web we weave..."): STATEMENT OF THE HONORABLE GEORGE MILLER CHAIRMAN, HOUSE INTERIOR AND INSULAR AFFAIRS COMMITTEE OVERSIGHT HEARINGS ON ALYESKA COVERT OPERATIONS NOVEMBER 4, 1991 (A few excerpts from this lengthy hearing appear below - Branton): "This is the first of two days of hearings before the House Interior Committee on the subject of covert surveillance authorized by the Alyeska Pipeline Service Company and conducted by The WACKENHUT Corporation. "On August 7 of this year, the Committee on Interior and Insular Affairs filed a written request for documents from Wackenhut and Alyeska in connection with allegations that the Wackenhut Corporation conducted undercover surveillance of Charles Hamel on behalf of Alyeska and its OWNER companies.

In letters to both Wackenhut and Alyeska, I expressed concern that the surveillance of Mr. Hamel was for the purpose of obtaining information on and/or interfering with Mr. Hamel's communications with this Committee. "Charles Hamel has been a source of information for Congress, state and federal regulatory agencies, and the media, concerning environmental, health and safety VIOLATIONS by Alyeska and its oil company owners (that is, ARCO or Atlantic Richfield. - Branton). Mr. Hamel has served as a conduit for whistleblowers, including Alyeska employees, to make public information on oil industry practices. At the same time, Mr. Hamel has at least two significant business disputes with ALYESKA and EXXON... "In the next two days, we will explore the issue of whether Alyeska's use of a 'bogus' environmental group formed by Wackenhut spies was an effort to disrupt and compromise a source of information for this Committee's continuing investigation of oil industry practices in Alaska... "In my view, it is important to find out why some of the largest and most powerful corporations in this country would resort to such elaborate 'sting' tactics to INVADE and DESTROY the privacy of Mr. Hamel, federal and state officials, environmentalists and ordinary citizens... "We believe that the testimony and the evidence presented in these hearings during the next two days will show that the covert surveillance operation involved the much more sinister and disturbing motives of SILENCING environmental critics and intimidating whistleblowers..."

TESTIMONY OF CHARLES HAMEL BEFORE THE UNITED STATES HOUSE OF REPRESENTATIVES OF THE UNITED STATES CONGRESS COMMITTEE ON INTERIOR AND INSULAR AFFAIRS 2226 Rayburn House Office Building Washington, D.C. November 4 & 5, 1991

(Note: The following is just one excerpt from the lengthy transcript of the hearing - Branton): "...In 1988, ARCO, EXXON and British Petroleum failed to tell this Committee about the existence of the Pt. McIntyre billion barrel oil field directly under the West Dock, virtually within sight of the Alyeska Pipeline, while they were testifying that Prudhoe Bay was running dry.

In fact, both ARCO and EXXON knew that they had discovered the Pt. McIntyre field years earlier. In 1989, my General Partner, EXXON, told me that our Pt. McIntyre leases were dry. I sold my interest in the leases for what EXXON told me was a fair price. Several weeks after selling EXXON my interests, the major discovery was announced. ONCE AGAIN, they LIED to you, they LIED to the Congress, they LIED to the public, and they DEFRAUDED us all." Here is an interesting report that I came across which suggests that the fascist conspiracy against America goes 'deeper' than some might dare to believe:

WAR OF THE CAVERNS, by Tom Lucas

If the importance of the caverns beneath Siloam Springs and Eureka Springs [CIA-Masonic-Mafia 'underground' drug capital in Arkansas...] is a

The Omega Files

bane of contention between the picturesque little towns, Hot Springs, Arkansas, would be the next logical choice for investigation. During the 1930 Prohibition days, it was frequently reported in a Chicago newspaper that Chicago gangsters traveled often to Hot Springs to go to the horse races and soak in the hot baths. It seems reasonable, based on what we think we know now, that during the lulls in recreational activities in Hot Springs, leaders of the various gangs made discrete trips to the caverns beneath the city to brag about their latest exploits and to bring offerings of gold. "To get a rough idea of what a cavern map of the U.S. would look like, simply pull out a road map of any state and identify all of the dense population centers, be they cities or hamlets. Where there is a city on the surface of the earth, there is a city in the caverns below that city...'as above, so below.' The co-relation breaks down as the size of the population centers dwindle... "In the early 1930's, the caverns of Hot Springs must have been the U.S. capital, or at least a regional area, for the marketers of illegal alcohol. "Cavern communities close to the surface are probably not completely self-supporting and require huge injections of funds to keep them going. These facilities lack the super-technologies of those caverns much deeper in the earth, and require much gold for trading with people within cities deeper in the Earth's crust.

An ounce of gold in the underworld has as much or greater buying power than on the surface because the deeper super-productive cities need all the gold they can get and are willing to make generous trades for gold. This relieves the near-surface caverns of the burden of secreting goods and services from the surface world which would be a real security headache. "Cities beneath cities, and some hamlets, require injections of wealth from the surface that doesn't leave paper trails to their caverns. Each cavern has to develop and specialize in some particular money-making scam, or any number of sting embezzlements to bring in a constant stream of traceless cash and gold.

"One cavern, for example, specializes in addictive drug sales, another bank embezzlement and fraud, another stock market riggings, government money transfer schemes, along with other more esoteric and less known ways of generating profit that must eventually be converted to cash and gold that cannot be traced. The expression underground cash economy is probably a semi-cryptic phrase that refers directly to installations beneath cities notorious for dealing only in cash and gold. (Note: The notorious 'inner world' researcher and writer Richard Shaver did state that organized crime syndi-

The Omega Files

cates were one of the larger elements operating within the secret cavern systems, and that the term "the underworld" — as a description of organized crime networks — is more than just a coincidence. - Branton) "When America was young, developing underground caverns beneath American cities having a flavor of anarchy similar to communities developing on the surface, did not at the time have formal relations with each other... not even "wild-west" sub-surface communities in the American West... "as above, so below."

"Over a period of time, cavern communities within regional areas geographically near each other found they had to get along with each other in a non-competitive manner, to encourage synergetic relationships which tended to raise the standard of living of each of the involved cavern communities. Each cavern specialized in an area of crime-monopoly expertise that wasn't in competition with neighboring caverns. If a regional area demonstrated it could keep surface dwellers in line — e.g., keep them thinking the 'right' thoughts, stifling all real creativity, via the under-ground's crack people-management teams and organizations on the surface in the form of police departments, public schools, controlling secret societies, quack medical fraternities, polished propagandists and moralists, a sufficiently initiated CLERGY, etcetera — then this regional area is allowed to incorporate into a semi-autonomous fiefdom that would eventually reflect on the surface as "a county" in the U.S... "As above, so below."

"These underground fiefdoms in the form of counties then combine to form states; states combine to form the nation... Today, 33 degree Masonry and the higher degree [33+] is getting ready for the final conflict between Rightwing Caverns [RWC] and Leftwing Caverns [LWC]. This [Hegalian/Machievellian] conflict will not be so much a battle between countries on the surface as it will a war of the caverns. Surface 33+ is clandestinely developing relatively unknown caverns beneath smaller communities which 33+ degree confidently feels will not be identified and destroyed once the conflict begins. Surface 32 degree and below are to be left on the surface to die with the rest of the 'profane'. The deal is, knowing a real holocaust is coming, 33+ is planning to abandon the old underground installations and flee to the new when the time arrives. It appears that both left and right wing factions will be responsible responsible for the sacrifice of huge segments of the Earth's above and below ground populations. (Take note of the fact that the Jesuit-created Scottish Rite and and the black gnostic serpent cult of

The Omega Files

the Illuminati of Bavaria — which both collaborated in the establishing of the "33 degree" system of Masonry — have their ultimate headquarters in ROME and BAVARIA, those two regions which made up the duel headquarters of the [UN]HOLY ROMAN EMPIRE. These were the same forces which brought about the Macheivellian conflicts between 'right' and 'left' wing factions in World War I and World War II. Now they are apparently planning for a third Machievellian global conflict — this one being nuclear in scope — ABOVE and BELOW the surface of the planet, a conflict which they intend to 'ride-out' in their secret underground strongholds and eventually emerge to control the upper AND lower 'worlds'.

It would be an elaborate "Helter Skelter" scenario — Helter Skelter being the term that mass-murderer Charles Manson used for his plan to incite a race war which he and his 'family' would ride-out in an underground cavern in the Mojave desert which he referred to as "the Pit". Once the holocaust had ended and most of those on the surface were dead, Manson and his followers believed that they would emerge from their hiding place and rule the world. If such a plan seems to be the product of an insane mind, then it would appear that Charles Manson was not alone in his insanity, which is a scary thought. Another thought — just what part do the alien Greys play in the 33+ Masons' plans? Incidentally, there are reportedly several levels above and beyond the 33rd degree, mainly those which interface with and collaborate with 'alien' fraternities or secret societies below and beyond planet earth. For instance the 'Alternative 2' and 'Alternative 3' forces who, in collaboration with the Greys, have exploited and oppressed numerous 'slave worlds' throughout this sector of the galaxy — according to one couple who in UNICUS magazine told of how they defected from the Alternative-3 agenda after a 'Federation' agent informed them of these facts. The Nazi 'Neu Schwabians' are deeply involved in these joint humanoid-reptiloid interstellar atrocities against the peaceful inhabitants of other colonial worlds. The atrocities of World War II were just the beginning, since the Nazi 'holocaust', if we are to believe some 'contactees', has spread beyond the surface of this planet, both within and without. As for the 33-plus levels of Masonry, according to former Dulce base security officer Thomas E. Castello — who possessed one of the highest security clearances at the base, Ultra-7 — there were several security clearances above his own that the 'higher initiates' held... such as UMBRA, STELLAR, and UMS - UNIVERSAL MILITARY SERVICE. In his writings Whitley Streiber tells of being taken during an abduction experience to another desert-like planet with ancient ruins and tall

The Omega Files

'Grey' type beings. He encountered American military personnel on this interplanetary excursion who were dressed in military kackies, carried camcorders and other unusual equipment. These military personnel would probably have possessed a security clearance similar to one of those mentioned above.

According to Castello, President Harry Truman was a 'High Archon' in the interplanetary lodges and one of the first U.S. Presidents to establish a secret American treaty with Greys from Alpha Draconis and Epsilon Bootes as well as with the subterranean Ashtar forces. George Bush was apparently at one point a 42nd degree Mason, according to another source who I believe to be reliable. He would have to had been considerably high in the degrees if he were involved with MJ-12 as is claimed. So the 33+ degrees of Masonry are the alien-interactive levels, and 'we' are meant to believe that there are ONLY 33 degrees and no more. The Scottish Rite's infiltration of the Masonic lodges challenged the domination of the more Judeo-Christian YORK Rite. The Scottish Rite can be traced back to the Jesuit college of Clermont in France, and at the core it advocates a global government and the destruction of all national boundaries, sovereignties and cultures; the dissolution of all traditional "family" structures making all children the wards of the world state; and the destruction of the idea that man has a soul — or rather that humans are merely evolved animals having no spiritual nature and therefore no need for God.

In other words a homogenized collective society which does not tolerate individual expression but instead enforces absolute conformity to the controlling establishment, kind of like the system which the Greys themselves live under. According to former 33rd degree Mason James Shaw, author of "THE DEADLY DECEPTION", the U.S. headquarters of the Scottish Rite is located in the "House of the Temple" in Washington D.C. and, according to some, it sits directly over an antediluvian system of 'Atlantean' tunnels and ancient underground chambers called the 'NOD' complex, which serves as a major NSA-Sirian-Grey center of collaboration. Some believe that the antediluvian or Atlantean alchemists or sorcerer-scientists had begun experimenting with elemental forces and that their experiments had gone out of control and created a temporal rift in the space-time continuum in the so-called 'Bermuda Triangle' region, opening up a hole between dimensions and leaving 'electromagnetic fallout' which has had adverse effects to this day. This was just prior to the global deluge which destroyed

The Omega Files

their island-continent. This 'House of the Temple' is, according to Jim Shaw, filled with murals, statues, and carvings of serpents. In other words it is a SERPENT cult.

This pagan temple actually sits at the northern point of the PENTAGRAM like street layout of downtown D.C., which is not surprising when we consider that much of the original construction of Washington D.C. was carried out by MASONS! After what was supposed to be the culmination of a lifetime of initiatory work, Shaw was excited about his 33rd degree initiation which was attended by two former U.S. presidents, a famous 'evangelist', and a Scandinavian king. He was anticipating a type of spiritual illumination, however the dead, dry ritual and the 'tomb like' atmosphere of the temple itself was far from inspiring. Following the disillusioning experience he left the building, looked at the entrance above which was written "THE SCOTTISH RITE OF FREEMASONRY", and, realizing that it was all a LIE he sadly said to himself, "It isn't Scottish, it isn't Rite, and it isn't Free!" He left the lodge and never returned, and from that day on became a Christian Evangelist and one of its most notorious critics. Some state that as part of the 33rd degree initiation one is challenged to blaspheme Christ, spitting on a cross or a Bible or something of the sort. If the initiate refuses to do so they are told "You have made the right decision", and remain forever in the 33rd degree. If they do commit the act of blasphemy however, they are told "You have made the right decision" and continue their ascension through the degrees beyond the 33rd. The lowest degrees are presumably 'Christian' and many share membership jointly in Masonry and Christian denominations. As one ascends higher, the Christian beliefs are slowly and almost imperceptibly subverted so by the time the 33rd degree is reached one has arrived on the verge of Luciferianism.

Those who have been through the degrees must admit that what they are being taught now is almost diametrically opposed to what they were taught in the lowest degrees. This is the work of the Scottish Rite which infiltrated the Masonic Lodges for the purposes of using them as a framework for the establishment of their Godless New World Order. In Masonry the LODGE is god, 'The Grand Architect of the Universe', which is simply another name for the Lodge itself. - Branton). "At the same time underground 33+ develops remote survival caverns — an activity generally unknown to underground inhabitants, including 32-, they are also developing caverns without support communities which, above, could pinpoint their survival

The Omega Files

caverns for target purposes...

Without support communities to obscure their activities, surface Masons are deprived of this advantage. "When one moves to a cavern without a support community above, it is similar to a surface dweller moving from the city to the countryside. Unless there is access to needed goods and services available at alien facilities much deeper in the earth, each time the remote cavern dweller needs something from the store he has to travel to a cavern with a support community above to get what is wanted. "While in the NAVY, I was told that only five men, who were sworn to secrecy, decided the targets for America's bombs; also that these five men were the only ones who know where the bombs were going! This means targeting information inside the ICBM's are sealed and not even technicians loading the programs know what is on them. Bombing instructions for nuclear bomber pilots are sealed. This means submarine captains do not know where their ICBM's are headed. All the captain does is tell the missile its location and the missile decides where to go.

Apparently an almost unlimited number of possible target guidance programs are generated and placed in a library made available to these five men. To be installed in missiles appropriate for specific targets, all is sealed and safely locked away. "I'm sure the method by which all this is done is complex and thought out in a way understood by none other than the five select men. I doubt the system has changed since my Navy days of years ago. The activities of these men and the targets selected are never audited. (Just as the secret agencies like MJ-12 are never audited since Congressional investigators are only allowed 'Top Secret' clearances — whereas MJ-12 and similar agencies operate at 'Above Top Secret' levels and beyond. In fact the charter for the NSA, for instance, states that the NSA is exempt from all U.S. laws which do not specifically mention the NSA within the text. So here is a job for you Congressional legislators... MENTION the NSA in every new or old regulatory law that might be applicable! - Branton). The person who told me this said there is no way of ascertaining if these five men are even on our side! Though the faces of the men may change over the years, the system of security remains the same. These five men must all be MASONS, which means there is much room for mischief. "300 U.S. citizens were made ready for the 1917 Russian Revolution. Taught the Russian language and leftwing socialist ideology, they were shipped off to Russia to form the first politburo. Plainly, this means that socialist Russia is a tool and

The Omega Files

puppet state of the United States (Or, more exactly the Masonic 'Banksters' operating within the U.S. — as for instance the Rockefellers, who played a major role in grooming the agents of the Communist-Socialist revolution in Russia AND the agents of the National-Socialist revolution in Germany.

Whether it is left-handed Socialism or right-handed Socialism — Socialism either way you look at it is TOTALITARIANISM! - Branton). Any recent reforms in Russia will NOT change the fact that she is still taking orders from [the Bavarian-backed 33+ Jesuit-Masons in] the U.S. [U.N.]. Although the front men may change, leftwing socialists are very adept at making reforms that increase their power. "All of which indicates that it is unlikely that the bulk of America's atomic arsenal is aimed at Russia, as claimed and, for the most part, it is unlikely that Russia's atomic arsenal is aimed at the United States. The only missiles targeted for the U.S. would be aimed at the underground installations of the most lethal of rightwing adversaries... After all, the effectiveness of our underground nuclear bomb-testing program is just that... a test showing just how efficiently each bomb design destroys underground caverns!... "Summarizing, it appears that both Russian and American nuclear arsenals stand ready to fire in concert. But at what? The answer is at all of the caverns which, occupied by the enemy of World War II (namely, the NAZIS - Branton), are awaiting the time to deliver THEIR nuclear missiles from sanctuaries beneath the ANTARCTIC, and from cavern strongholds beneath SOUTH, CENTRAL and NORTH AMERICA. (Note: The 33+ themselves are neither against the 'right' nor 'left' wing forces, but rather control the leadership of each, so as to set the two forces against each other in a Machievellian or Hegalian scenario — with more than a little help from their reptiloid and grey alien advisors. This plan seems to have been traced back to the MASONIC 'Pontiff' Albert Pike [who called himself 'the vice-regent of Lucifer' on earth] and his JESUIT 'deputy' Guisseppi Mazzini. According to Des Griffin, Pike and Mazzini established the 22 Illuminati 'Palladium' lodges for the express purpose of creating the right-wing Nazi and left-wing Communist movements and to lay the foundation for three world wars which they hoped would wear-down the masses to the point where they would accept a New World Order dictatorship as the only peaceful alternative. From the alien perspective, the New World Order would offer easier control and massive population reduction at the same time.

As I have suggested, we can also surmise that the 33+ Masons 'leading' the right wing factions and the 33+ Masons 'leading' the left wing fac-

The Omega Files

tions are all working closely together along with their reptilian allies beneath and beyond this planet. When and if the final conflict breaks out, we can expect the high-ranking 'leaders' of both sides of the Machievellian conflict to leave the so-called left-wing Communist Socialists and the so-called right-wing National Socialists to their fate, with the hope and expectation that they will slaughter each other and eliminate all resistance when they — the Roman-Bavarian 33+ Jesuit-Mason Banksters and their alien 'hosts' in Orion and Draconis as well as some collaborating factions from Sirius-B / Hale-Bopp, etc. — emerge to take control of the planet. In reference to the Sirian collaborators, a major irony exists in the fact that the Sirius-B zealots connected with the Hale-Bopp complex — who are so determined to stage a mass landing on earth — may be largely motivated by the fact that several of their allied underground colonies on earth and in this system have been and are under attack by the Reptiloid-Grey collectivists.

Apparently they believe that by supporting their secret-society allies here on earth — who are in turn intent on establishing a New World Order — they will be in a better position to defend themselves and their ancient bases and colonies here from the Draconians-Greys. Yet, they are in fact serving what they have been led to believe are "Ascended Masters" within the Hale-Bopp complex itself, unaware that their beloved "Ashtar" hierarchy has long since been infiltrated by Orionite Dracos and Greys. In a similar manner, the Orion-backed Jesuit Lodge had managed to infiltrate the Sirian backed Masonic Lodge on earth via the Jesuit Scottish Rite, and just as the Sirians have been duped into submitting to the agenda of the Orionites in Hale-Boop, the Masons have been duped into forming an alliince with the Jesuits in the form of the Bildeberg society. If the Masonic Lodge and our own Constitutional U.S. Government can be infiltrated by Draconian-Orionite interventionists, then are those from Sirius-B who live in an even more collectivist system any more exempt from the same threat? Maybe one day they, AND WE, will learn that the Draconians are playing for keeps and that there is NO level of deception to which they will NOT sink in order to get their way. Just like us, the Sirians and their Masonic representatives on earth have been so concerned about defending themselves from an 'enemy without', that they AND WE have ignored the infiltratration of the 'enemy within'. - Branton) "This explains why the U.S. and Russia have such a large surplus of atomic bombs. Caverns tend to be nuclear proof, except for direct hits which mean that at least one bomb is needed per cavern, and perhaps several just in case the first one fails to make it.

The Omega Files

All those bombs going off will have a negative environmental impact on all life on the surface; but the 33+ plan to be safe and snug in their holes. -Branton) "Both sides could fire all their arsenals at once; but this is unlikely to happen. World War II will be PROTRACTED [like a chess-game] and both sides will agree to a standard set of rules for war. "As the war progresses and the world's standard of living drops, squabbles over remaining resources will become frequent, and pointed. States will fight states, counties will fight counties, towns will fight towns, all of which will reflect the political biases and inclinations of controlling caverns beneath. "Did you know that only group organisms such as ant hills and termite colonies — and masonic controlled men — indulge in mass warfare? Nothing else in nature does. "All group organisms, such as bee hives, use sex odors [via the queen bee] to induce conformity in the hive or colony. [Scottish Rite] Masonry is most similar to the termite colony in that both chew away at the foundations of civilization and neither can stand the light of day.

"Masonry may not use sex odors to induce conformity and absorption into the group organism but it does use mesmerizing, hypnotic rays that may have sexual content to it. Selfless devotion to service, faceless anonymity, slavish devotion to a noble ideal... for the good of the whole, work without compensation, profitless causes, these are the value-philosophical ideals of an and in an ant hill, a termite in a termite colony...and a mason in a masonic organism. "Interesting is how cleverly encyclopedias talk about springs but never caverns, and that De Sota was more curious about caverns than springs. The tunnels I recently learned of that lead off from basement rooms in the old KNIGHTS OF PYTHIAS TEMPLE in Springfield, Missouri, which is in the heart of the Ozarks, gives pause for a lot of wonder and conjecture. Until recently, I thought only a few surface dwellers knew and had access to the Underworld, but it now appears to be common knowledge among those of a specific segment of the population... It's just that those who talk don't live long." More of what the 'Aryan elite' plan for America and the world was revealed in a lecture given by the late Phil Schneider, who was murdered [strangled to death] by persons unknown shortly after giving this speech: "I love the country I am living in, more than I love my life, but I would not be standing before you now, risking my life, if I did not believe it was so. The first part of this talk is going to concern deep underground military bases and the black budget. The Black Budget is a secretive budget that garners 25% of the gross national product of the United States. The Black Budget currently consumes $1.25 trillion per [2] years. At least

The Omega Files

this amount is used in black programs, like those concerned with deep underground military bases. Presently, there are 129 deep underground military bases in the United States. "They have been building these 129 bases day and night, unceasingly, since the early 1940's. Some of them were built even earlier than that.

These bases are basically large cities underground connected by high-speed magneto-leviton trains that have speeds up to Mach 2. Several books have been written about this activity. Al Bielek has my only copy of one of them. Richard Souder, a Ph.D architect, has risked his life by talking about this. He worked with a number of government agencies on deep underground military bases. In around where you live, in Idaho, there are 11 of them. "The average depth of these bases is over a mile, and they again are basically whole cities underground. They all are between 2.66 and 4.25 cubic miles in size. They have laser drilling machines that can drill a tunnel seven miles long in one day. The Black Projects sidestep the authority of CONGRESS, which as we know is illegal. Right now, the New World Order is depending on these bases. If I had known at the time I was working on them that the NWO was involved, I would not have done it. I was LIED to rather extensively.

"Basically, as far as technology is concerned, for every calendar year that transpires, military technology increases about 44.5 years. This is why it is easy to understand that back in 1943 they were able to create, through the use of vacuum tube technology, a ship that could literally disappear from one place and appear in another place. My father, Otto Oscar Schneider, fought on both sides of the war. He was originally a U-boat captain, and was captured and repatriated in the United States. He was involved with different kinds of concerns, such as the A-bomb, the H-bomb and the Philadelphia Experiment. He invented a high-speed camera that took pictures of the first atomic (Hydrogen or H-Bomb - Branton) tests at Bikini Island on July 12, 1946. I have original photographs of that test, and the photos also show UFO's fleeing the bomb site at a high rate of speed. Bikini Island at the time was infested with them, especially under the water, and the natives had problems with their animals being mutilated. At that time, General McArthur felt that the next war would be with aliens from other worlds. "Anyway, my father laid the groundwork with theoreticians about the Philadelphia experiment, as well as other experiments. What does that have to do with me? Nothing, other than the fact that he was my father. I don't agree with what he

The Omega Files

did on the other side, but I think he had a lot of guts in coming here. He was hated in Germany. There was a $1 million reward, payable in gold, to anyone who killed him.

Obviously, they didn't succeed. Anyway, back to our topic — deep underground bases. "Back in 1954, under the Eisenhower administration, the 'federal' government decided to circumvent the Constitution of the United States and form a treaty with alien entities. It was called the 1954 Greada Treaty (Eisenhower administration — established contact-landings at Holloman AFB, New Mexico; and Muroc-Edwards AFB, California in 1954. This was a year after the 'Greys' had established geosynchronous orbits around our planet within two 'planetoids' that had been engineered to serve as operational bases for later abduction, implantation, cattle mutilation, base construction, and infiltration operations. - Branton), which basically made the agreement that the aliens involved could take a few cows and test their implanting techniques on a few human beings, but that they had to give details about the people involved. Slowly, the aliens altered the bargain until they decided they wouldn't abide by it at all.

Back in 1979, this was the reality, and the fire-fight at Dulce occurred quite by accident. I was involved in building an ADDITION to the deep underground military base at Dulce, which is probably the deepest base. It goes down seven levels and over 2.5 miles deep. At that particular time, we had drilled four distinct holes in the desert, and we were going to link them together and blow out large sections at a time. My job was to go down the holes and check the rock samples, and recommend the explosive to deal with the particular rock. As I was headed down there, we found ourselves amidst a large cavern that was full of outer-space (or "inner-space"? - Branton) aliens, otherwise known as large Greys. I shot two of them. At that time, there were 30 people down there. About 40 more came down after this started, and all of them got killed. We had surprised a whole underground base of existing aliens. Later, we found out that they had been living in our planet for a long time... This could explain a lot of what is behind the theory of ancient astronauts. (Note: This report seems to reveal a limited 'perspective' on the overall 'Dulce wars' based on the experience of one man. It appears however from a number of sources as if there was much more involved in the overall scenario than what Phil Schneider describes. For instance from Phil's description it would appear as if his team broke-in to the base 'accidentally'. It could have been that IN RESPONSE to the cap-

The Omega Files

tured scientists mentioned by Thomas Edwin Castello and others, special military forces and agents intentionally attempted to break-in to the underground alien bases through a "back door" so-to-speak, yet Schneider may have not been aware of this part. Other reports would suggest that the conflict was more complex than this, involving more than one firefight. According to Thomas Castello, John Lear, Bill Cooper, and other sources, the "Dulce Wars" involved AT LEAST a hundred highly-trained special forces, including Delta force Black Berets, Air Force Blue Berets, Division 5 FBI, CIA, and Secret Service.

Because of the "cover-up", special forces units with the necessary security clearances for this type of operation were rare. Needless to say, this "war" did not have the full backing of Congress and the American people, and this no doubt contributed to the loss of the 66 special force personnel who died in the conflict. Following the confrontation, the U.S. 'government' withdrew from all negotiations with the Greys and a rift began to develop within the Intelligence Community. It appears as if this split can be traced back to Kirtland AFB in New Mexico, which became divided over what to do about the Dulce situation and the aliens in general. Col. Edwards and the Wing Commander wanted to support Paul Bennewitz in a full-scale investigation of Dulce and they petitioned the White House, which at first agreed and told them to go ahead with the project... that is until forces 'elsewhere' in the intelligence community began to bring pressure against the White House and Kirtland AFB to drop the whole thing. Kirtland AFB Col. Richard Doty seems to have been torn between two intelligence agendas, explaining his seemingly schizophrenic reversals in policy regarding Dulce and related matters. Some segments of U.S. intelligence wanted to declare war on the Greys and develop SDI weapons that could be used against them in space and underground, whereas others — apparently motivated by more sinister motives — desired to continue negotiations. Two years following the Dulce wars, AQUARIUS and MAJI re-established negotiations with the Greys at Dulce for the purpose it would seem of gaining continued access to mind control technology for their New World Order agenda. - Branton) "Anyway, I got shot in the chest with one of their weapons, which was a box on their body, that blew a hole in me and gave me a nasty dose of cobalt radiation. I have had cancer because of that. "I didn't get really interested in UFO technology until I started work at Area 51, north of Las Vegas. After about two years recuperating after the 1979 incident, I went back to work for Morrison and Knudson, EG&G and other companies. At Area 51, they were

The Omega Files

testing all kinds of peculiar spacecraft. How many people here are familiar with Bob Lazar's story? He was a physicist working at Area 51 trying to decipher the propulsion factor in some of these craft. "Now, I am very worried about the activity of the federal government. They have lied to the public, stonewalled senators, and have refused to tell the truth in regard to alien matters. I can go on and on. I can tell you that I am rather disgruntled. Recently, I knew someone who lived near where I live in Portland, Oregon. He worked at Gunderson Steel Fabrication, where they make railroad cars.

Now, I knew this fellow for the better part of 30 years, and he was kind of a quiet type. He came in to see me one day, excited, and he told me "they're building prisoner cars." He was nervous. Gunderson, he said, had a contract with the federal government to build 107,200 full length railroad cars, each with 143 pairs of shackles. There are 11 sub-contractors in this giant project. Supposedly, Gunderson got over 2 billion dollars for the contract. Bethlehem Steel and other steel outfits are involved. He showed me one of the cars in the rail yards in North Portland. He was right. If you multiply 107,200 times 143 times 11, you come up with about 15,000,000. This is probably the number of people who disagree with the federal government. No more can you vote any of these people out of office. Our present structure of government is 'technocracy', not democracy, and it is a form of feudalism. (I would venture to say that it is more like a techno-monarchy, since several of the U.S. presidents since Truman have been placed in office with Rockefeller financial-media backing, suggesting that these same presidents were inclined to favor certain Rockefeller corporate agendas over the interests of the American people. The Techno-Monarchy would constitute those parts of the Military-Industrial Complex or M.I.C. that are largely influenced by Rockefeller and European Black Nobility interests. When the American Union was young, the Continental Congress was fearful that the roots of Monarchy might rise within the new Republic. There were critics who suggested that we should not even have a Chief Executive or a President for this very reason, however by majority vote they installed George Washington as the first U.S. President with the hopes that all those who came after him would follow his example of selfless devotion and patriotism. Unfortunatelly the Continental Congress was wrong, and had overestimated the integrity of those U.S. 'Presidents' who would come later. - Branton). It [our present form of government] has nothing to do with the republic of the United States. These people are god-less, and have legislated out prayer in public schools. You can get fined up to $100,000 and two years in prison for praying in school.

The Omega Files

I believe we can do better. I also believe that the federal government is running the gambit of enslaving the people of the United States. I am not a very good speaker, but I'll keep shooting my mouth off until somebody puts a bullet in me, because it's worth it to talk to a group like this about these atrocities. "There are other problems. I have some interesting 1993 figures. There are 29 prototype stealth aircraft presently. The budget from the U.S. Congress five-year plan for these is $245.6 million. You couldn't buy the spare parts for these black programs for that amount. So, we've been lied to. The black budget is roughly $1.3 trillion every two years. A trillion is a thousand billion. A trillion dollars weighs 11 tons. The U.S. Congress never sees the books involved with this clandestine pot of gold.

Contractors of [these] programs: EG&G, Westinghouse, McDonnell Douglas, Morrison-Knudson, Wackenhut Security Systems, Boeing Aerospace, Lorimar Aerospace, Aerospacial in France, Mitsubishi Industries, Rider Trucks, Bechtel, *I.G. Farben*, plus a host of hundreds more. Is this what we are supposed to be living up to as freedom-loving people? I don't believe so. "Still, 68% of the military budget is directly or indirectly affected by the black budget. Star Wars relies heavily upon stealth weaponry. By the way, none of the stealth program would have been available if we had not taken apart crashed alien disks. None of it. Some of you might ask what the "space shuttle" is "shuttling". Large ingots of special metals that are milled in space and cannot be produced on the surface of the earth. They need the near vacuum of outer space to produce them. We are not even being told anything close to the truth. I believe our government officials have SOLD us down the drain — lock, stock and barrel.

Up until several weeks ago, I was employed by the U.S. government with a Ryolite-38 clearance factor, one of the highest in the world. I believe the Star Wars program is there solely to act as a buffer to prevent alien attack — it has nothing to do with the "cold war", which was only a toy to garner money from all the people — for what? The whole lie was planned and executed for the last 75 years. "Here's another piece of information for you folks. The Drug Enforcement Administration and the ATF rely on stealth tactical weaponry for as much as 40% of their operations budget. This in 1993, and the figures have gone up considerably since. The United Nations used American stealth aircraft for over 28% of its collective worldwide operations from 1990 to 1992, according to the Center for Strategic Studies and UN Report 3092. "I don't perceive at this time that we have too much more than six

The Omega Files

months of life left in this country, at the present rate. We are the laughing stock of the world, because we are being hood-winked by so many evil people that are running this country. I think we can do better.

I think the people over 45 are seriously worried about their future. I'm going to run some scary scenarios by you. The Contract With America. It contains the same terminology that Adolph Hitler used to subvert Germany in 1931. I believe we can do better. The Contract With America (or is it the "Contract ON America"? - Branton) is a last ditch effort by our federal government to tear away the Constitution and the Bill of Rights. "The black helicopters. There are over 64,000 black helicopters in the United States. For every hour that goes by, there is one being built. Is this the proper use of our money? What does the federal government need 64,000 tactical helicopters for, if they are not trying to enslave us. I doubt if the entire military needs 64,000 worldwide. I doubt if all the world needs that many. There are 157 F-117A stealth aircraft loaded with LIDAR and computer-enhanced imaging radar. They can see you walking from room to room when they fly over your house. They see objects in the house from the air with a variation limit of 1 inch to 30,000 miles. That's how accurate that is.

Now, I worked in the federal government for a long time, and I know exactly how they handle their business..." On Oct. 20, 1991, California researcher Michael Lindemann, founder of 'The 20/20 Group', gave a lecture before a large crowd of interested investigators. During the course of his lecture wherein he discussed the Military-Industrial Complex's underground bases outside of Lancaster, California, he made the following statements: "...How many of you have seen the book 'BLANK CHECK'?... It is not a UFO book. I strongly recommend that you read the book 'BLANK CHECK' so that you can understand something about how these projects are funded without your say so, indeed WITHOUT THE SAY SO OF CONGRESS. Most citizens don't know for example that the National Security Act of 1947 made it illegal to ever say how much money is spent on the CIA. Indeed all of our tremendous alphabet soup collection of Intelligence Agencies. Whether your talking about the CIA, or the NRO, or the NSA or the DIA, etc., all of them are in the same category. "You cannot say how much these things cost. All you can do if you want to find out is add-up the numbers on the Budget that aren't assigned to anything that actually means anything. There are these huge categories that have tens of billions of dollars in them that say nothing but 'Special Projects...' And every year the Congress dutifully passes this bloated

The Omega Files

budget that has some $300,000,000,000 or more with HUGE chunks of cash labeled like that: 'Special Projects,' 'Unusual Stuff.' — Ten billion dollars. O.K., well where does the 'unusual stuff' money go? Well, it DOES go to 'unusual stuff', that's for sure, and one of the places it goes is that it goes into the underground bases. Indeed TIM said recently since the publication of his book [BLANK CHECK]...

MORE Black Budget money goes into UNDERGROUND BASES than ANY OTHER kind of work. "Now I don't believe that 35 billion, which is the approximate size of the black budget money that you can find by analyzing the budget, I don't think that comes CLOSE to the real figure because there is absolutely unequivocal evidence that a great deal of additional money was generated in other ways, such as the surreptitious running of guns and drugs. And one wonderful example of that is coming to light with the B.C.C.I. scandal which I hope you've heard of... a number of very high-ranking American officials are caught in the undertow of the BCCI tidal wave... Even though these guys are tying to pull 'fast ones' on an immense scale they are getting caught. These things don't always work. Indeed they are very, very vulnerable. Indeed this whole 'end game' is very vulnerable and that's why they feel it requires such secrecy.

The American people wouldn't stand for this stuff if they had the information, and that's the reason why we have to get the information out and take it seriously because it really is a matter of our money and our future that's being mortgaged here. "But my friend who worked in the underground bases, who was doing sheet-rock was down on, he thinks, approximately the 30th level underground... these bases are perhaps 30-35 stories deep ['ground-scrapers']. As I say they are not just mine shafts, these are huge, giant facilities... many city blocks in circumference, able to house tens of thousands of people. One of them, the YANO Facility [we're told... by the county fire dept. director, the county fire dept. chief who had to go in there to look at a minor fire infraction] there's a 400-car parking lot on the 1st level of the YANO Facility, but cars never come in and out, those are the cars that they use INSIDE. "O.K., so... a very interesting situation down there. Our guy was doing sheet-rock on the 30th floor, maybe the 30th floor, underground. He and his crew are working on a wall and right over here is an elevator door. The elevator door opens and, a kind of reflex action you look, and he saw three 'guys'. Two of them, human engineers that he's seen before. And between them a 'guy' that stood about 8 to 8 1/2 feet tall. Green

The Omega Files

skin, reptilian features, extra-long arms, wearing a lab coat, holding a clipboard... "I tend to believe that story because, first of all because we have other stories like it, but more importantly because he walked off that job that very day. And he was getting paid a GREAT deal of money... If your basically a sheet-rock kind of guy, if you can do sheet-rock in a place like that then you get paid way more than standard sheet-rock wages, you can count on it. "So, he walked off that job. His buddy on that same crew turned into an alcoholic shortly after. This is an extremely upsetting thing. You know, it wasn't like this alien jumped out and bit his head off or anything, it was just standing there for a few minutes, the doors closed. He has a feeling that that elevator was malfunctioning, otherwise he never would have seen that except by accident..."

Several people have referred to the underground as well as the operational 'connections' between the Dulce base in New Mexico and the Dreamland base in Nevada, connections that exist via Dougway, Utah and Page, Arizona. From Dreamland/Area 51/S-4 these underground systems reportedly extend towards the Edwards AFB/Lancaster/Tehachapi region where so many Military-Industrial-Aerospace operations are being carried out. If alien forces are intent on taking control of this planet, then it would be logical for them to target our most strategic military-industrial weapons research and development center. This might involve actual 'infiltration' of our military-industrial complexes and control of the line-of-command through mind control of specific and strategic personnel. In many cases patriotic Americans have become caught in the middle of this 'underground war' between loyal American military personnel and alien or alien-controlled 'personnel', as in the Dulce and the Groom wars themselves. The 'deeper' one descends into the underground 'alien empire' the greater the security and therefore the greater the 'control' will be. Michael Riconosciuto, a former Wackenhut employee, claims that at Area 51 when one goes past a certain level of security they are either dead or disappear. Riconosciuto's father Marshal Riconosciuto was a Hitler-supporter and a close friend of Fred L. Crisman, who was involved with the Maurey Island Incident, was an agent of Military-Industrial Intelligence, and was in turn a close friend of Clay Shaw who Louisiana District Attorney James Garrison accused of being the CIA-Mafia go-between in the John F. Kennedy assassination. Garrison might have convicted Clay Shaw if not for the fact that Garrison's star witness David Ferry was killed a few days before he was to testify at Clay Shaw's trial. Anyway, Michael Riconosciuto told reporters that when he worked for

The Omega Files

Wackenhut at the Nevada Test Site before he was 'framed' on drug charges and put in a Federal Prison, he and several others tried to get damning evidence and documents out of the base on a helicopter, data apparently dealing with unconstitutional biogenetic activities, alien interaction in the underground facilities, etc. This helicopter was shot down before it could leave the base and the five people on board were killed. How many brave freedom-loving Americans have to DIE before we finally wake up from our apathetic skepticism and realize that WE ARE AT WAR!?

Must we have a repeat of the Holocaust, and only after the fact hear such pitiful excuses like those that followed World War II?: "Yes, we heard the reports about the concentration camps, but they seemed too fantastic to be believed, so we didn't bother bombing the ovens or the train tracks leading to the death camps..." Or maybe: "Underground bases and concentration camps that have undermined America, where Nazis and Aliens are working together in a joint effort to impose a global dictatorship on this planet? Come on, how were we supposed to have believed something so fantastic?..." When all is said and done I will probably be seen as one of America's greatest heros or one of the nations most notorious fools.

To tell you the truth I could really care less. I would rather be seen as a fool rather than risk the lives of thousands or possibly millions of people who might turn out to be the potential victims of a cosmic conspiracy which I 'perceive' to be taking place, one which has specifically targeted America and her citizens. So then, at the risk of being a fool, I'll just go for broke and expose those specific areas where I 'perceive' the 'collaboration' maintains underground strongholds, based on what I have learned through years of research, personal experience, and interaction with others who have their own stories to tell about such an 'underground invasion' of North America... Within the United States, the following joint operational bases — operating under the control of Bavarian and Draconian intelligence agencies — have been identified by various researchers, beginning with the major facility near Dulce, New Mexico. Other facilities of this nature include Page, Arizona; Dougway, Utah; Nevada Test Site; the Madigan facility near Ft. Lewis, Washington; Deep Springs, California; Mt. Lassen, California; Lancaster, California; Montauk, Long Island; the Denver International Airport; Granite Mountain - Little Cottonwood Canyon, Salt Lake City, Utah; Sleeping Ute Mountain on the Ute Reservation of SE Utah; and Creede, Colorado. Other underground facilities for the New World Order itself are [apparently] oc-

The Omega Files

cupied exclusively by lower-ranking levels of the collaboration which are nevertheless controlled by the 'serpent cult' of humanoid and reptiloid collaborators in the 'joint operational' facilities. Many of the 'closed' military bases in the United State possess underground facilities which are occupied by U.N. troops from various countries. Several Federal Buildings in many major cities also reportedly have underground facilities equipped with massive military weapons stashes, such as the Oklahoma City Federal Building which contains a 15 level base underneath, which was revealed during the initial local reports of the bombing of the federal building there — although these references to the underground tunnels were censored by the time the story reached national and international audiences. Since Oklahoma City and Airport are intended to be a major FEMA / U.N. 'relocation' processing center, one has to ask just which 'side' had stashed the underground arsenals there, the American, or New World Order government? Also FEMA itself maintains SEVERAL underground facilities, many of them located beneath major airports throughout the United States... Could America be facing a four-fold invasion force in the future... via air, sea, land as well as an 'invasion' from the underground networks of the Military-Industrial Complex?

THE UNITED NATIONS IN THE UNITED STATES

The following information comes from a research source which has investigated actual UNITED NATIONS preparations, WITHIN THE UNITED STATES, to deal with any resistance to a 'New World Order' takeover.

Take note that FEMA is a major New World Order front with SEVERAL extensive operational underground bases which, like underground Trojan horses, exist beneath strategic locations throughout the United States: "'FINCEN' CONFIRMED PRE-DEPLOYMENT LOCATIONS: south and east-central California; west-central Montana; north Texas; west-central Wisconsin; north-east Illinois; south-east Michigan; central Indiana; south-west Ohio; north New York; south Delaware; south Maryland; north-east Virginia. north-east North Carolina; central, south Florida.

"ALL FINCEN EQUIPMENT IS BLACK, FINCIN UNIFORMS, HELICOPTERS, ETC. FINCEN ARE FOREIGN MILITARY AND SECRET POLICE BROUGHT INTO THE UNITED STATES FOR DEPLOYMENT AGAINST THE U.S. CITIZENS. MOST IDENTIFIED FINCEN UNITS ARE AT COMPANY STRENGTH (160+). SOME ARE AS LARGE AS BRIGADE STRENGTH (2600+) "FINCEN'S

The Omega Files

MISSION IS:

"A) House to house search and seizure of property and arms.

"B) Separation and categorization of men, women and children as prisoners in large numbers.

"C) Transfer to detention facilities of aforementioned prisoners. "CONFIRMED MJTF [Multi-Jurisdictional Task Force] POLICE LOCATIONS: northwest Washington; central, south California; south-west, south-east, north Wyoming; north, north-west, south-west Nebraska; north Texas; south-east Missouri; west-central, south-east Wisconsin; north-east Illinois; central, south-east Michigan; central Indiana; north-central Kentucky; south, south-west Ohio; north, south-east New York; south-central North Carolina; west-central Georgia; south-east Florida; central(?) Alaska.

""THE MJTF IS THE VELVET GLOVE ON THE IRON FIST" — MOTTO ON THE COVER PAGE OF THE MJTF GUIDELINES AND AUTHORIZING LEGISLATION. "The MJTF Police is made up of:

"1) MILITARY - Converts those National Guard Units that are not banned by the president, into a National Police Force.

"2) Converts all surviving local and state police to national police.

"3) Converts street gangs into law enforcement units for house to house searches [L.A., Chicago, and New York are in the process now]

"MJTF POLICE MISSION:

"1) House to house search and seizure of property and firearms.

"2) Separation and categorization of men, women and children as prisoners in large numbers.

"3) Transfer to and the operation of detention camps in the U.S. [43+ Camps]

"UNITED NATIONS COMBAT GROUPS CONFIRMED LOCATIONS: east-central, south California; north-west, west, south-west Montana; south Arizona; north Texas; east Michigan; north, south-east New York; north New Jersey; north-west, north-central, north-east North Carolina; west-central Georgia.

"UNITED NATIONS BATTLE GROUPS ENTRANCE TO UNITED STATES PASSED UNDER PRESIDENTIAL EXECUTIVE ORDERS SIGNED 11 NOVEM-

The Omega Files

BER (11/11) 1990 (Note: There are those who are convinced that WITH the Assassination of President John F. Kennedy a 'coup d'etat' took place within the Executive branch of the America government via Internationalist groups who are determined to destroy the U.S. Constitution, and that the 'presidents' who were manipulated into office since that time — mostly C.F.R. and T.L.C. members — have signed numerous un-constitutional 'executive orders' designed to pave the way for America's assimilation into a global dictatorship. If this is the case, then American's have the CONSTITUTIONAL RIGHT to resist this FOREIGN U.N. - N.W.O. government, a right which is also laid down in the DECLARATION OF INDEPENDENCE.

As for the Kennedy assassination itself and those behind it, Louisiana District Attorney James Garrison in an interview with Playboy magazine made the following statement in regards to Lee Harvey Oswald: "...Our office has positively identified a number of his associates as neo-Nazis. Oswald would have been more at home with Mein Kampf than Das Kapital." Ironically, the Mafia agent who was assigned to kill the 'patsy' Oswald, Jack Ruby, was one of these "neo-Nazis" according to Garrison. - Branton)

"DETENTION FACILITIES AUTHORIZED THROUGH FEMA AND AUGMENTED BY DOD BUDGET AMENDMENT PASSED WITH 1991 FISCAL BUDGET: "north, south-west, south-east Wyoming; north-west, north-east, south Nebraska; north, central(?) Texas; central Wisconsin; central, south-west, south, south-east Michigan; north-east, west-central, south Indiana; north-west, north-east, central, south Ohio; west, north, east New York.

"A) Each site can detain between 32,000 to 44,000 people min.

"B) It is indicated that the Texas and Alaskan sites may be much larger and more heavily armed.

"C) For the areas west of the Mississippi, OKLAHOMA CITY is the central processing point for detainees and can handle up to 100,000 people at a time.

"D) The Eastern processing center is not yet identified at this time. "DETENTION FACILITIES — 23 FEMA Authorized and stationed; 20 DOD [Department of Defense] Budget authorized and stationed — 43 TOTAL. Note: In Red China an untold number of people are suffering in Communist 'Laogai' camps as slave laborers; in Soviet Russia it was the 'Gulag' camps. In Nazi Germany the 'Concentration' camps were not only used as slave camps, but also as extermination camps to carry out the genocidal plans of American

The Omega Files

CORPORATE and European MILITANT 'Nazis'. I have only one thing to say concerning these plans for confinement camps here in America, and I'm sure that many of our Jewish-American citizens who share this country with us — that is with ALL of us of all national backgrounds whose ancestors came from all parts of the world in order to be free from tyranny — will agree with me whole-heartedly when I repeat their battle-cry: "NEVER AGAIN!!!"

THE FEDERAL EMERGENCY MANAGEMENT AGENCY

The following is from the Patriot Archives ftp site at: ftp://tezcat.com/patriot If you have any other files you'd like to contribute, e-mail them to alex@spiral.org. Although an excellent article, the January 1995 edition of 'Monitoring Times' magazine published only a tiny portion of what FEMA has been tasked by Executive Order to perform. FEMA was brought into existence by E.O. All the frequencies I have for FEMA follow my comments here: Federal Emergency Management Agency [F.E.M.A.] [and other emergency agencies]: F.E.M.A. [Federal Emergency Management Agency] has been authorized for the past 15 years by Presidential Executive Orders to confiscate ALL PROPERTY from the American People, separate families in the current 43 internment camps [already built and operational by the way, 5 of which are located in Georgia. The largest can confine somewhere on the order of 100,000 American citizens], called relocation camps by the 'government', for assignment to work camps; declares martial law and TOTALLY OVER-RIDES the U.S. Constitution. Presidential Executive Orders that are related or control this are given at the end of this. Two of the state prisons here in Georgia are currently empty, although manned by a minimal number of staff, have been setup and intentionally unpopulated by prisoners just to support this political policy. Concentration [internment] Camps. An Executive Order signed by then President BUSH in 1989 authorized the Federal Emergency Management Agency [F.E.M.A.] to build 43 primary camps [having a capacity of 35,000 to 45,000 prisoners EACH] and also authorized hundreds of secondary facilities. It is interesting to note that several of these facilities can accommodate 100,000 prisoners. These facilities have been completed and many are already manned but as yet contain no prisoners. [Remember all the TALK of over-crowded prisons that exist...]. In south Georgia there are several state prisons that except for a few guards, are completely devoid of prisoners. Under F.E.M.A., the Executive Orders which are already written and is the current law of the land, calls for the COMPLETE suspension of the United States Constitution, all rights and liberties,

The Omega Files

as they are currently known.

The following executive orders, which are in the Federal Register located in Washington DC for anyone to request copies of, call for the suspension of all civil rights and liberties and for extraordinary measures to be taken in, as most of the orders state, "any national security emergency situation that might confront the government." When F.E.M.A. is implemented, the following executive orders will be immediately enforced:

E.O. 12148 - FEMA national security emergency, such as: national disaster, social unrest, insurrection, or national financial crisis.

E.O. 10995 - "... provides for the seizure of ALL communications media in the United States."

E.O. 10997 - "... provides for the seizure of ALL electric power, petroleum, gas, fuels and minerals, both public and private."

E.O. 10998 - "... provides for the seizure of ALL food supplies and resources, public and private, and ALL farms, lands, and equipment."

E.O. 10999 - "... provides for the seizure of ALL means of transportation, including PERSONAL cars, trucks or vehicles of any kind and TOTAL CONTROL over all highways, seaports, and waterways."

E.O. 11000 - "... provides for the SEIZURE OF ALL AMERICAN PEOPLE for work forces under federal supervision, including SPLITTING UP OF FAMILIES if the government has to."

E.O. 11001 - "... provides for government seizure of ALL health, education and welfare functions."

E.O. 11002 - "... designates the postmaster general to operate a national REGISTRATION of all persons." [Under this order, you would report to your local post office to be separated and assigned to a new area. Here is where families would be separated].

E.O. 11003 - "... provides for the government to take over ALL airports and aircraft, commercial, public and PRIVATE."

E.O. 11004 - "... provides for the Housing and Finance Authority to relocate communities, designate areas to be abandoned and establish new locations for populations."

E.O. 11005 - "... provides for the government to TAKE OVER railroads,

The Omega Files

inland waterways, and public storage facilities."

E.O. 11051 - "... the office of Emergency Planning [has] complete authorization to put the above orders into effect in time of increased international tension or economic or financial crisis."

All of the above executive orders were combined by President NIXON into Executive Order 11490, which allows all of this to take place if a national emergency is declared by the President. The burning and insurrection in Los Angeles in the case of Rodney King could have executed [and partially did execute] these Executive Orders.

Executive Order 12919: "National Defense Industrial Resources Preparedness" signed by CLINTON June 3, 1994, delegates authorities, responsibilities and allocations of F.E.M.A.'s Executive Orders [last entry] for the confiscation of ALL PROPERTY from the American people, and their re-location and assignment to 'labor' camps. The Executive Order also supersedes or revokes eleven (11) previous Executive Orders [from 1939 through 1991] and amends Executive Order 10789 and 11790. This executive order is A DECLARATION OF WAR AGAINST THE AMERICAN PEOPLE by the [Secret] Government of the United States in concert with the UNITED NATIONS. Operation Dragnet. Janet Reno can implement this operation upon receiving one call from the President. Arrest warrants will be issued via computer to round-up over 1 MILLION PATRIOTIC AMERICANS who may 'resist' the NEW WORLD ORDER. Americans who are not 'politically correct.' Specifically mentioned are CHRISTIANS or those who read the Bible. Cultist Definition by Janet Reno, Attorney General USA Concentration/internment camps have already been built to accommodate these American prisoners. See above paragraph as these internment camps have been setup and are run by F.E.M.A.

(Note: In reference to Christians, just where should they/we stand in regards to defending America? Should Christians take up arms if necessary? Apparently the Founding fathers of the American Republic believed so, so long as it was in order to DEFEND their country, their women and children... and NOT in order to engage in offensive warfare for the sake of conquering and exploiting others, which to me would be "living by the sword" or you could say "making a living" by the sword. This could be exemplified by the Germans who initiated unprovoked invasions of their neighbors to meet their economic needs during World Wars I and II.

The Omega Files

One might ask, what about all the Orthodox Jews and Greek Orthodox Christians who went to their deaths like lambs to the slaughter without resisting during World War II? Why didn't they fight more zealously to defend themselves? That is a hard question and one that I don't have an answer for. It may have simply come down to a lack of unity of faith and understanding of the threat. All I can say is that from my study of the Old and New Testaments, I find no passage that forbids us from defending ourselves from aggressors — at least in a national sense, however we ARE forbidden to become the unprovoked aggressors ourselves or engage in conflicts which are offensive rather than defensive oriented. The offensive attacks against the native Americans for instance, resulting from the Anglo invasion of North America, can NOT be justified through scripture, and such policies and mistreatment of the native Americans, the continuous betrayal of treaties, and the stealing of their God-given land in the past have or will doubtless have an adverse affect on America's destiny UNLESS reparations are made to the native peoples — for instance a restoration of historical territories. Perhaps the Greys felt justified in repeatedly violating our government's secret 'treaties' with them because 'we' had done the exact same thing to the native Americans?

Perhaps we in part DESERVED the abuses that the Greys have inflicted upon us? Perhaps our nation's destiny will be largely determined by how we treat the native Americans from here on out, whether or not we begin to honor ALL of the treaties that 'we' had made and broken in the past? Could it be? On the other hand, if OFFENSIVE warfare is forbidden by God, then DEFENSIVE warfare against a foreign invasion of American soil — or an internal threat to our freedoms, as guaranteed in the Bill of Rights WOULD, from my perspective, be justified. In Psalm 125:3 we read how the rule of the wicked is a DIRECT VIOLATION of the will of God: "...For the wicked shall not rule the godly, lest the godly be forced to do wrong." A perfect example would be the Lutherans of Germany who all-too-often capitulated to the Nazi's who themselves were backed by Luciferian cults which the Christians should have resisted. Instead, many of these backslidden Christians in Germany grudgingly supported the atrocities of their Nazi leaders, and by default the extermination of millions of Jewish, Gypsy and Slavic men, women and children. Why could Martin Luther himself stand alone against hundreds of pompish religious hypocrites at the council of Worms in Germany and boldly accuse them of blasphemy to their faces, yet many of his Protestant followers — not detracting from those few brave souls who DID resist — gave-in right and left to the Nazi Satanists, and in some cases even contributed to the atrocities of World Wars I and II?

So in short, if a situation exists wherein an offender or a defender must die — one or the other so that the other could live — then the defender would be the one who should keep his or her life. In warfare, the INVADER should be considered a 'murderer' for killing a human being; whereas if the INVADED took the life of an invader, it should be considered 'execution' in retribution for the murderous acts of the invaders themselves. All of this would be justified in the name of and according to the rules of the society which gives the defending citizens the power to defend his or her country, just as one is authorized to use deadly force against an unwelcome intruder into their home if they feel their life is being threatened. The only exception to this would be an offensive invasion of an allied country which has been invaded by an enemy force, or the SELECTIVE invasion of an enemy country in order to rescue allied citizens who are being held within a targeted region — as in underground bases for instance? — in which case the invasion should be considered a form of self-defense on behalf of their own citizens, so long as the invader REMAINS in a mode of 'offensive defense'. - Branton)

OPERATION ROLLING THUNDER.

Reno and Benson have mentioned this operation which comprises county-wide sweeps of house to house, dynamic entry, search and seizures for all guns and food stockpiles by B.A.T.F., state national guard, activity duty soldiers, as well as local police. This function is also run and coordinated through F.E.M.A.

Public Law 100-690 banned almost ALL RELIGIOUS GATHERINGS [not yet enforced..]. (Note: When and if this is enforced, this will be a blatant defecation upon the BILL OF RIGHTS, and in this event every true American is allowed — and in fact it will be his and her Patriotic DUTY — to implement the clause within the DECLARATION OF INDEPENDENCE to OVERTHROW such an alien or FOREIGN tyranny-structure which has like a tape-worm infested the governing 'body' of America. - Branton); grants no-knock search and seizures without a search warrant; expands the drug laws to include EVERY American.

This will generally be the prelude, or in addition to, a F.E.M.A. operation and contingency plan implementation. The Omnibus Crime Bill of 1990.

The Omega Files

Ensures confiscation of all private property via money laundering, environmental violations of the Clean Water and Air Act, and extends as far as child abuse. This act also coordinates activities through F.E.M.A. and the Department of the Army, Commanding General, U.S. Forces Command, Fort McPherson, GA which is the executive and implementing agency upon initiation of many of these acts. The responsible agency within U.S. Army Forces Command was what used to be known as the Deputy Chief of Staff for Operations, Plans Division [DCSOPS, Plans], which was changed several years ago to J-3 after the Headquarters became a joint headquarters. They keep on file copies of all F.E.M.A. Emergency Management Operation Plans, including those plans developed by the Army to support the F.E.M.A. plan to eliminate the U.S. Constitution upon implementation. According to current plans, the Constitution will be 'temporarily' discontinued and shelved until the real or perceived and declared 'threat' has been neutralized (ask yourself — who or what is the REAL threat that needs to be 'neutralized'? - Branton). But once 'shelved,' as with almost every other action of the Government, it STAYS shelved.

The Crime Bill of 1994. Banning of all military weapons which are necessary to the formation of a militia [when needed], denies other military equipment to the people's militia units (that's OK... the average American gun owner can legally acquire this 'equipment' from off the DEAD BODIES of UN/FEMA-backed gestapo forces when they break-in to our homes to steal our personal property or try to take us and our families prisoner without due process of law. - Branton), prelude to confiscating ALL guns in the hands of private citizens, DESTROYS the 1st Amendment, and makes virtually every American an outlaw. See above comments concerning the house-to-house search. The agency responsible for the actual implementation and search is the Department of the Army in concert with local and state police, including F.E.M.A., FBI, BATF, and other Federal Agencies. SECRET UNDERGROUND BASES. There have been documented over 60 secret, VIRTUAL CITIES, UNDERGROUND, build by the government, Federal Reserve Bank Owners (such as the 'Rockefellers', etc. - Branton), and high ranking members of the Committee of 300 [some of these under-ground areas can be seen in Kansas City, Missouri and Kansas City, Kansas].

In additional, there exist underground Satellite Tracking Facilities which have the ability to punch your 911 address into the computer and a satellite can within seconds bring a camera to bear on your property to the point that those monitoring can read a license number on an automobile in your driveway. These facilities have as of Oct. 1, 1994, been turned over to the [foreign power of the] UNITED NATIONS. (Note: Forget the license plate, according to information released by Norio Hayakawa, this satellite technology is now so sophisticated that they can CLEARLY read every word on your driver's LICENSE supposing it were in view of the satellite. - Branton)

THE BAVARIAN ILLUMINATI

At this point we will discuss present plans by the Bavarian Illuminati and other Bavarian cults to stage an invasion of America under the cover of a United Nations 'New World Order' operation to "restore order to America" in the event of an internal emergency, a "staged" emergency of course. The REAL motive would be to destroy every last vestige of patriotism and resistance to the New World Order.

For those who are not familiar with George Washington's famous vision at Valley Forge, I would highly recommend that you locate a copy since the vision correctly predicted the outcome of the Revolutionary war, the Civil war and it's outcome, and the 'third trial' that America must pass through before it enters into its ultimate destiny.

Following this war according to Washington, no power on earth, in heaven, or in hell would be able to stand against her divine destiny. Compare this prophecy with the prophecy in Revelation chapter 12. Could America be the 'wilderness' mentioned in that chapter? Also compare that prophecy with the fact that America and Israel harbor more Jewish citizens than any other nations on earth, more or less equally distributed between the two. Washington, in this angelic vision, saw a dark red cloud rise out of Europe, the Middle East, Africa and Asia. This cloud carried a massive army with it and this army then invaded American soil and commenced to engage the citizens of America in battle, as the nation was engulfed in the dark cloud. He saw most of the major cities in flames. The Americans rallied their forces in a common defense and from their newfound unity of purpose they continued the fight, according to the vision. According to other private visions that are not as well known, yet which confirm Washington's own vision, the Rocky Mountains and the Great Plains west of the Mississippi will apparently be the heart of the "Free America" zone where the true Americans will make their stand, and those areas east of the Mississippi River will be the hardest hit by the occupying forces. Those border areas north, south and

The Omega Files

west of the Rockies / Great Plains may also be threatened, however Washington's vision did not go into detail on this, neither did he see exactly how long the battle would last. In the vision he was shown that near the end of the war when the American resistance seemed to be "well nigh overcome", Divine Intervention would bring about an American victory as "legions of white spirits" descended to join the Americans in battle. The broken ranks would be re-fortified and the American militia would go on the offensive and eventually drive the enemy into the sea. This would apparently coincide with the destruction of the power-base of the New World Order in Europe, which would also be the result of Divine Intervention in keeping with the Apocalyptic prophecies of the book of Revelation.

Just who were these "white spirits" that General Washington saw in his vision?... I recall an interesting sermon I heard from a Pentecostal evangelist years ago. He claimed that he was friends with some government scientists with high-level security clearances. It seems as if they had detected, with powerful electronic telescopes, a brilliant and beautiful 'star-like' object emerging from the 'vortex' within the Orion NEBULA. This nebula is several hundred light years BEYOND the Orion open cluster itself, which is in line-of-site between Sol and the Nebula. From our perspective this awesome nebula is the middle star in Orion's "dagger" which hangs from Orion's "belt". Some have interpreted this to be the area that Lucifer referred to as the "Sides of the North", which was the ultimate target of his war against the Creator and his vain desire to conquer the heavens and the throne of the Almighty One. Others have referred to this vortex in the Orion nebula as the Eternity Gate, because they believe it leads to the Eternal Realm of the Creator which exists beyond our time-space-material universe. This brilliant object however is on a direct course to the Sol system and earth, according to these scientists, which means that it will eventually pass through the core of the Orion cluster. This does not mean that the Angelis forces who are believed to reside in this awesome "City of Light" must wait for this to take place to wage their "war in heaven" against the Unholy Six Empire of Orion — as some Federation worlds refer to it because of the six draconian-controlled star systems which make up its core — being that the Angelic "light beings" can travel at the speed of thought and enter any point in time-space instantaneously.

However even though this City of Light is on a direct course to earth, at its present rate of speed, according to this Evangelist, it will not arrive

The Omega Files

here until sometime around 3000 A.D. or the end of the "Millennium", all according to the perfect timing of the Creator. This is EXACTLY when the book of Revelation states that the New Jerusalem will arrive and descend to earth. Revelation states that this CITY OF LIGHT — home of the Son of God Melchizedek [an immortal being described in the Old Testament, to whom Abraham paid tithes], also known as Jesus the Christ, and also the home of His Angelic command forces under the Archangel Michael — is some 1500 miles high and 1500 miles wide, foursquare. Some suggest that this would be a large 'cube'. However I recall reading the story of some Chinese Christian children years ago who experienced simultaneous visions of the New Jerusalem as a vast three-leveled PYRAMAL city of light. Of course pagans have used 'pyramids' for their own purposes, yet this does not necessarily mean that the Almighty does not use this form as well, especially when we consider the tendency of pagans and fallen angels to counterfeit that which the Almighty One has done. So a pyramidal city of light would also be just as tall as it is wide, even though the interior of the city will not necessarily be limited to the time-space-material restrictions of this omniverse, being that the interior of the New Jerusalem Command exists in the realm of ETERNITY... The "war in heaven" and the war on earth will apparently NOT be just a physical war, but a physical AND spiritual war between Lucifer and his draconian denizens operating through the pagan New World Order, and Michael and his angelic warriors backing the Judeo-Christian American Republic.

In this sense, as the conflict between Free America and the New World Order increases, the CHAPLAIN will be just as important if not more so than the GENERAL, since this war will involve simultaneous attacks against all three levels of our beings — spiritual, psychological, and physical. As these events become more common, gone will be the Darwinist THEORIES which would deny that humanity and nature possess any spiritual attributes. You could say in a sense that all of this will amount to a 'Holy War' against a fascist-satanist empire and its draconian backers. In other words the distinction or barrier which formerly existed between the spiritual and physical worlds may very well collapse as the two become one. There will no doubt be a large number of traitors and infiltrators living in America who will try to betray the USA to the invading forces, not being true Americans, but most of these will no doubt be forced to take one side or the other when the final confrontation occurs, and that confrontation IS inevitable. And it will probably be a surprise attack when Americans least expect it. Some

The Omega Files

have suggested that the invasion is being planned for winter and around Christmas Eve, which might make sense. It would not be very logical to stage such an invasion on the 4th of July. Although Divine intervention will bring about an end to the New World Order, the question would not so much be whether the draconian conspiracy against planet earth — working through the UN/NWO — will or will not succeed.

The question is how many of US will survive to the end. I firmly believe that this will depend on our own collective choices and our willingness to work together as Americans, regardless of color or creed, being unified around the National standard and holding fast to the inspired documents upon which the United States of America was founded, or in the case of the other American Republics... holding fast to the democratic principles that all men are created equal and that the citizens of any given nation have the right to determine through electoral freedom the course and nature of their government and laws. We must strive as a unified force to defend, by the grace of God, our fellow citizens — men, women and children — with whom we share this oppressed yet nevertheless "last bastion" of freedom, America.

THE FINAL INVASION OF THE UNITED STATES?

The following information was released January of 1997 by Dr. Al Overholt. Titled, "THE FINAL INVASION OF THE U.S.??", the document reads: From the INTERNET, 12/96 [quoting:] The following, about a possible planned 'invasion' of the U.S., is, I know, the sort of alarmist thing one hears from time to time. Yet it ties in with other events that make it not readily dismissible.

(1) U.S. forces sent to Bosnia, not here in the USA to protect us.

(2) U.S. forces going to Zaire, further diminishing National Security.

(3) Gulf War Syndrome, decimating U.S. military.

(4) Gradual infiltration [known] of GERMAN military into the U.S. Like I say, the following might be only alarmist claptrap. Then again.... *caveat lector*. This means, "reader beware." In other words, it is up to the reader to form her/his own judgments as to the following. [End quoting] From: Stop All Federal Abuses Now! S.A.F.A.N. Internet Newsletter, No. 129, November 15, 1996 (Take note on how the New World Order is trying to incite civil war between British Columbia and French Quebec, Canada, and use this emergency as an excuse to activate unconstitutional executive orders in America.

The Omega Files

This has not been the first attempt to create an "emergency" that would "justify" martial law in America, and if this one fails, then it will certainly NOT be the last attempt. I take this report very seriously, being that my own ancestors were Frenchmen who became British citizens and later immigrated to America. Just WHAT force would try to create a civil war between French Quebec, British Columbia and America? Could it be, just possibly, that same "force" which was responsible for killing hundreds of thousands of French, British and American allied soldiers during World War I and World War II? - Branton)

THE COMING INVASION OF AMERICA INTERNET: Posted by Roger D. Cravens (rbg@CCDOSA1.EM.CDC.GOV

The following is most of the message printed in THE PROPHECY CLUB NEWSLETTER from Intelligence sources in Canada and New England, [quoting:] Preparations for the COMING INVASION OF AMERICA by Russian/NWO FORCES are progressing rapidly in Canada! As candidly admitted to me by many Canadians [including author and lecturer Grant Jeffery of FINAL WARNING and many other books explaining the coming New World Order takeover] Canada it totally sold out to the NWO and its heinous agenda of world domination. (Note: I would suggest that this statement is somewhat extreme. Certainly those ADVOCATES of a New World Order operating within certain executive levels of Canadian government are sold out to the agenda, but no more so than the advocates for the NWO operating within various executive levels of the AMERICAN government. It is obvious that the majority of Canadians AND Americans desire to maintain their national independence, and it is THESE who the advocates of the New World Order are apparently willing to sacrifice in the devastating civil wars that they have 'planned' for America and Canada. We must realize that just as there is an electorate AND a secret government within America, the same holds true with Canada as well. - Branton)

America has long been a thorn in the flesh of the NWO planners, because of our Christian heritage and its isolation from Europe. With little over three years left to move this Western Hemisphere into their NWO agenda by the year 2000, they are making rapid use of Canada's [NWO advocates'] willingness to betray America into their control. How is this taking place? Canada has opened her doors wide to NWO forces, including GERMAN, RUSSIAN AND CHINESE. As Grant Jeffery admitted to me personally one month ago, "we have MORE GERMAN MILITARY FORCES IN CANADA NOW

The Omega Files

THAN WE DO CANADIAN MILITARY FORCES [emphasis mine]!" Indeed, for next to Dease Lake, Canada, Germans have been handed a military air base for their use. They are actively practicing bombing and strafing runs for the coming Invasion of America...much as they are doing down at Holloman AFB, which has been permanently turned over to the Germans (in NEW MEXICO). The traitorous NWO elements within our own government are fully aware of the motives of these GERMAN NWO FORCES both in Canada and America and welcome their presence into the Western Hemisphere as part of the solution to subduing patriotic Americans who simply refuse to surrender national sovereignty to a foreign power. Russian and Chinese forces are also very active in Canada. They are "re-building and strengthening railroad tracks for the anticipated heavy use of railway transportation of incoming military personnel from the West Coast" [both Russian and Chinese forces] as well as transporting military vehicles and armaments and food supplies. New tracks are also being laid between border states and Canada. Those people who are arrested as resistors or dissidents will also be transported in specially prepared prisoner boxcars to the death camps already established near the border, such as the one near Cut Bank, MT. The death camp outside of Cut Bank has been conveniently located right off a major AMTRACK express line in the anticipation of transporting resisters and dissidents conveniently to their deaths by rail.

Reports have been received from INTEL sources nationwide which indicate that certain boxcars are quietly being renovated from the inside so that they can be used for prisoner transport to such death camps. Preparations noted by eye-witnesses include shackles being bolted into the walls to restrain those taken prisoner until they reach their final destination. From our intelligence source in Florida, we know that Russian train engineer experts are already being trained in how to operate American engines and how our rail system functions... Russian railway procedures differ from American. As least fifty Russian engineers are in training presently in Jacksonville, Florida. Many others are apparently being trained in other locations as well. (Note: Some have alleged that the sudden 'fall' of the Soviet states and the Berlin wall was planned in advance as part of an agenda to merge the East and the West into a so called democratic-socialist/communist-socialist New World Order. East and West Berlin would be at the forefront for the reunification of Eastern and Western Europe and in turn — they hope — the rest of the world. Germany has also led the way for European unification by establishing an 'open border' policy and encouraging other

The Omega Files

European countries to do the same. This may sound benign on the outside but considering the facts it may be a ruse to 'unify' Europe under German control, which was actually Adolph Hitler's goal.

However in this case the unification is being accomplished through economic means rather than military means. The control is still in Germany but it is more subtle. The Third Reich established German MILITARY control of Europe. The "European Economic Community" or E.E.C. established ECONOMIC control. In most cases, in this world it is the ECONOMIC forces which control 'governments'. Sad, but true. Notice how the term "Economic" has now been removed, and the New World Order has been re-named the "European Community". Very clever! In other words the unification is no longer just along economic lines but is becoming increasingly political, since the member nations have been pressured into submitting to an E.C. constitution along MORE THAN mere economic lines. France and England have been pulled into this alliance, in spite of two devastating world wars with the country that is secretly orchestrating the E.C., aka the New World Order. Come on France and England, get a clue!!! Germany is not only the largest federated state in the E.C., but in 1990 was the LARGEST economic power in the WORLD, with a trade surplus totaling over $58 billion. With almost no foreign currency reserves in 1949, Germany had accumulated nearly $80 billion in reserves by 1989, compared with the $38 billion in the U.S.A. and $41 billion in Great Britain. A rather incredible "comeback" for a country that had waged two world wars for the sole purpose of offensive conquest, wars that had cost the Allies a HEAVY price in blood and resources. Of course Germany is also the LEADING economic power in the E.C. as well, possessing 35% of the Economic power-base of the European Community according to the GROLIER ENCYCLOPEDIA. So just WHERE does the real power lie in the E.C. / N.W.O?

Considering that the German Black Nobility — who have controlled vast financial empire's for over 1500 years and have ruled the [un]Holy Roman Empire for centuries — were the same ones who sent Vladimir Lenin from GERMANY to Russia to start the Communist Revolution, AND the same powers who backed Adolph Hitler... then it is not surprising that Communist East Germany would merge into Democratic(?) West Germany with such ease. It should not be surprising, therefore, to learn that GERMAN troops In the United States AND Canada play a MAJOR role in the planned invasion of North America — since after all most of the New World Order agenda had

The Omega Files

its roots in Bavaria region of Germany. Most do not realize that Adolph Hitler's second book, after he wrote MEIN KAMPF, was titled — believe it or not — "THE NEW WORLD ORDER". - Branton)

Already seen being transported on these train lines are huge power generators to various locations in Canada, in anticipation of the planned power outages that will be triggered deliberately both in Canada and America as the planned takeover methodically takes place. Incredibly, we now have information that [All emphasis mine, below] THE RUSSIANS HAVE FINALLY SUCCEEDED IN BRIDGING THE GAP BETWEEN SIBERIA AND ALASKA THROUGH A VAST UNDERGROUND TUNNEL! (The Bering Sea between Alaska and Asia is UNDER 100 miles wide at its narrowest point, so this would not be an inconceivable undertaking - Branton) Although documented in more than one newspaper report in Western Canada, THE AMERICAN NEWS MEDIA HAS REMAINED SILENT ON THIS FEAT. RUSSIAN CIVILIANS (???) ARE KNOWN TO BE COMING THRU THIS TUNNEL, 100 PER MONTH, PLUS HEAVY MILITARY ARTILLERY. ALSO, THERE IS YET ANOTHER TUNNEL THAT HAS BEEN BUILT FROM SIBERIA TO NORTHERN CANADA, THIS ONE BEING USED FOR RAILROAD TRANSPORTATION PURPOSES. (Note: It is interesting that several underground tunnels have been discovered by American troops which originate in North Korea and run under the border, emerging at different points in the border region of South Korea. Some of these tunnels are well-built and modern and could accommodate massive troop movements. It appears that North Korea may be planning something for the future, possibly in conjunction with the Russian-Chinese plans mentioned above? A U.S. Air Force Officer who wrote an expose on U.N. betrayal of America forces during the Korean and Vietnam 'wars' has stated that based on intelligence data he has gathered, those Vietnamese 'boat people' who 'escaped' to America AFTER — not BEFORE — North Vietnam took control of the South, were and are die-hard Communists. The reason for this is that when the North took control of the South of Vietnam they immediately hunted down all known Anti-Communist activists and sympathizers and exterminated them.

In other words the 'boat people' who left Vietnam FOLLOWING the 'purge' were mostly Communist infiltrators masquerading as people who were 'escaping the Communists'. The USAF officer claimed that these infiltrators are involved in a plan to bring down America, and that they have been accumulating and storing huge weapon stashes in anticipation for the

The Omega Files

time when they will be called in to action to join their comrades in their war against America. - Branton) The extent of the American Government's [the corporate fascist military-industrial 'government' as opposed to the Constitutional or electorate 'government'] betrayal of her citizens can be further evidenced in the fact that these Chinese and Russian forces are RECEIVING PAYMENT FOR THEIR PRE-INVASION ACTIVITIES THROUGH THE INTERNATIONAL MONETARY FUND... ISSUED ON AMERICAN GOVERNMENT CHECKS. In anticipation of the coming invasion from Russia and China [and German - U.N forces, etc.] Canada has even gone so far as to disband its Western Coast Guard Division, thus they are open to amphibious invasion of America from the West. This was openly evidenced recently through the presentation of a documentary report over the BBC television in London which detailed amphibious assault forces practicing war maneuvers and strategy in the Formosa Straits. When BBC newsmen were permitted to interview these soldiers in training, they repeatedly asked them the following question. "What are you preparing to use this training for?" The shocking, consistent reply was "FOR THE COMING INVASION OF AMERICA!" When it became clear that a gaff in security was created by airing this broadcast over television in England, its scheduled re-broadcast for the next day in London was hastily canceled. (So then, for our readers in our West Coast and especially Hawaiian Naval bases, TAKE NOTICE. You are the last line and front line of defense against such an action. Remember Pearl Harbor, and learn from the mistakes of the past!!! - Branton)

SPECULATE NO MORE ON THE SUSPICIOUS SUICIDE OF ADMIRAL MICHAEL BOORDA [FORMER DIRECTOR OF THE U.S. NAVAL FORCES]. I WAS INFORMED HE WAS TERMINATED BECAUSE OF HIS REFUSAL TO CO-OPERATE IN THE COVERT PLAN BY OUR TRAITOROUS NWO FORCES WITHIN OUR OWN GOVERNMENT TO ASSIST IN THE COMING INVASION OF AMERICA. WHEN HE REFUSED TO GO ALONG WITH THE PLAN TO COVERTLY BRINGING CHINESE FORCES INTO AMERICA THROUGH USE OF OUR OWN NAVY VESSELS, ORDERS WERE GIVEN FROM ON HIGH TO TERMINATE HIM.

The message is clear. This message is to inform those who may not know the magnitude of the New World Order and its massive agenda. BE WISE AND INVESTIGATE FOR YOURSELVES. We are not getting the truth from agents of government. Examples are Vietnam, Waco, Ruby Ridge, Militias, TWA800, Oklahoma, etc. Beware and prepare! God Bless America.

The Omega Files

[WE CERTAINLY WON'T STOP IT WITHOUT HIS HELP.] We need his blessing. ARE WE GOING TO WAKE UP IN TIME TO STOP THIS?? [The following accompanied the above information, in the newsletter from which these reports were taken...]

The following articles are excerpts taken from advertisement flyers put out by Serge Monast. They have short news-bites of VERY INTERESTING INFORMATION THAT I FEEL IS WORTH PONDERING. For those who haven't heard yet — Serge Monast was recently deaded [killed] for his daring exposes of the Elite. His son was kidnapped shortly before he was [killed], also because of his exposing their dastardly deeds and plans to make most of us their slaves... SOON!! I don't have any information whether or not any of his reports are available since he has transitioned to the heavenly realms. — Al. FEMA: RED IRON PLAN — NATIONWIDE STATE OF EMERGENCY — NATIONAL STATE — SOVEREIGNTY ENDANGERED... Excerpted from THE INTERNATIONAL FREE PRESS AGENCY 'REPORT', 12/96, [quoting:] FORWARDED MESSAGE: FROM: U.N. Military Confidential Source. Sender: Int'l Free Press Agency, Fax: 1 (819) 888-2949 Reply to: Int'l Free Press Agency, Fax: 1 (819) 888-2949 To: Please forward this crucial information to all networks — World, National Date: December 3rd, 1996; Time 15:00 GMT EXTREMELY URGENT... RED ALERT CONFIRMED HIGH U.N. SENSITIVE MILITARY INFORMATION. NOTE: PLEASE PAY CLOSE ATTENTION TO THIS ONE... KNOW THAT FOREIGN TROOPS ARE IN STANDBY... THEY ARE DAGGERS POINTED AT THE HEART OF OUR HOMELAND AND SOCIETY... THIS IS REAL... THAT'S ONLY THE BEGINNING... RED IRON FEMA PREPAREDNESS... FEMA: RED IRON FEMA PLAN/NATIONWIDE STATE OF EMERGENCY / NATIONAL STATE SOVEREIGNTY ENDANGERED... STORM WARNING IN AMERICA... Department of the Army, FEMA, FBI, BATF, State and Local Police and other Federal Agencies involved [knowingly OR unknowingly]... the R-EMAP regions correspond exactly, by location and number, to the FEMA regions... R-EMAP, an EPA program, stands for Regional EMAP... UN's Global Biodiversity Assessment (GBA) for UN's Foreign Troops Global Training Centers & Detention Facilities Areas... Bring about national disaster BY ALL MEANS, social unjustified unrest into "Black communities", national financial crisis as a result of massive budget cuts, national social crisis blamed upon Militia and Religious Groups before the end of 1997... 1 million patriotic Americans who may resist the New World Order and Americans who are not "politically correct" are already listed and targeted to be arrested... [Specifically mentioned are Christian followers of those who run talk-shows

The Omega Files

throughout the country and Churches not under federal control]...

Very high secretive United Nations Military Plans... Never released before... TOP CONFIDENTIAL at high political level... also concern RUSSIAN AND FOREIGN TROOPS DEPLOYMENT AND OCCUPATION OF U.S. TERRITORY UNDER UNITED NATIONS MILITARY COMMAND... FEMA - U.N. Multi-Jurisdictional Police/military operation "TO NEUTRALIZE ALL PATRIOTIC AND CHRISTIAN ORGANIZATIONS IN AMERICA BEFORE THE END OF 1997"... ...FEMA canceled their scheduled Aug./Sept. 1996 "exercises" and changed it to the period between Jan./March 1997 which link to "PHILADELPHIA PHASE III" — to start in Eastern Canada during the same period... High-ranking politicians and military involved... Strong link between main roads to be used by foreign troops stationed in MEXICO and CANADA and Detention facilities areas, Biodiversity areas, some Military bases and railroad centers... [End quoting]

COUNTDOWN TO THE 1997 NORTHERN SHOWDOWN

Excerpted from RED ALERT REPORT, Aug. '96, [quoting:] International cross-checking verified sources and other absolute reliable and "unprecedented" sources of documentation [DATED JUNE 1996] tell us that this time is for "REAL". No fiction, no imagination, no process of deduction, the "TOP SECRET" scenario we now have in our hands is just BEYOND EVERYTHING EVER IMAGINED BEFORE. We can surely state that no one else anywhere has the "FULL COMPLETE PICTURE" with all accurate details of what has been carefully planned at the highest level of the world Politics and Economic Elite for something (BIG) to happen in 1997 which will disrupt life of millions of people. With full, well documented documents strongly supported by various serious unknown Politics and Military hard evidence files copies and actual documents for a major prearranged "Chaos", WE KNOW: * "WHY, HOW and WHEN a "DECLARATION OF A NATIONAL STATE OF EMERGENCY" in the U.S. will emerge during night time, and which are the 19 States that will be placed under "MARTIAL LAW"? * WHAT will be the precise "MILITARY AGENDA" in the targeted States for FEMA, Foreign UN Battle Groups, FINCEN, MJTF and BATF troops? * WHAT are the names of these — people — in Canada, in the U.S. and throughout the world who planned and finalized the 1997 scenario?? You might think you know something. Beware of what you always think which might not be this time what will really happen. * KNOWLEDGE IS THE BEST PROTECTION. * NO ONE CAN PROTECT THEMSELVES IF THEY ARE UNAWARE HOW THEIR RIGHTS ARE THREAT-

The Omega Files

ENED. [End quoting]

RECENT NEWS FROM THE PARTISAN RANGERS OF OHIO Excerpted from Serge Monast's International Free Press Agency, "THE PARTISAN RANGERS OF OHIO", 8/14/96, [quoting;] United States Military Command Office... (Mag. Gen. Darren Day) CANADA: On August 14, 1996, the Canadian Serge Monast was interviewed on the Steve Quayle SW radio program (9400); our Col. Watchman supplied a summary as follows: "The Russian ID system is probing before invasion to test the strength of police units; create havoc, such as riots, to see what the reaction is; see the reaction of the people; create confrontations with the militia and Patriot groups to test their response. THE EAST COAST IS THE START OF THIS INVASION. New Brunswick, Nova Scotia, brand new unit specializing in "search and seizure", "roundups" — COLD WAR WEATHER AND ARCTIC-PREPARED. The 82nd Airborne, Mountain Division, Watertown, NY, same preparedness — with these two units they can close off the St. Lawrence sea-way. Invasion routes: from Nova Scotia through Maine, across the borders. * "The Champion Paper Co. is cutting [trees] on the mountains closest to the Canadian border, creating a clear area to the border before the mountains. They're also spreading herbicides. 'Satellite motion-sensor detection equipment to be installed in area.' *

"Phase One of Project Philadelphia is about two-thirds completed: rise in prices, shortages of food, power outages, civil unrest... expect a price doubling in your staple food items. *

"Phase Three — Quebec Hydro shutdown; this is the 6th largest electric power [plant] in the world, and controls ALL ELECTRICITY EAST OF THE MISSISSIPPI... Scheduled to go down any time from Jan./March. An "induced" outage during the cold of winter (winter of '97 - '98 or a following winter? - Branton) would create the most hardships and be a major "emergency" crisis condition... * There were two very high ranking Quebec hydro engineers aboard RON BROWN'S plane. Keep your eyes on Canada. [End quoting]

CONCLUSION AND PHILADELPHIA PHASE III

And from an article titled "TOP-SECRET NEW WORLD ORDER PLAN", from the same publication: "...Television commentator Bill Moyers found out during a fifteen-day, globe-spanning trip in the company of David Rockefeller that just about a dozen or fifteen individuals made day-to-day decisions that regulated the flow of capital and goods throughout the entire

The Omega Files

world." He quotes Bill Moyers himself as saying: "David Rockefeller is the most conspicuous representative today of the ruling class: a fraternity of men who shape the global economy and manage the flow of its capital. Rockefeller was born to it, and he has made the most of it. But what some critics see as a vast international conspiracy, he considers a circumstance of life and just another day's work.... In the world of David Rockefeller it's hard to tell where business ends and politics begin." Cannot we say the same thing about the Executive branch of the U.S. Government? It's hard to tell where politics ends and the 'corporate' military-industrial 'government' begins. Later in the same publication, in reference to "PHILADELPHIA PHASE III", we read: "The basic scenario finalized at the June 1996 meeting in Toronto, and completed with other reliable sources, is as follows: (1) Quebec makes its Unilateral Declaration of Independence between January and March 1997. This situation provides the "trigger" for the catastrophic and irreversible "breakup" of Canada and the "Declaration of a National State of Emergency" in the Eastern and Northeastern part of the United States. (Note: Those British citizens within British Columbia AND Quebec can prevent a civil war by doing the last thing that the New World Order advocates expect, that is they can do NOTHING. If you refuse to go to war against your Canadian brothers and sisters of Quebec then there will be NO civil war. The only ones left to fight will be the German military units occupying Canada — you know, the same guys who killed Frenchmen, Britons AND Americans in the last two world wars. Whether or not you believe Quebec should have its independence, you must ask yourself — what would be more preferable... an independent Quebec, or a devastating civil war that will end in the destruction of both British Columbia and Quebec and the assimilation of ALL of Canada into the New World Order? If war breaks out between the New World Order and North/South America, the Republics of British Columbia and Quebec will have to either side with the NWO or America.

There will be NO neutrality in such a war. Either Canada, Mexico, Central America, South America, etc., will be completely taken over by the New World Order — meaning that their cultural distinctiveness and national independence will be forever destroyed — or they will join as allies with the United States of America in a type of Union of American Republics, independent Republics, yet united in a common front to defend these last bastions of freedom and liberty on earth from the onslaught of a neo-Nazi "New World Order" dictatorship. IF we choose that side which we KNOW is favored by Almighty God, then we will have Divine protection and guidance. Remem-

The Omega Files

ber that those satanic cults which motivated the atrocities of Nazi Germany are the VERY SAME FORCES which are promoting the New World Order. And if you think Nazi Germany was bad news, you can bet that this time around they will have learned from their 'mistakes' and will be far more determined this time to succeed. So we must also learn from the mistakes of OUR past and be even more determined to succeed than our would-be enemies. Remember what George Washington revealed in respect to his vision of America's future. If we try to build and maintain a society — in spite of our past mistakes and lack of vigilance against the enemies of freedom from without and within —, a society which is based on justice, mercy, truth and indeed a "nation under God", then all of the powers of heaven and the angelic forces will be behind us. I myself am a non-denominational Christian Patriot who believes in Jesus as the only spiritually begotten Son of God. If we are honest with ourselves, then we must admit that the greater majority of those who formed the U.S. Constitution held the same belief. I don't believe that a certain 'denomination' should be given political favoritism, but I do believe that this country was founded on the Judeo-Christian ideal that all men are created equal and that God is no respector of persons. Those who believe that they are somehow superior to their fellow man are not truly Christian Patriots and would probably be more comfortable with the self-deifying pagan belief systems which gave rise to Nazi Germany and which in turn have given rise to the New World Order and its hierarchy of leaders who consider themselves to be the "Master Race".

So again, there is no neutrality in this war whether it be political, philosophical or spiritual neutrality. So, as Joshua once said... "choose ye this day whom ye will serve". - Branton) (2) A six-way [Canadian] civil war erupts, involving, in its first stage, the Cree Indians, Quebec population and the Canadian Forces; and in its second stage, the population of Quebec and Canada at three different levels: a war of French against English Canadians, a war between French Catholics and English Protestants and a war of identity." At this point please allow me to offer a number of relative comments regarding the draconian agenda on and beyond planet earth, following which we will return to the PHILADELPHIA III scenario: In regards to a potential conflict between Catholics and Protestants, the Charismatic Catholics might be helpful in preventing such a potential 'religious war', due to their emphasis on Christ as the Savior. The Jesuits in the Catholic Church tend to emphasize the deification of Mary, the Saints, and angels whereas the Masons in certain Protestant Churches tend to emphasize the deification

The Omega Files

of self through fraternal advancement. Taken to the extreme, both of these organizational structures can be turned towards polytheistic idolatry rather than Christ-ianity. It may be that the Jesuit-Masons will try to turn the Catholics against the Protestants and vise versa, encouraging the other to accuse the other of 'blasphemy'. Such accusations, if provoked, will of course be nothing more than blind hypocrisy on both sides. However, focusing on Jesus Christ of Nazareth as the only begotten Son of God would serve to bring all 'Christians' together. This would be true 'Christ-ianity', as opposed to its counterfeit... 'Church-ianity' or idolatry. Churchianity is apostate Christianity, or a 'church' which has lost its spiritual aspect and focus on 'things above', and has reverted instead into an idolatrous economic and politically based organization, one which exploits spiritual passions and beliefs for the sake of promoting the political and economic agendas of the leaders. BEWARE of those churches who would lead you to believe that a human religious leader or religious leaders are mandatory 'mediators' between us and Christ. If you don't believe that CHRIST ALONE is the savior then you have no right calling yourself a 'Christian', since you are trusting in fallible humans for your salvation.

Now of course one has the FREE AGENCY to choose just what to believe, whether they accept Christianity or not, and I'm certainly NOT trying to take your right of self-determination away from you. We DO have the right to choose our destiny, but along with that right comes the responsibility of accepting the consequences of our choices. The Pharisees — those who crucified Jesus of Nazareth — were a perfect example of a religious institution which lost its inward spiritual essence and became nothing but an empty eco-political shell. Jesus had threatened the Pharisees' economic and political hold over the Jews, and so in collaboration with the Romans they were determined to kill Him. However in doing so they unknowingly fulfilled the prophecy in Isaiah chapter 53. The Jesuits, who were behind the inquisitions of Europe — during which hundreds of thousands of Christians were slaughtered — and who according to writer Edmond Paris served as 'advisors' to the Nazi S.S. in their 'inquisition' against the Jews, are another example. If I am not mistaken, then it would seem that if an organization ceased from spreading a message of spiritual regeneration for the benefit of others and rather turned to killing hundreds of thousands of European Protestants and Meso-American Natives for the sole purpose of preserving their eco-political empire, then it would seem that this would not be an institution which is based on the teachings of Jesus, and therefore not 'Christian'. The Jesuits

The Omega Files

never were Christians nor even Catholics. Ignatius Loyola had a previous arrest record in Spain for subversive activities as a gnostic, and had manipulated himself into the Vatican through flattery by promising an un-discerning Pontiff his devotion as the head of a 'militia' that would serve to protect the interests of the Popes and of the Vatican. The Jesuit infiltration of Catholicism AND the Masonic infiltration of Protestantism incidentally was planned well in advance by the Bavarian cults. The Bavarian 'serpent' cults control both Jesuitism and Masonry in spite of the apparent outward animosity between the two. In turn they control the Bilderberg society, which at the core has a council or 39 initiates, or 13 Black Nobility, 13 Wicca Masons and 13 Maltese Jesuits.

Another example of Jesuit-Masonic collaboration is the Scottish Rite of Masonry itself. As an interesting note, some contactees refer to an ancient conflict involving Orionite 'Greys' and Sirian 'Nordics'. The Orionites and Sirians allegedly fought for control of the ancient Egyptian ruling fraternities, and this later developed into a war between the [Un]Holy Roman Empire/Jesuits/Nazis who were backed by the Orionites, and their opposition within the British Empire and its Masonic lodges who were backed by the Sirians. With the Orionite infiltration of the extraplanetary 'Ashtar' collective or the 'Melchizedek' lodges, and with the infiltration of the Masonic lodges on earth by the Orion-backed Bavarian Jesuit/Illuminati/Thule societies, the unsuspecting Ashtarians and Masons were manipulated into serving the agendas of the Orionite and Jesuit infiltrators, respectively. This is why humans from Sirius-B who had formerly been at war with the Orionites could be turned to serving the agendas of Orionite agents — operating in and around the Hale-Bopp 'comet' — who had infiltrated the Sirian's 'Ashtar' collective. To these Sirians, they weren't dealing with 'Draconian-Orionites', but with 'Ascended Masters'. Hale-Bopp is apparently an Orionite 'Trojan Horse', intent on supporting a New World Order to be ruled in part from the CLUB OF ROME's joint Illuminati-Grey Alien base under Pine Gap, Australia. All of this has been prepared in advance through the joint Nazi-Grey abduction and implantation of millions of people throughout the world — see the quote at the beginning of this file. Am I insane? Is all of this merely the ramblings of a lunatic? I suppose time will tell, however this is what my 'other worldly sources' have 'told' me, and is followed-up by what others have been saying. Think about it, if a hostile alien force had its sites on earth, would they arrive as part of a mindlessly destructive 'INDEPENDENCE DAY' invasion, or could we credit them with a bit more intelligence — although

The Omega Files

no less malevolence — by carrying out a type of 'Operation Trojan Horse', to coin a phrase from well-known Ufologist John Keel? Perhaps they would plan well in advance to bring the planet to a state where resistance would be minimal... massive abductions, mind control, infiltration, underground staging bases, genetic projects to create alien warriors who could operate well in the environment, overtures to foolish and greedy planetary rulers so as to gain their cooperation, multi-leveled deception and psychological warfare, a global government that would facilitate an easier takeover — taking control of the leaders of an already-existing power-structure rather than destroying the old structure and creating a new one. And perhaps a main invasion force arriving in the tail of a 'comet' so as not to attract too much fear and negative reaction — and when the so-called 'comet' passes the planet they could attempt to send out powerful transmissions to activate implants and subliminal programming within abductees...

I believe that it's time that the 'battle lines' are drawn. If we do not know who our friends and our enemies are 'out there' — that is, those creative and 'free' POWER STRUCTURES as opposed to those destructive and 'slave' POWER STRUCTURES existing upon, below and beyond this planet — then we are more likely to BECOME the enemy by default. The collectivist Ashtarian and Masonic lodges, with their 'all-inclusive' philosophies, tend to cloud the LINE between self-centered elitist agendas as opposed to agendas based on service towards the overall good of others. The only real thing that the collectivists are 'unified' in is their self-centeredness, and in the collectives only those 'selves' which are strongest will survive, and these 'selves' in turn will tend to siphon the individuality from the weaker 'selves' around them. It's like the black hole which many astrophysicists believe exists at the center of the galaxy. It is the largest black hole in the galaxy, and even though other smaller 'black holes' exist around it, these tend to be pulled in to and assimilated by the super-black-hole. I wonder if this has anything to do with the Nazi occult worship of the 'Black Sun', which is in essence the worship of the black hole at the center of the galaxy? The collectivists would also attempt to spread the gnostic lie that there is no 'good' nor 'evil', but just 'experience'. From my perspective, evil is a "service to self" mode and good is a "service to others" mode, so since these two modes OBVIOUSLY exist, the occult "channelers" for instance who spout this sort of rot are proven to be LIARS. This lie that there is no 'battle-line', so-to-speak, between good and evil because neither really exists, only serves the agenda of evil. So then, we must draw the 'galactic battle lines' between those alliances which

The Omega Files

strive to adhere to a service-to-others / non-interventionist philosophy and those alliances which choose to adhere to a service-to-self / interventionist philosophy. Also we will include the collectivists who claim that they don't 'take sides' but are neutral. I am sorry, but in this cosmic conflict which our galaxy finds itself in there is NO neutrality. It's like Switzerland, they were 'neutral' in World War II. But of course their 'neutrality' did not prevent them from protecting stolen Nazi gold in their bank vaults.

If one is not for the side of service-to-others, then they are by default on the side of service-to-self, which leads to collectivism, since in a self-centered collective the most selfish tend to assimilate the weaker of their own kind. Collectivism is therefore a form of interventionism, since it violates and invades the individuality and personal sovereignty of others, whether on a planetary, national, local, or individual basis. Individual-Collectivism can be useful, like the INTERNET for instance because the individual has control over their interaction with the collective and can 'log-on' and 'log-off' at any time they chose. When a collective however INVADES a persons individuality, as the Ashtar and Grey collectives do by implanting permanent micro-electronic devices WITHIN the person, invading their personal boundaries, then that collective is a dictatorship of the worst form as it violates the God-given sovereignty of those who are 'assimilated' or born into such a collective. Once the collective has violated ones personal boundaries by ones personal CHOICE, then they are in essence 'selling their soul' to the collective — in this case their 'soul' being their identity, emotions, sovereignty, free agency, etc. This puts the person's soul at extreme risk. For instance, an impending example of this on this planet would be a computer chip implanted into one's right hand or in their forehead in order to be a part of a planetary economic collective, as prophesied in Revelation Chapter 13. If one succumbs to such a temptation they would in essence be giving up their soul and identity in exchange for physical gains. Once the soul is COMPLETELY 'assimilated' into such a collective there is no turning back because personal will and free choice have been forfeited. The exception would be someone who is 'assimilated' against their will via deception, or through force and ignorance as with a child. Even though I myself have been implanted with psionic mind control devices, and at least one hemisphere of my mind assimilated into the Ashtar 'collective', this was done without my full conscious agreement but through deception and trickery. Because of this, I have retained a 'conscious identity' and a will which has been able by the grace of God to 'fight back', even though the 'psychic

The Omega Files

battles' have been VERY difficult at times, a virtual psychological HELL.

Based on what has been learned from a number of contactees, it would seem as if the Reptiloid-Grey interventionist-collectivists have succeeded in conquering several human colonial worlds in the past through 'Trojan horse' type strategies. Most of these have been quasi-collectivist societies whose global leaders have discouraged national, cultural and individual distinction, and who have sold themselves over to the alien agenda for self-centered motives, succumbing to the deception and propaganda of the aliens. Once the Reptiloid-Grey collectivists however set their sites on planet earth, they were faced with a whole new challenge. Because of planet earth's national, cultural and individual diversity and because the situation on earth was unpredictable as a result of this, the alien[s] were forced to gain more of a following of collaborating human elite than they normally would in order to establish their global dictatorship. This global 'New World Order' government would more easily facilitate the planet's assimilation into the alien collective. In anticipation of this, the aliens began to support and infiltrate the international fraternal networks [the Lodge, or Masonry] several centuries ago. Being that the United States of America was the strongest supporter of individual sovereignty and freedom — individual distinctiveness, freedom and creativity being the mortal enemy of the collective — they established several 'Trojan horse' underground bases in America behind the guise of "technology transfer", below various strategic areas. Even though representatives from several 'Federation' worlds — who were well aware of the nature and strategies of the Reptiloid-Grey collectivists because of ages-old conflicts with the same — warned the NSA-controlled executive branch of government against having anything to do with the "Greys" who were entering the system in staging bases that had been constructed within 'engineered' planetoids, the NSA ignored their overtures. The NSA, which may have already maintained a secret alliance with the reptilian collectivists due to its 'Nazi' roots, continued with the "interaction" projects, heedless to the warnings of the Federationists. The technology exchanges occurred, however needless to say the super-technology could only be used and operated by the aliens themselves, or by agents or scientists working for the fascist corporate-industrialists [rather than the Congressional-Electorate government] who were completely programmed and mind-controlled by the alien "hive".

Those within the collaboration who showed signs of resistance against

The Omega Files

the agenda had a tendency to disappear or die prematurely. The Reptiloid and Grey interventionists managed to infiltrate and take control of the deeper subterranean human collectivist [Ashtarian] colonies, although as they continued the planetary takeover from the bottom up [the same strategy they use to take over the minds of human abductees — from the 'deeper' collective unconscious level to the 'outer' individual conscious levels], they met with some resistance from more individualistic American military forces who had access to the underground network, as well as from non-collectivist Federation forces. Through selective implantation and assassination, further dubious treaties, technology exchanges and "false flag" strategies — i.e. feigning benevolence — the resistance was for the most part subdued. Several 'Trojan horse' bases that were used to gain control over specialized fields of military-industrial research and development under the guise of the technology-exchanges were established beneath the following areas: Montauk - Camp Hero, Long Island [quantum-hyperspace mechanics & microwave mind-control]; the Denver International Airport [transportation & human containment]; Little Cottonwood Canyon - Dougway, Utah [cloning & cybernetics]; Mercury - Area-51, Nevada [nuclear & antigravity]; Lancaster - Tehachapi, California [aerospace & computing]; and Ft. Lewis - Madigan, Washington State [bio-medical & bio-replication]. And of course the major base which supervises the activities taking place in all of the above, the ancient underground facilities below the Dulce - 4-Corners area of New Mexico. It was inevitable that draconian collectivism and human individualism would eventually clash within the joint-operational underground networks, and it seems to have began in 1975 during a 'demonstration' by the Greys of an antimatter reactor within the underground levels of the Area. There were a large number of human scientists and security personnel present in the underground chamber where the demonstration was taking place. The Greys DEMANDED that the military officers either disarm themselves or leave the room. One military officer, offended by this display of alien arrogance on a planet where the aliens were supposed to be 'visitors', questioned the order. This led to a conflict of interest which erupted into a military altercation, which ended with the death of one Grey alien and several dozen human scientists and security officers. Although there were apparently no further confrontations at that base [at that time], the incident was NOT forgotten, and may have sowed the seeds of a resistance movement which escalated within the "Dulce" [pronounced "dul-see"] base 4 years later in 1979, which became known as the DULCE WARS.

The Omega Files

The resistance was led by the late[?] Thomas Edwin Castello, who was in contact with personal friends until the mid-1990's at which point he disappeared. Castello was head of Security at the multi-levelled base, and joined with 9 other workers initially in an effort to sabotage the biomedical atrocities that were being perpetrated on abductees who were being brought to the base... some temporarily, but others permanently. Others joined the resistance, and even a few tall "reptiloids" which did not agree with the policies of their collective and who had developed a degree of individual emotionalism as a result of their close association with the humans, also joined. There were apparently traitors in the midst of this resistance, although just who it was is uncertain. The resistance grew as the result of the discovery that the "White Draco" leaders of the base had broken the "treaty" and were holding several thousand abductees against their will in more remote alien-controlled levels of the underground network, in cages or in cryogenic containment, so that their body parts could be used for various biogenetic experiments, or worse. Several of the scientists who had discovered the "Grand Deception" were found out and taken captive and held in peripheral sub-bases such as those beneath the Ute Reservation of SW Colorado and SE Utah, and at least two major altercations broke out. In one conflict, several special forces were sent in to rescue the captive scientists and abductees. This mission was a miserable failure, except for the fact that over 200 aliens were killed and some 66 special forces out of 100 that were sent in also died in the firefight. Another attack was apparently ordered by the leaders of the fascist collaboration, who ordered the assassination of all members of the resistance, Americans, Nordics, Reptiloids... Most of the members of the resistance were slaughtered in cold blood, although a few escaped, Thomas Castello being one of them. Whether or not these attacks were ordered by two different intelligence agencies, or one schizophrenic [MJ-12] agency, the fact remains that these overall events led to a major split within the American intelligence community, and this may have contributed to a similar resistance that DID result in the sabotage and cessation [for a few years at least] of the Thule Society/CIA-NSA/Orion Grey projects at the Montauk base six years later in 1985. The Reptiloid and Grey collectivist-interventionists of Draconis and Orion became desperate as the situation grew increasingly out of control. Time was running out, and the alien collectivists faced the danger that their centuries-old agenda to infiltrate and conquer the surface nations of planet earth was falling apart at the seems. All efforts were directed towards the infiltration of American and global society in general,

The Omega Files

and the destruction of the U.S. Constitution and implementation of the New World Order via their collaborator agents on earth.

On a more personal note. For several years I have personally experienced unusual re-occurring "dreams" of interacting with aliens in underground basing systems. Some of these apparently had to do with certain Ashtarian/Telosian-Shastan/Aghartian semi-collectivist colonies which have since been stressed by, if not infiltrated and taken over by, the draconian collectivists. At one point in 1995, a clear and distinct "voice" in my mind told me that I was "a CIA agent". Fearing my sanity, I ignored the "voice", however I was painfully reminded a few days later when I was told by a close friend — an abductee whose father worked on the Los Alamos Manhattan project — that in more than one abduction experience "I" myself had come and taken her to some underground facilities below the foothills of the Western Rockies in the Salt Lake Valley of Utah, where we encountered alien beings. The beings presented themselves as being benevolent, but this might have been a facade, that is, unless I subsequently recieve proof of the fact. During one of these experiences she asked "me" why I had security access to all of these underground facilities. According to her — I kid you not, I did not mention a thing about the "voices" in my head a few days earlier — "I" reluctantly told her during this abduction episode of hers that it was because I worked for the CIA! I do not "consciously" recall this particular incident, whether as a "dream", or whatever. I do however recall having several "underground dreams" wherein I saw the tall and in some cases small alien humanoids she mentioned. According to several contactees, during abductions alien beings often impose — through a form of technosis — a state of consciousness similar to that which one experiences while in the dream state, so that upon awakening the abductee is led to believe that the experience was all a dream, even though evidence often exists suggesting that something did happen during the night. In my friends case it was strange bruises and markings on her body that were not there when she went to sleep. After hearing this confession by my "other self" of being a CIA agent, she became violently angry and the next morning recalled the emotions relative to the event and in turn the event itself. Both of us have also met other abductees who were experiencing "double lives", a conscious life and a suppressed life in an altered state of consciousness, interacting with aliens of all types. Several of these people — who happen to live in the Salt Lake Valley — spoke of being involved, in their nocturnal "alternate" lives as an abductee, with some kind of violent space war taking place between two groups of aliens who maintain underground bases and strongholds within the Rocky Mountains, with each side determined to root out the opposition... Some have suggested that some of the Greys want to break free from the Draconian-controlled Orion Empire, and may be training human abductees to fight their erstwhile draconian overlords in that capacity if such a revolution occurs.

If this were to occur, due to the collective itself, it might be the individualist Hubrids who lead such a resistance, along with Greys who may have developed some degree of independent emotional expression due to their close contact with the more emotionally-individualistic Hubrids. It would seem however that by commandeering the unconscious lives of abductees and training them to fight a war — against the Draconians, or in the case of "collectivist" Greys against the Federation, the U.S. Government, or what have you — the Greys are doing to abductees on earth exactly what the Draconians have done to them. They have made them the unconscious puppets of their collective agenda. As they say, abuse tends to breed abusers. I would NOT suggest that our military come to the aide of any Greys and Hubrids [Hu-brids being hy-brids born with a human soul-matrix] who are trying to defect from the Draconian collective UNLESS the Greys/Hubrids fully submit themselves to a Congressional or a joint Congressional/Federation council if such can be established. The reason for this would be to ensure that all human forces and operations are FULLY monitored by Congress. There WILL no doubt be Greys — the Grey-Reptiloid hybrids for instance — which WILL attempt to sabotage such a resistance or feign themselves as being part of the resistance, when in fact they would be working for the Draconian elite. Such collectivist-Greys might try to gain the assistance of a human agency, excusing their former abuses with something like "we didn't have a choice, we were just following the orders of the Dracos... but now we want to rebel and break away from the Draconians with your help." Even if there were an element of sincerity in the desire for individualist Greys/Hubrids to break free, the collectivists themselves might use the situation to gain a stronger foothold in our society... as they have done with the 'treaties'. Even if some of the past treaties were implemented by Greys with semi-ethical motives, which I strongly doubt, then the collectivists themselves would step in and betray these treaties and use them as Trojan horses to establish more control within human society, which they HAVE done. For this reason, ANY such resistance must be absolutely CONTROLLED AND DIRECTED by Congress or a Congressional/Federation council. Any Grey

The Omega Files

or even Reptiloid that has just recently acquired individuality and partly severed itself from the collective "hive" could certainly NOT be trusted to make key life-and-death decisions involving humans, since they would no doubt retain some level of residual "collective programming".

Supposing one government agency makes a deal with the Greys to "fight" their enemies the Draco... It could be that yet another government agency might be manipulated into an opposing agenda in what would amount to a galactic Machievellian scenario. It fact it may have already happened. Contactee Alex Collier claims to have learned from Andromedan-Pleiadean non-interventionists — who have 'blockaded' our system to prevent outside malevolent forces from taking advantage of our present planetary chaos and changes — that at least one agency has sent out a call for help to alien civilizations to come to our defense and assist us in rooting out the Greys that have become entrenched in our planet. One group responded. Wouldn't you know it, it was the Reptiloids from Alpha Draconis, whose forces are apparently en-route to earth according to Collier. Also, a large armada from Sirius-B is reportedly on its way to the Sol system and due to arrive around 2004, and these may or may not be allies with the Draconians. Hopefully they are not. There are some reports which seem to imply that the large Sirius-B armada may be arriving to defend their own bases in the Sol system and beneath planet earth, that are being stressed or attacked by the Grey-Reptiloid interventionists with whom the Sirians have had conflicts in times past. As for the Alpha Draconians, if and when they are allowed into our system/planet, they will NOT do anything about the Greys, simply because the Draconians SENT THEM HERE in the first place. My only suggestion is to declare our planet, or at least the "upper" and "lower" Continental United States, a "VERMIN FREE ZONE" — that is, NO GREYS, NO REPTILOIDS, NO INSECTOIDS — PERIOD! In order to enforce this we must DEMAND access to the interplanetary and subterranean technology now possessed by the largely alien-infiltrated Military-Industrial Complex.

Those members of the Masonic M.I.C. fraternity must realize that this is their only solution, otherwise they will remain stuck between the proverbial rock and a hard place... with the threat of total assimilation — along with the individuality-killing New World Order — into the alien collective on the one hand, and the threat of an invasion of their Military-Industrial underground by angry patriotic Americans on the other hand. Returning to the incident involving my "alternate identity", the day following this "ab-

The Omega Files

duction" incident — wherein my alter-ego "spook", or programmed "sleeper agent" you might say, came and took my friend to an underground base — she noticed a black automobile with what looked like government agents sitting in it, parked across the street from her house, and she had the definite feeling that they were observing her. What I found interesting is that my friend informed me that in her experience "I" was left-handed [or right-brain dominant — the right brain being responsible for "non-verbal" mental functions] whereas in my conscious life I am right-handed [left-brain dominant — the left-brain being responsible for "verbal" mental functions]. Having heard previously that those possessing an alternate personality often harbor THE alternate identity in the hemisphere opposite from the one in which they are consciously dominant, I put two-and-two together. I have a strong impression that this alternate identity is NOT entirely an individual personality, but more of an implanted "receptor" for an alien collective mind, you might say. I've heard of abductees who have been taken aboard ships within the "Ashtar" collective. They tell of being psionically linked to a powerful intelligence outside of themselves, and as a result of this they are able to perform activities that they normally would or could not do... fly a starship for instance, or rather it would be a case of the "central mind" flying the ship THROUGH them. Contactee Israel Norkin states that the core of the Ashtar collective operations is a 20-mile-long space-based computer mainframe, a MASSIVE artificial intelligence... I have often wondered just when and where this alternate identity was induced into my subconscious mind [apparently by the CIA-Alien collaboration], yet that has continued to elude me, however all of this has served to convince me of just how far the infiltration of our society has progressed, and how it has affected me on a personal basis.

I know of several abductees whose "alternate lives" with Aliens has virtually drained their normal waking lives in a devastating manner, leaving many of them mental and emotional wrecks, which in turn severely affects their abilities to maintain a productive career or social life. If this has been true in my own life, and the lives of other abductees who I know, then how many more people have had their lives sabotaged in this manner by alien infiltration of the subconscious levels of their existence? As an example, my friend who I have mentioned above had a photographic memory when she was a teenager. However after the abductions began, she has had nothing but memory problems galore! I sometimes wonder if these aliens-fascists are deliberately sabotaging our abilities as human beings in order to

The Omega Files

keep us operating at minimal potential, and facilitate continued control over us on an individual, national and global basis. With the understanding that I am NOT the only one who has been a victim of this type of INTERVENTION, you can perhaps understand my zeal in getting this information out to as wide an audience as possible, and above all to those suffering abductees whom a skeptical society has ignored and ridiculed. Just remember, in spite of those who do not understand — not having undergone the overall abuses that we have, for which they should be eternally thankful — there are millions of people in America and around the world who DO understand. I do hope and pray that the information within this file will help YOU to break free from the influence of the "Intruders" and re-claim your personal sovereignty. Remember, you have the POWER to claim your INDEPENDENCE from these collectivist parasites. Their weapon is to DECEIVE you into believing that you must submit and that you have no choice in the matter. THIS IS A LIE!!!

I would strongly recommend however that in standing your ground, that you put your faith in a power that is infinitely greater than the entire alien collective... that is Almighty God. My own attempts to break free from the control of the alien collectivists has been a long and painful process, however I am convinced that the Almighty, and to some extent ethical other-worldly forces, have helped me along the way — possibly more than I can ever know. Once the 'enemy within' was exposed however, and I began to resist the process of alien infiltration of my unconscious mind, I was in a sense able to 'defect' from the collective with some rather damaging information — damaging to the continuity of the 'collective' that is. The collectivists are taking a chance by connecting individualist humans to their collective via psionic implants, as there is always the possibility that the implants might work both ways. That is, if the abductee becomes aware of how he or she is being manipulated and controlled on an unconscious level, then that person's individual nature may out of self-preservation feel that his or her personal sovereignty is being threatened and they might try to take back control. In so doing, they might succeed in 'probing' or 'interrogating' the collective, violating its innermost secrets and thereby threatening its security. This is why the aliens are depending so much on mind control and memory repression via technosis and electro-chemical dissolution of memory, and whatever other methods they use to impose mind control. I will say for a fact that if I can fight back, then other abductees who have been implanted or even those who have been born into the Ashtar collec-

The Omega Files

tive below or beyond this planet can also fight back and re-claim their individual identities and independence, especially with the help of Divine Intervention. Since my personal discovery of the Ashtarian-Draconian conspiracy to 'assimilate' the people of this planet, I have found some remarkable similarities between my perceived reality and certain aspects of the science fiction media. It would seem that the collective unconscious of humanity here on earth perceives certain things on a more subtle level that emerge in the form of inspiration at the conscious level, for instance the possibility of being 'assimilated' into an alien control network. And yes, STAR TREK was right on — at least in regards to this part of alien reality — although a scientifically sophisticated race would use micro-miniaturized mind-control devices integrated into the brain's central nervous system rather than the slow and bulky cybernetic devices depicted in the series and movies. I had to laugh at the movie MARS ATTACKS, because there was so much truth in it in regards to how certain leaders and 'Grey hugging' abductees have dealt with the aliens.

The apparent need for people to worship the super-technology of the Greys in spite of their abuses against our society, is incredible. In some cases — as with certain mind-controlled 'Stockholm Syndrome' secret government agents themselves — it comes down to just plain FEAR of the power of these creatures. In other words they love them because they are afraid NOT to. We can liken this to the early serpent cults, such as the ancient Neolithic cults which existed on the island of Malta, who built intricate underground temples — for instance the Hypogeum of Hal Saflienti which some actually believe connects at the lowest levels to a massive 'alien' underground system — in which they sacrificed tens of thousands of humans in ancient times in order to APPEASE the serpentine 'gods' of the underworld. Incidentally, in the late 1930's over 30 school children disappeared without a trace within the Hypogeum of Hal Saflienti catacombs of Malta along with their teachers and guides, an incident which was reported in NATIONAL GEOGRAPHIC magazine for August, 1940. On a more human level there was the British Prime Minister Neville Chamberlain, who in essence turned Czechoslovakia over to Adolf Hitler in a pitiful attempt to APPEASE this dictators appetite for conquest. It had the opposite effect however, and only served to increase Adolf Hitler's appetite and boldness for conquest and his disdain for weak-willed leaders like Chamberlain. It would be wise to learn from the mistakes of the past. Then there are the legends, whether they have any basis in fact or not, of the Dragons and Dragonslayers of old. For instance there

The Omega Files

was the leader of the city of Selene, Libya whose community — according to legend — was plagued by a fire-breathing dragon. He attempted to 'appease' the beast with livestock, until the livestock were all depleted and the villagers began casting lots so that the chosen ones could be sacrificed and the city could be spared temporarily from further devastating attacks from the dragon. One day the Kings own daughter was chosen, and although grief-stricken the King nevertheless allowed her to be tied to the post outside the city. As the dragon approached, a knight on a white horse and clad in silver armor approached from another direction. It was the notorious Christian Dragonslayer Saint George. With his steel lance and a shield with a red cross emblazoned on a white background reflecting the bright sunlight, the Knight swiftly approached the dragon and impaled it through. Legend says that Saint George married the princess of Selene and they lived happily ever after, as could be expected for a traditional storybook ending. Even if the legend is more symbolic than fact, it nevertheless holds many truths that may be learned today in our dealings with certain 'alien' and/or 'totalitarian' agendas.

In short, APPEASEMENT IS NEVER THE ANSWER. It is merely a form of CAPITULATION or surrender. The Ashtarian 'collectivists' below and beyond this planet for instance believed that by 'appeasing' their enemies and allowing them access to their societies, that these malevolent entities might be 'converted' to the side of reason. This may have been successful in a few instances, however there are those forces who are so degenerate — like spiritual black holes that have lost every vestige of 'light' within themselves — that they will NEVER turn from the side of evil. And so, throwing ones pearls before such 'swine' will merely increase their appetite for more 'pearls', and thier disdain for those who cast them. In respect to the Reptiloids and Greys, I would personally offer my interpretation of the prophecy in Genesis 3:14, which from my perspective would indicate that the Reptiloids have become a reprobate race with no hope of attaining any degree of spiritual integrity, having completely annihilated as a race any degree of spiritual virtues which they might have originally possessed. History has PROVEN over and over and over again that the Reptiloids/Greys are, in spite of their vast collective intellect, creatures that are irrepairably turned over to base predatory animal instinct, and have lost ALL sense of individual conscience... having in essence become the absolute slaves of those "astral parasites" — if you will — who control them. A physical form capable of developing advanced technology yet NOT capable of maintaining any degree of self-motivated spiritual maturity or conscience to 'tame' such lower predatory instincts should NOT be tolerated in this universe. They should not be tolerated any more than an AIDS virus, which knows nothing other than conquest and destruction, should be tolerated within a human body. These reptiloids SHOULD PAY for what they have done to our people as well as to millions if not billions of men, women and children on other colonial worlds throughout the galaxy.

I cannot stress this conviction too much! Of course I am referring here only to bi-pedal reptilian entities capable of developing technology, AND NOT TO the MANY genetic hybrids who have been born with a human soul-matrix, nor to non-bipedal reptiles. Also, any bi-pedal Reptilian that is severed from the collective and has been 'tamed' so-to-speak should not be included in this extermination, however it SHOULD be forbidden from procreating after its kind. Genesis 3:14 states that this is the decision of the Almighty — and after all IT IS 'HIS' UNIVERSE — which was decreed for the sake of the rest of humankind and the creation. Otherwise, if the problem were allowed to continue, the insatiable predatory drives of these unnatural creatures of unbounded appetite and evil WILL eventually cause their corrupting influence to spread throughout the whole galaxy and universe, and this would eventually mean the end of all human life as we know it... since the Reptiloids and Reptilian Greys have NEVER shown any interest — as an interventionist-collective — in respecting human life anywhere in the universe. Nor have they shown ANY interest in making peace with humankind, except in the case of false overtures of feigned 'peace' WHICH ALWAYS, BUT ALWAYS has resulted in the inevitable betrayal and destruction of the human society with whom they have established a 'peace treaty'. The Genesis prophecy was not necessarily fulfilled at the time it was spoken. As it is with numerous prophecies, this one would not be completed until a later time... Isaiah 65:25 states that the completion of this prophecy will occur sometime during the Millennium. All of the above was confirmed by Dr. Paul Bennewitz, who was one of the most notorious and original investigators of the Grey Alien presence operating within the base underneath the Archuleta mesa near Dulce — and also the canyons near Los Alamos — New Mexico. Bennewitz was later 'committed' to an Albuquerque Mental hospital with the help of William Moore and other CIA-backed 'Ufologists' who emphatically denied that the abductions, cattle mutilations, and underground bases existed. It is interesting that part of the alleged deal between the CIA and the Alien Greys was that in exchange for technology the CIA had to cover-up

The Omega Files

the reality of the abductions, cattle mutilations, and the underground bases.

While in the mental hospital, Bennewitz was electroshocked into submission, and when released he publicly stated that he had "no more interest in UFOs". Before this however, Bennewitz had stated that, from his own experiences with the 'ALIEN' [he used the word in a collective sense because most of the aliens there are like individual 'cells' in a vast controlling collective organism] he came to the firm conviction that THE ALIEN was irreparably deceitful and that the ONLY way that the alien/aliens could be dealt with or reasoned with is to deal with them as one would with a MAD DOG! The alien collective — being completely sold over to their base animal instincts and to the will of the Luciferian controllers of the collective — only respect one form of authority. That is, BRUTE FORCE! In light of the Luciferian connection, I would say BRUTE SPIRITUAL FORCE as well. If as some claim the true behind-the-scenes controllers of the 'draconian' collective or HIVE are the rebel angels themselves, then aside from technological and psychological attack they would use sorcery or black witchcraft to attack our spritial nature. If these rebel angels are irreparably committed to evil, then their 'puppets' who we know as the 'Greys' or 'Reptiloids' may be about as repentant as these infernal beings are themselves, unless of course the Greys/Reptiloids are some how able to break free from the grasp of the 'Luciferian collective'. As I stated earlier, it is important for us to know where the 'battle-lines' exist in this immediate sector of the galaxy surrounding our own Solar system, which naturally is the sector where the most ancient of all the galactic cultures exist... planet earth of course being by far the oldest of all worlds in this sector. I should state that some of the other-planetary cultures claim to travel interdimensionally, and have spoken to their 'contactees' of 11 'densities' and a 12th that is now spontaneously manifesting within the Omniverse. The Omniverse itself would consist of our Matter Universe as well as its Anti-Matter TWIN or DAL counterpart Universe, and also the 12 densities which make up the Omniverse, including our own '3rd density' reality.

In some of these densities 'time' reportedly flows at different rates. In some of these dimensions three 'days' on an other-dimensional world would be equivalent to three 'hours' on 3rd dimensional earth. In other words a culture on planet earth may have been established at the same time as one established within another 'realm' by 'ancient astronaut' fraternities for instance, yet one civilization would be 'older' that the other. These 'ancient

The Omega Files

astronaut' colonies were allegedly composed of the most advanced minds of the ancient world [earth], or people who were initiated into those secret scientific lodges whose agents continually searched out those whose intelligence rose high above the average. The motives of some of these scientific fraternities may have been honorable, that is keeping dangerous knowledge out of the hands of the warring masses to prevent their self destruction. The motives of others were not so honorable, and boiled down to nothing less than intellectual or fraternal snobbery and elitism. These ancient 'brain drains' would have kept the general population of earth in a state of constant technological atrophy whereas the 'scientific fraternities' would go on to develop their sciences by pooling their knowledge and resources, commencing to colonize other realms below, beyond, or even parallel to planet earth — by phase-shifting into other densities through Philadelphia-Montauk type technology, lets say for instance into a dimensional density with a three-day to three-hour ratio as described above. Therefore using this ratio, a culture established on planet EARTH in 1000 B.C. might be 3000 years old in 2000 A.D., whereas a culture established in a peripheral dimensional density at the same point in 'time' might conceivably be 78,000 years old in 2000 A.D., 'relatively' speaking.

The 'solidity' of such a dimensional reality would not be as concrete as our own according to some theories, because space and time must work together. If you increase TIME, then SPACE must give up some of its 'ground' in the process, and vise versa. So objects and events in such a dimensional reality might be more 'fluid' or 'dreamy' than in the concrete 3rd dimensional reality because 'space' and 'matter' must capitulate some of its territory over to 'time' in a give-and-take manner. However ALL dimensions interact with each other at the more subtle levels of reality. Events in one dimension effect the outcome of events in others... in a type trans-dimensional cause-and-effect. There are some contactees who suggest that the concept of TIME as we know it is flawed. In other words the 'future' would not necessarily be in FRONT of us and the past BEHIND us, but the ETERNAL NOW would exist in the SAME SPACE yet in different phases or frequencies. One symbolic representation might be to say that TIME is rather a woven conglomeration of EVENTS. These events can be seen symbolically as WATER in its various PHASES. That is, the so-called 'future' might be seen in general as events that are in a GASEOUS state. These events have SUBSTANCE but they are not "concrete" or "set". The so-called 'present' could be seen as LIQUID. Present events are more solid than gaseous events, yet are still fluid

The Omega Files

enough to be manipulated, channeled and formed by Divine or human will. The so-called 'past' would generally be those events that have become SET or SOLID, like ice. They are set and cannot be undone. Now there may be SOME events 'before' us that are SOLID, and SOME events 'behind' us that are GASEOUS you could say, and the PRESENT or the ETERNAL NOW could, like water, intersect any point within the event-chain where "gaseous events" have yet to phase into "solid events". So it would not so much be past-behind and future-ahead as it would be a case of cause-and-effect EVENTS that are in a transitional state from a GASEOUS PHASE to a LIQUID PHASE to a SOLID PHASE.

IF time travel were possible, and one were to go into the past and try to change a CONCRETE event, some believe that this will result in what is called a paradox, or two SOLID events occupying the same SPACE. Now since two SOLIDS cannot occupy the same THIRD DIMENSIONAL Space, the new event which would be challenging an already existent SET EVENT in the same time-space could not possibly retain its solidity or remain in that same space. So in essence a PARADOX cannot exist within the concrete third density. If this time traveler were to insist on changing a SET event and REMAINED in the 'past' or in that part of the 'event-chain' to see what would happen if they 'broke the chain' — according to some of those involved with the Philadelphia and Montauk projects for instance — he or she would simply create a localized quantum field and this field and its occupants would simply be shoved off to the side and out of the third density and into a peripheral dimension where paradoxes can exist due to the 'fluid/dreamy/surreal' nature of objects and events in that reality. He or she would in essence phase-out into a "gaseous thought form state" along with all others who may have happened to be phased-out of the third dimension in this manner. This is apparently nature's simple way of dealing with 'paradoxes'. The more one tampers with 'time' [in essence being removed from the 'event-chain'] the less grounding they will have in 'space-matter'. We might conceive that one can tamper with time and create so many paradoxes that they are shifted into a density with almost NO concrete matter at all. At this point they would as has been suggested, exist as little more than dematerialized 'thought forms', which in my book would probably not be a very exciting existence.

So don't be too quick to give-in to certain "channeled" entities who would like for us to give up our ground or our hold in the 3rd dimension —

The Omega Files

or 'material' reality — and become involved in a "collective new age ascension" into the 4th and 5th dimensions. It may be that they don't WANT us inhabiting the 3rd dimension simply because doing so gives us a great deal of influence over the other dimensions. 3rd dimensional Matter or Material is not 'evil' as certain gnostic cults believe, matter is merely a tool. It can be used for good. Or it can be used for evil. So although we should be vigilant in defending our planet, I believe that we should also be vigilant in defending our dimension as well! So then, at this point I will detail what I 'perceive' to be the 'interstellar borders' in this sector of the galaxy, based on what I've learned from my own 'cosmic' experiences and sources as well as through many other confirmations. The following is based on years of research and interaction with abductees and contactees, and by reviewing elusive but dramatic consistencies within thousands of books, documents, files, etc. Essentially these 'borders' as I 'perceive' them are as follows.

The ANDRO-PLEIADEAN Federation, the "non-interventionists", have major alliances within the following star systems: Taygeta Pleiades, Vega Lyra, Iumma/Ummo/Wolf 424, Tau Ceti, Epsilon Eridani, Procyon, Alpha Centauri, etc. The DRACO-ORION Empire, the "interventionists" [abductors/mutilators, etc.] are dominant in Alpha Draconis, Epsilon Bootes, Zeta II Reticuli, Rigel Orion, Bellatrix Orion, Polaris, Nemesis, etc. Nemesis by the way is a 'dark star' or a protostar outside of the Sol system in the direction of Orion, yet nearer than Proxima Centauri, which was not massive enough to attain stellar fusion. Instead it condensed into a huge solid frozen sphere that has been detected by our IRIS satellites. Nemesis is reportedly the major staging center for Draconian - Orion operations against the Sol system and has been the source of many of the 'engineered' planetoids, like Geographos and *Phobos [*where reside 2000 "original Greys" which serve as the biogenetic sources for the millions of Grey clones operating in the Sol system. Phobos is also where the 109 members of the original human "personnel exchange" program really ended up, according to contactee Alex Collier — where they were used as fodder for further biogenetic experimentation], and also other planetoids which have cruised through the Sol system since at least 1953. Many of these planetoids have made unpredictable 'course alterations', and in 1953 two of them simultaneously established stable geosynchronous orbits around planet earth, strongly suggesting that they are being 'controlled'. These have apparently served as staging bases for the Grey/Reptiloid collectivists in their abduction, mind control, implantation, genetic, animal mutilation, underground base, and infil-

The Omega Files

tration projects on earth. As confirmation of the above, The MELBOURNE SUN [Melbourne, Victoria, Australia], August 25, 1954 issue, carried an article titled "THE NEW SATELLITES", which stated: "Two meteors [asteroids?] had become satellites of the earth and WERE REVOLVING WITH IT 400 to 600 miles out in space, the latest issue of the American Magazine 'AVIATION WEEK' said yesterday.

The magazine said that the discovery of the satellites threw the air force into confusion this summer. Alarm over the sightings ended only after they had been identified as natural rather than manmade." Another possibility may be that they were both 'engineered' natural objects such as hollowed-out planetoids. The simultaneous arrival of two LARGE asteroids, NOT 'meteors', combined with the fact that both took up a geo-synchronous orbit [synchronized with the revolving of the earth and positioned always over a particular geographical location], would be an incredible 'coincidence' indeed. According to 'inside' sources, the NSA established radio contact with the 'Greys' operating within these planetoids and this led to the 1954 Edward's/Muroc/Holloman AFB landings and treaty negotiations — under the Eisenhower administration — with the space-based Greys and Reptiloids, even though previous treaties [Truman, etc.] were signed with the humanoid [Telos/Ashtar/Agharti/Melchizedek] groups under Mt. Shasta, California and the Reptiloid-Grey Draconis-Bootes-Orionite connected groups under Mt. Archuleta, near Dulce, New Mexico. According to former Dulce base security officer Thomas Castello, the Shasta treaty dates back to the Grover Cleveland presidency. This would also include the 'Agharti' and 'Silver Fleet' Ashtar forces below central Asia and the 'Posidean' colonies below the Matto Grosso and surrounding regions of the Brazilian underground. It was apparently Truman who later established or updated the treaty with the subterranean — Archuleta? — Greys just after World War II, in addition to the already existent treaty with the Greys that the Bavarian government had established VIA the Gizeh [Phoenix?] empire as early as 1933. In addition to the ANDRO-PLEIADEAN Federation and the DRACO-ORION Empire, the THIRD major interstellar alliance within this sector of the galaxy is believed to be the CORPORATE-COLLECTIVE — also known as the ASHTAR or ASTARTE collective which has ties with the ancient humanoid-reptiloid collaborations of Egypt, India and Babylon. This alliance has major centers of influence in Altair Aquila, Sirius-B, Arcturus, Aldebaran, Zeta I Reticuli, Bootes Centaurus, and of course Sol, etc. The collectivists, who consist of various humanoid, reptiloid, insectoid, etc. races — may be either interventionists

The Omega Files

or non-interventionist depending on which 'side' they are allying themselves with at any given 'time', the Andro-Pleiadean non-interventionists OR the Draco-Orionite interventionists. So much for my perceptions of the geopolitical workings of the immediate sector of the universe, based on what I've learned from various 'galactic intelligence' sources. Let us now return to the Sol system and continue with what has been learned from more 'down to earth' intelligence and research sources. Let us focus for a moment on the subject of the Jesuit-Masonic collaboration... It was a collaborative cult of Jesuits and Masons, in the form of the "Knights of the Golden Circle", who at the behest of the Black Nobility infiltrated both the northern and southern governments during the American civil war.

The Black Nobility were fearful that a strong and independent America would threaten the economic domination of the world which the European elite held. Their agents in the north and the south drove a wedge between the Yanks and Rebels and helped to foment and precipitate the war. Just as there was a legitimate argument in the Viet Nam war, Communism... there was also a legitimate argument in the civil war — slavery in a country where all men were supposed to be equals. However these outward tensions were being aggravated and manipulated by the New World Order agents behind-the-scenes. Before returning to the Philadelphia III revelations, I'd like to share just one more source of information in relation to the above. The following information is taken from the book "TRIBULATION 99: ALIEN ANOMALIES UNDER AMERICA" (sub-title: THE SHOCKING TRUTH ABOUT THE COMING APOCALYPSE), by Retired Air Force Colonel Craig Baldwin. "...Baldwin has been tracking the Quetzal conspiracy for well over a decade. Despite the risk to his personal safety, Baldwin continues to make public his astonishing findings through screenings and lecture tours worldwide." (1991 — Ediciones La Calavera., P.O. Box 1106., Peter Stuyvesant Station., New York, N.Y. 10009-1106). The following is a paraphrase of some of the highlights of Baldwin's research: — The "Quetzal" conspiracy involves an alien species of reptilian hominoids that have been collaborating since ancient times with a renegade branch of degenerate Mayan cultists. In more recent times the Nazi's have apparently joined forces with this unholy alliance and are working with them to undermine South and North America. — One of the servants of the Quetzal conspiracy was the NATIONAL SOCIALIST president of Guatemala [beginning 1951] Jacobo Arbenz, who was actually — according to Baldwin — an infiltrator from the Quetzal collective. He plotted the takeover of the United Fruit Co., and confiscated large tracts of

The Omega Files

land throughout Guatemala. It is said that members of his secret cult [tied-in with the aliens] re-instituted the ancient Mayan practice of human sacrifice.

Over 40,000 Guatemalans disappeared mysteriously during his leadership. Several bodies were later found in the craters of extinct volcanoes throughout the area, as if they had been mutilated and then dropped from the air. — The Quetzals, whose major base is in Antarctica (near the Nazi's "New Berlin" base? - Branton), have infiltrated South and Central America via a system of caverns and tunnels and have done the same throughout North America. One of these areas was under the Nevada desert. Nuclear tests [intentionally?] shattered some of their major underground facilities, and the Quetzal's vowed retaliation. — The U.S. government sent 20,000 M-16 assault rifles to the Guatemalan Army. According to Baldwin this was to fight continued Quetzal infiltration and activity in and under that country. Over Guatemalan 100,000 soldiers reportedly died in conflicts with the inner-terrestrial forces. — Antarctica and its "vortex" area is the major headquarters from where the Quetzals/Nazis or Reptilians/Fascists plan a planetary take-over "from the bottom up". The Quetzals are named after the Mayan "Serpent" god Quetzalcoatl. — Alien programming is being broadcast on the 666 megahertz frequency [the same wavelength as human thought], throughout the U.S. and the world. — At least 6 space shots [satellites] as well as the Challenger Space Shuttle itself were destroyed by Quetzal-backed [Illuminati?] occult forces in an attempt to sabotage America's overt space program. A particle-beam weapon used by this fifth column in collaboration with an alien base near Port Salinas, may have been used to destroy our space vessels. — The Quetzal [joint Reptilian - renegade Mayan - and Nazi] forces have attempted to take over Central American governments via infiltration: Nicaragua, Granada, Chile, Guatemala, El Salvador, Panama. They have undermined these areas through a system of artificial tunnels and natural caverns which they control. Chilean president Salvador Allende was also implicated in the conspiracy. Baldwin also discusses scalar wave earthquake generators that were focused on the fault lines of Chile and tuned to their EM frequency to produce instability, resulting in massive earthquakes. These scalar waves were detected by I.T.T., which controls Chile's communications network. — Henry [Operation Paperclip] Kissinger placed his ex(?)-NAZI friend Walter Ralph into the leadership of Chilean Intelligence after Allende's fall. Klaus Barbi was still alive in Bolivia at the time.

The Omega Files

Allende's former ambassador to the U.S. dies while driving down embassy row on Sept. 21, 1976, when he mysteriously "bursts into flames". So then, bringing the conspiracy back to the human-collaborator level of this "cosmic conspiracy", we now return to the "Philadelphia III" agenda: The planned Civil War by the Elite of the New World Order has also been related for a time in well analyzed and proved "prophecy" documents in recent Canadian history. (3) The Cree Indians, unwilling to remain in an independent Quebec, rise up in the "UNGAVA REBELLION", appeal to the Canadian Government to honor Crown treaties with the Cree, and attempt to retain their lands and loyalty to Canada while the English Canadian community of Quebec appeal to the Federal Governnent to protect them against the rise up of political tenseness and violent acts they are victims of. (4) As an act of desperate political pressure, the Cree Indians then seize the massive James Bay hydro-generating facilities located in Northern Quebec, and sabotage them, causing immediate massive power outages in Quebec which ripple through the grid, "down" all Southeastern industrial areas of Ontario and also the ENTIRE East and Northeastern coast of the United States. Nineteen American States, including the District of Columbia, will be directly affected by the massive BLACKOUT, which will follow the sabotage of the James Bay hydro-generating facilities in Northern Quebec. These States are: Maine, New Hampshire, Vermont, New Jersay, Rhode Island, New York, Massachusetts, Connecticut, Pennsylvania, Maryland, Delaware, Virginia, North and South Carolina, Kentucky, Tennessee, Indiana, Michigan, Ohio and the District of Columbia, paralyzing all activities in Washington. Within the first hours of this massive BLACKOUT the President will trigger and implement over a dozen Executive Orders including EO 11490 which will install Martial Law and suspend the constitutional rights into the targeted States. (Note: If and when this happens, ignore these so-called "Executive Orders". If they are unconstitutional then they are ILLEGAL and are not worth the paper they are written on.

Nevertheless, BE CAREFUL because at this point the New World Order will have outwardly declared war on the Constitutional Republic of the United States of America, if they have not already done so just by establishing such so-called 'Executive Orders' - Branton) FEMA, U.N. BATTLE GROUPS, FINCEN, MJTF and BATF would then go into action, firearms would be confiscated while all constitutional rights and guarantee would be suspended. (Can't you just see it? The U.N. gestapo units break into the homes of your typical Joe Redneck American, who says, "You want my gun, eh? OK

The Omega Files

here... have my LEAD too... BLAM!" As far as I'm concerned, these invaders should be treated just like any THIEF that might break into a home. After all if your a PATRIOT, you'll probably end up in one of their DEATH CAMPS anyway if they "arrest" you, according to their current agenda. The owner and potential victim in such an ATTACK would be justified in defending their home with deadly force. Maybe when the gun-grabbers start dying off right and left, then the New World Order will justify an outside invasion of American soil in order to "Restore Order" in America as part of a U.N. military action. It doesn't matter how many gun-grabbing pawns or occupying forces are killed in the process, what is important is that the Black Nobility elite get their New World Order. To hell with the 'pawns', the so-called 'elite' would say, they are merely a means to an end. If only the Communist forces involved in the U.N. operations knew that their TRUE leaders are what they despise the most: that is "Corporate Imperialists" or international bankers with fraternal roots in Bavaria who have "bought-out" these U.N. member countries as a result of long and carefully planned agendas involving massive loans to these same countries. Fully aware that these loans would be hoarded and misused by the greedy leaders of these countries and that as a result these loans could never be re-paid in full, the "Banksters" in turn demanded access to various national resources OR military forces within these debtor countries as reimbursement, and the sovereignty of these nations have slowly been assimilated into the global UN/NWO power structure. If there was one major mistake that the founding fathers made — and no doubt it was because many of them were wealthy businessmen — it was their failure to place in the U.S. Constitution sufficient safeguards to prevent the Electorate government from being subverted by Corporate imperialists.

The problem has been with the media, and the International Banking forces which control the media. Another problem was in giving too much power to one man — the President of the United States. History has proven that the media has a MAJOR influence on forming public opinion, if not engaging in all-out propaganda and mind control. The International Banking interests controlling the media have the power to build-up candidates of their own choosing and tear down those who they do not like. Once their hireling is in office they, incredibly, have the power to appoint their own UNELECTED Executive staff. Not only this, but they have the power to enact 'EXECUTIVE ORDERS', to sign over the ECONOMIC or MILITARY RESERVES of the nation to PRIVATE unelected organization, to create secret intelligence agencies manned by UNELECTED persons, and to VETO decisions made

The Omega Files

by Congress — who should be the REAL governing power. Where did we go wrong? When did we cease from being a Democracy and begin sliding into the sewers of a FINANCIAL-FRATERNAL-ELITIST-MONARCHY, the kind of government that the founding fathers of the American Union detested so much? - Branton) Specific troops dressed with flat black uniforms and unmarked units will be brought in by UH-60 Blackhawk helicopters. They will then be deployed on line and "swept" though towns, building by building, block by block, and remove [by force if necessary] the civilians from towns. Each search team will carry three lists: A Black List, a White List, and a Grey List. The names on the Black List will be removed in total from their residences and business by force, hog-tied by flex cuffs, and placed on the unmarked black helicopters for removal to some unknown, pre-programmed destination. Those on the White List [collaborators?] will be removed "for their own safety" and flown out, and those on the Grey List will also be removed for their own safety -- but the troops have been told that they should "be watched because they weren't sure which list they fit on yet." So under this type of full state of emergency, thousands of Americans [guilty of hate, environmental, financial or gun control "crimes"; or "criminal" violation of any of tens of thousands of new government regulations; or resistance to the New World Order] will be likely to be imprisoned [this is why George Bush moved in recent years to double U.S. prison capacity].

These specific troops that will remove pre-identified civilians from given areas and will confiscate firearms, "subversive elements", remove certain groups for political and/or religious reasons [targeted groups will be gun owners, certain religious groups, and other groups or organizations considered detrimental to the "peacekeeping" or "peace-restoring" missions of an occupying force, or the objectives of the current government body]; these troops will make massive use of mechanized infantry, assault units, light infantry units, MPs, and they all will be connected with the Special United Nations Task Forces. These "special units" will consist of Rhodesians, East Germans, Bulgarians, Hungarians, Estonians, Afghans, Pakistanis, Ghurkas and South Africans, brought in from countries that, of late, had professional armies which no longer exist, or have downscaled their force structure, and have provided a surplus of military troops for the opposition; and been placed under the auspices of the U.N. for "special activated operations". Such troops will be useful for such operations because they will not have families here, and they have been secreted and sequestered aboard remote NON-ACTIVE MILITARY RESERVATIONS to keep them away from

The Omega Files

the civilian population and from discovery. (Note: Just exactly how many U.S. Military bases have been 'deactivated', I do not know for certain. I have heard from one source that there are over 200 non-active U.S. Military Bases which were "officially" closed "once the Cold War ended", and were "no longer needed". I cannot state how accurate this number is nor whether this refers to bases world-wide or just in the United States. I would suspect world wide. We should remember however that several sources claim that a large number of the U.S. military bases, whether active or inactive, possess extensive underground base counterparts. Many of the U.N. occupying forces are reportedly stationed in such underground facilities until they are called into action. In a sense, America has already been INFILTRATED and UNDERMINED, if not INVADED by U.N. - N.W.O. forces. - Branton).

They [the hidden NWO forces] also will not owe the local population any form of loyalty or concern. They have the mentality of occupation forces in a hostile environment. Their actual possible/probable opposition locations are in larger facilities such as Fort Lewis, Washington. These troops are considered mercenaries or blackshirts. The scenario these troops will likely use is practice to insert forces by "fast-rope" in a vertical insertion into a confined area such as a downtown, suburban or industrial area where no adequate helicopter landing zones (LZs) are available. "MARTIAL LAW" is a system of government under the direction of military authority. it is an arbitrary kind of law, proceeding directly from military power and having no immediate constitutional or legislative sanction. It is only justified by 'necessity', and supersedes all civil government.... Martial law is built on a "no settle" principle, but is arbitrary and, in truth, no law. SUSPENSION of the writ of habeas corpus [i.e. right to trial by judge and jury and protection from illegal imprisonment] is a major element of martial law. As Justice Blackstone wrote: "In this case, the nation parts with a portion of its liberty and suspected persons may then be arrested without cause assigned." In light of the above, when the FEMA - U.N. gestapo forces come knocking down your door without your consent and without warrant, steal your guns, your computers and personal belongings under the pretext of a 'National Emergency' — or even attempt to 'relocate' you and your family elsewhere in opposition to your rights as laid out in the U.S. Constitution and the Bill of Rights — then this will NOT be an act of the Law, BUT AN ACT OF WAR!!! You have the right to resist as laid out in the DECLARATION OF INDEPENDENCE. Read these documents, because they are the FOUNDATION and LIFEBLOOD of the American Republic. In the end, the last line of defense of the Ameri-

The Omega Files

can Republic — or that system of government which is laid out in the U.S. Constitution, Bill of Rights and the Declaration of Independence — will not be those who are guilty of HIGH TREASON within 'our' government who have sold America over to the New World Order. It will be THE CITIZEN'S MILITIA, which is authorized by the 2nd Amendment. And for all you military, police and government officials who have sworn to uphold and defend the U.S. Constitution against ALL ENEMIES FOREIGN AND DOMESTIC... When and if a National Emergency is declared, and when you begin receiving conflicting instructions from the 'Elected' Senatorial-Congressional 'government' AND FROM the 'Unelected' Military-Industrial 'government', then it will be UP TO YOU personally to determine which instructions will serve the interests of YOUR American Republic, and which will serve the interests of THEIR New World Order...

POSTSCRIPT

Although this file has dealt mainly with Nazism, we should not forget the evils perpetrated by so-called 'communism' in Russia, China, Southeast Asia and elsewhere. Many sources agree that during the course of the 'Cold War', Communism was responsible for over 200 million human deaths. Nazism was directly or indirectly responsible for the over 50 million deaths resulting from World War II, and an unknown number of deaths in third world countries as a result of underground covert warfare which the Nazified CIA carried out following the second world war. I've dealt more with the modern-day Nazi conspiracy than I have with the modern-day machinations of Communism simply because the evils of Communism were exposed all throughout the Cold War period, whereas the Nazi's kept a much lower profile. HOWEVER, we must NEVER forget that both the 'right' and 'left' arm of "the Beast" [or the 'right-wing' and the 'left-wing' of the 'Dragon' if you prefer], are BOTH ultimately controlled by the same entity, which is as you may have guessed the joint human-alien "Cult of the Serpent", as exemplified by those forces at work within their supreme planetary headquarters — their Eastern Command Center under PINE GAP, Australia; and the Western Command Center under DULCE, New Mexico! If we are to believe all of the above, then there is in fact a Machievellian national/global socialist conspiracy being jointly carried out by Corporate American and Cultic European 'Commu-Nazis' — for want of a more descriptive term. If the 'Bavarian Empire' cults are attempting to implement a totalitarian national-socialist and/or global-socialist takeover in America as they did in Germany through Adolph Hitler

The Omega Files

and in Russia through Vladimir Lenin, then they must be preparing everything in advance. Having learned the mistakes of the last fascist 'Holocaust' and communist 'Purge', they would be determined NOT to allow the FINAL HOLOCAUST OR PURGE to fail.

Could revelations like these lead to all-out civil war between the infiltrators within the secret underground "Corporate government" AND their enemies within the open and constitutional "Electorate government" — whom these self-proclaimed 'elite' are determined to destroy? They have already declared 'war' on American Patriots in no uncertain terms, even to the point of carrying out a coup d'etat of the Executive Branch of government in 1963 with the murder of President John F. Kennedy — who in essence gave an executive decree to "dismember" this illegal, secret, and unconstitutional national-socialist/global-socialist government [exemplified by JFK's order to "dismember" the CIA], an order which has yet to be carried out in the U.S. Once this fascist-communist network is dismembered within the CIA and NSA, the legitimate operations of the CIA could be moved to other branches of Military Intelligence — possibly to Navy Intelligence or divided among the four military branches. We might "rationalize" keeping the CIA-NSA as is and "converting" them to agencies subject to full Congressional oversight. However I would personally suggest that one should not "put new wine in old wineskins". At the very least, they should be given a complete overhaul and the names of these agencies should be changed, out of respect for the memories of all those whom these agencies have destroyed. The JFK assassination, however, was only the tip of the iceberg in regards to the over-all damage that these draconian-backed planetary traitors have done to the forces of FREEDOM here in America. From my own perspective, I'd prefer a two-sided WAR over a one-sided HOLOCAUST or PURGE any day. Unfortunately due to the ignorance and apathy of earlier administrations, we may have more-or-less guaranteed one or the other...

APPENDIX:
Important Documents on Nazi UFOS and Other Related Subject Matter

Source material from various researchers and organizations provided to help assist in the verification of the Nazi UFO theory. Such documentation centers around a number of first hand experiences and sightings of the so-called 'Too Fighters" by Allied pilots.

August 10, 1998
By Louise Lowry

ALL RIGHTS RESERVED: (permission is granted to reproduce or redistribute this edition provided that attribution is made to the Author or Authors noted)

Website: www.jbgraphics.com/thestrange/

Nazi UFOs

1 Source: alex constantine < alex@DIRECTNET.COM>

An interesting series of articles: new information, or misleading propaganda? You be the judge!

Over the last few months new information has emerged relating to the terrestrial origins of flying saucers in the USA - a fact which surprises few researchers.

Despite the argument that German scientists had no more advanced technology than the allies, one American was very clear as to the technical achievements of Nazi scientists: Major General Hugh Knerr, Deputy Commanding

General for Administration of US Strategic Forces in Europe, wrote to Lieutenant General Carl Spatz in March 1945:

"Occupation of German scientific and industrial establishments has revealed the fact that we have been alarmingly backward in many fields of research, if we do not take this opportunity to seize the apparatus and the brains that developed it and put this combination back to work promptly, we will remain several years behind while we attempt to cover a field already exploited."

It is possible to look into the area of German flying saucers without reference to so-called "established" sources.

These authors are often targeted for attack by skeptics and include Allen Harbinson, who has contributed to the subject through his exciting series of Project Saucer novels and the more recent non-fiction paperback "Projekt UFO" and Renate Vesco, whose research appeared in the late 1960s as a paperback with the title "Intercept But Don't Shoot" and later as "Intercept UFO". Vesco appears to have cooperated with "hidden knowledge" writer David Hatcher Childress in the production of "Man-Made UFOs - 50 Years of Suppression". In addition to these books, which are interesting though imperfect in their presentation (and omission) of the evidence, there are also two books written in the 1970s by Ernst Zundel under the pseudonym "Mattern Friedrich' which were popular for a short time within the far-right political community and may still be available.

Zundel himself is a controversial figure for a number of obvious reasons which include support for anti-Semitic groups, his publication of books and magazines denying the holocaust, and his links with most of the influential neo-Nazi groups in Germany, Britain, the USA and Canada. His most important book on the subject of German flying saucers is entitled "UFOs: Nazi Secret Weapons".

Despite the fact that Zundel is a character with whom we have little or nothing in common from a political point of view, his espousal of far-right politics neither means that every piece of information in his two books is wrong nor that they should be ignored. It is important to realize that Zundel's main purpose in writing and dissemination these books was not primarily an attempt to advocate the supposed "superiority" of Nazi technologies but to make a fast buck. In short, Zundel did it for the money, and he has made it quite clear that these publications are, in his view, not to be taken 100% seriously. The skeptics point to Zundel as a major source on German secret projects despite the fact that there are several other books and articles, including primary material, that have no link with such questionable politics. Where we have a situation where skeptics will use any tactic, we can expect them to claim that any use of contemporary German-language material is evidence of "apology" for Nazi war crimes. This is not the case although we do not any longer intend to look over our shoulder every time we mention German pre-war or wartime technology. We research this subject in order to shed new and important light on the fundamental reality of man-made flying saucers.

The final point to bare in mind regarding this subject is that the victors of any conflict have a head start in writing the history books and, in the case of the immediate aftermath of the Second World War, burying or spiriting away evidence, documents, plans and blueprints, actual technology and a variety of other materials that the allies did not, and do not, want the public to know about - for a variety of reasons that may become apparent.

Despite the fact that the man-made origins of flying saucers are of the greatest implications in terms of our understanding of postwar history, "man-made UFO" researchers have to some extent been deliberately ostracized and smeared.

Nevertheless, a great deal of new information has emerged in recent years and there is still more to come. The suggestion that fifty years after the end of the Second World War new information cannot emerge because this period has been the subject of the most intense scrutiny is an illogical one. For any number of reasons information can stay buried and, beyond mere speculation, we know that files relating to the Second World War remain locked in the deep dark vaults of the Public Records Office in Kew, London. Remember this - records are routinely held for 30 years and can be held for 50, 75 and 100 years after the event. By the time they emerge they may have been altered, edited or sanitized to "protect" the identity of those responsible for the implementation of policy. One simple example that comes to mind is the emergence in recent years of new and credible information about the German nuclear research program underway during the Second World War. Much of this has been the result of research undertaken by Philip Henshall who has also contributed a great deal to our understanding of advanced German weapons projects through his books on the rocket research facilities at Pennemunde on the Baltic coast.

Even before the allies landed in Normandy in June 1944 special groups of language and technical research specialists had been organized in order to recover as much of the technological hardware and research data relating to advanced German weapons. This effort was dedicated to getting hold of much more than data on the V2 rocket - the most obvious and well-known example of German scientific expertise. Already, through an intelligence estimate passed to the allies via a Norwegian source and known as the "Oslo Letter", the allies were aware of other weapons under development and in operation by axis powers. These included radio-controlled bombs, huge guns, rocket launchers, new radar systems, long-range bombers and torpedoes. It would seem that they might also have been interested in a circular-wing aircraft with Vertical-Take-Off-and Landing (VTOL) capabilities. In short, an early and relatively primitive flying saucer...

The mind reels.

The major media ignore or pooh-pooh these theories, for fear of appearing to take seriously the perspective of the radical fringe, or, depending upon your point of view, for fear of blowing their cover as agents in the master plot. Indeed, the media rate high on conspiracy theorists lists of bad guys. But imagining Brokaw, Jennings and Rather, along with the editors of The New York Times and The Washington Post, giving secret handshakes and chanting verses from the Bible backwards hardly seems realistic.

But conspiracy theories riddled mainstream thought as well. Recently, filmmaker Oliver Stone joined the ranks, portraying in his film "JFK" a CIA/vice-presidential coup behind the Kennedy assassination, attempting, like so many others, to blame the evils in the world upon a hidden group of powerful masterminds. And then some see a conspiracy in the Clinton Whitehouse behind the Vince Foster suicide, and another to trade an accommodating foreign policy with dictatorial Indonesia for hard cash. The list goes on.

And while few of us can assert with certainty what actually goes on behind closed doors in this world, the unifying factor of all the above is unsubstantiated evidence and, not infrequently, a shortage of common sense. How, for instance, could so many people in media and government be kept quiet about the bad guys in power for so long?

But why, then, the sudden shredding of the social fabric of generations? How, other than pointing to an insidious conspiracy, does one explain the pervasive, subversive or even predatory force to which the world has apparently fallen victim? Some of the answers, ironically, may arise in the world of science and government, the very halls of power and intellectual authority conspiracy theorists point to as part of the problem.

Not long ago, Harvard professor John Mack articulated the unspeakable, as far as science and academia are concerned, when at a meeting of skeptics and intellectuals, he declared that we, modem civilization, are the first society in history without a belief in the invisible. Mack's remark came at a particularly trying moment, as he defended himself against a hostile crowd of peers for having taken seriously, and then clinically investigated, claims of alien abductions, spooky accounts of otherwise normal individuals being kidnapped by strange beings, presumably from other worlds, victims of telepathic mind control. The kind of stuff you won't hear about on network news (check your Cable listings, though), the idea of interstellar boogey men moving between dimensions didn't sit well with Mack's stodgy colleagues. Their collective reaction springs from their adherence to absolute materialism, the belief system of modem science and academia, the theory that says all things in existence derive from matter (including that ever-elusive commodity called consciousness), the foundation of Western scientific thought since the turn of the last century.

But as we near the next millennium, evidence of the existence of an invisible resounds from quiet corners in the halls of established power, validating what the ancients took for granted and claimed to have mystically experienced. From sources as disparate as Nobel Prize - winning physicists to whistle blowers at the United States Army's Defense Intelligence Agency (DIA), we hear testimony regarding the existence of other dimensions, where those who seek to point the finger of blame for life's insanities might find some answers.

Into The Invisible

Modem physics, to its own amazement, allows for and even professes the existence of dimensions parallel to our own. Physicist David Bohm, a protege' of Albert Einstein, revealed to the world the scientific basis for what he called nonlocality, an essentially conscious medium he saw as the foundational reality behind all appearances, time and space. Nobel laureate Steven Weinberg, and other notable physicists, speak of the existence of a multiverse, in which our reality is one of many existing in non-time/non-space, a principle echoing from such disparate sources as Carl Jung, the famous psychologist, and now, the Pentagon's Defense Intelligence Agency.

Ex-DIA operative David Morehouse's in-depth forays into he shamanistic realm of out-of-body experience, where he and other specially trained colleagues practiced remote viewing for intelligence gathering purposes, and then remote influence in order to change the way people think, reveal in a methodical manner the existence, not only of extrasensory perception, but of an otherworld where forces of good and evil dwell, according to early rocket projects, there is little doubt that Miethe would have been a target too. Nevertheless, his work near Prague put him out of reach and only through Miethe's own efforts did the allied teams get their hands on him.

The Plot Thickens

Blaming secret and powerful bad guys turns up everywhere. We've heard about evil-doing multinational corporations being responsible for the world's woes, one or other of the political parties, or the military industrial complex. The Catholic Church has been blamed, said to conspire with the Mafia and international financiers, and then, lamentably, Jews,

Human beings search and grasp for a way to understand the incomprehensible, moral and social decline in the form of teen suicide, child pornography and sexual abuse, an astronomical crime rate, the ding epidemic, terrorism, etc. Some blame David Rockefeller, his Council on Foreign Relations and Aspen Institute for Humanistic studies, and the infamous yet utterly bland Trilateral Commission, reportedly in cahoots with space aliens, all this being part of an intergalactic conspiracy. And until the fall of communism, some declared that a high-level capitalist/communist conspiracy dominated American foreign policy and international trade, a secret, elite partnership between the United States and the Soviet Union.

In order to make some progress in terms of this research it seems necessary to avoid using the standard sources -Vesco and Harbinson - even though some of their information is valid as we have seen. Other sources are equally significant interest in both Vertical-Take Off and-Landing (VTOL) and circular wing aircraft interesting. One source indicates that from the mid 1930s there was. This led to a number of designs one of which was the Focke-Wulf VTOL..

Professor Heinrich Focke was particularly interested in emerging helicopter and autogyro technologies and was involved in the design and production of the FW6, Fa223, Fa226, Fa283 and 284 models during the war. The creation of the jet engine encouraged him to design a propulsion system known as the "turbo-shaft" still used in most helicopters today. In 1939 he patented a saucer-type aircraft with enclosed twin rotors. This was a revolutionary development described as follows:

"The exhaust nozzle forked in two at the end of the engine and ended in two auxiliary combustion chambers located on the trailing edge of the wing. When fuel was added these combustion chambers they would act as afterburners to provide horizontal propulsion to Focke's design. The control at low speed was achieved by alternately varying the power from each auxiliary combustion chamber."

This was by no means the only circular aircraft.

Another similar aircraft was the troubled AS6 partly designed by the leading aviation expert in Germany Dr. Alexander Lippisch whose work at the Gottingen Aviation Institute was legendary and whose impact upon postwar UFOs' cannot be underestimated. His revolutionary "DM" series of small triangular aircraft were built and flown in conjunction with students at Dannstadt and Munich Universities (hence the DM prefix) and used rocket propulsion. The plans for these were transported to the USA after the war. His most advanced design was undoubtedly the Lippisch Supersonic Flying Wing which, although never built, strongly hinted at the triangular 'UFOs' of the 1980s and 1990s.

The information about the AS6 (V1) emerged in an article written by Hans Ebert and Hans Meier based to a certain extent upon information and a photograph provided by German aviation expert Wolfgang Spate. (Spate was the former Commander of Operational Test Unit 16 during the War and more recently recognized as a leading aviation expert. He served in the refounded postwar Luftwaffe.) The article, entitled "Prototypen -Einselschicksale deutchser

Flugzeuge, Der Kreisflugler AS6 Vi", was included in a the respected Luftfahrt International in 1980. In certain respects the AS6, built by Messerschmidt, was based upon similar thinking as the Zimmerman V173 "flying flapjack" - designed for use by the US Navy from 1942. The "flying flapjack" was far more successful and developed at the Chance-Vought works in Connecticut and despite its' supposed limitations was a propeller-driven aircraft designed to be flown from an aircraft carrier, hence the need for Short Take off and Landing (STOL) capability. The flapjack was able to fly at low speeds of approximately 40mph. The flight envelope was 40-425 mph and a more advanced version, the XF5U 1, was also tested.

One other important feature of these circular wings was an early 'stealth' capability. The Horten brothers Reimar and Walter, known for their many successful flying wing prototypes, had developed a composite wing made of plywood held together by sawdust, charcoal and glue intended to absorb radar waves for use in their HIX model.

In 1946 Chance-Vought was using a similar technique. A skin called 'metalite' was used in one of its' circular wings. Thomas C. Smith, former President of the Woodstream Corporation and a Penn State graduate engineer at the time, reported that he had seen a 'flying saucer' (XF5U1?) taking off vertically from the Chance-Vought facilities in Stratford, Connecticut at the time and that it had used this composite. This was reported last year.

This means that the circular wing or 'flying saucer' had a limited stealth capability years before the use of Radar Absorbent Materials was considered for other advanced aircraft...

We can certainly dismiss all the nonsense so prevalent in various media on the subject of German flying saucers which relates to the development of circular-wing aircraft as the result of "occult" or "mystical" beliefs. The truth is that the circular wing was designed for technical reasons.

Whilst it is likely that any information relating to the limited A56 would have been taken by the allies for examination at a later date it would seem that there is some evidence to suggest that a more advanced jet-powered flying saucer was at least designed, if not built, from around 1943 onwards. The first source is Flight Captain Rudolph Schriever who came forward in 1950 and claimed that he had worked with a small team at facilities near Prague with a view to developing a flying saucer-type vehicle. The Schriever story first emerged in "Der Spiegel" magazine dated March 30th 1950 entitled "Untertassen-Flieger Kombination":

"A former Luftwaffe captain and aircraft designer. Rudolph Schriever, who says engineers throughout the world experimented in the early 1940s with "flying saucers" is willing to build one for the United States in six to nine months. The 40 year old Prague University graduate said he made blueprints for such a machine, which he calls a "flying top", before Germany's collapse and that the blueprints were stolen from his laboratory. He says the machine would be capable of 2,600 mph with a radius of 4,000 miles, Schriever is a US Army driver at Bremerhaven."

This is a most credible story. Schriever claimed that the model built for testing was completed in 1944 with a view to flying it in 1945. Nevertheless, the Russian advance ended any hopes of a test-flight.

A 1975 Luftfahrt International report took these claims seriously and noted that after Schriever's death in the late 1950s papers found amongst his belongings had included technical drawings of a flying saucer.

Schriever seemed to argue that although a saucer had existed it had not flown. This is contradicted by a possible eyewitness, George Klein.

He claimed after the war in an interview, given on November 18th 1954 to the Zurich-based "Tages Anzeiger", that he had actually seen a flying saucer test on 14th February 1945 and that the craft had performed remarkably well reaching an altitude of 30,000 ft in 3 minutes as well as a high speed of hundreds of miles and hour. Despite the fact that subsequent information leads us to conclude that a jet-powered flying disc was developed at the end of the war Klein spoke of a "ray-guided disc". Despite this fanciful claim some of the things he said made more sense. For instance, he claimed that some of the work on the flying saucers had taken place at Pennemunde. Pennemunde was of course the focal point for the development of the A4/V2 rocket. Interestingly, Klein also claimed that the necessary stability for the saucer had been attained through the use of a gyroscope. This is exactly the method used in the later German rockets developed by the Von Braun/Dornberger team. What is more, the entire rocket effort moved to the Mittlewerke underground facilities near Nordhausen in the Harz Mountains. It is claimed, by several other witnesses, that a flying saucer was tested in the vicinity of Kahla In Thuringia in early 1945.

The evidence presented above seems to have been taken seriously not only by mainstream magazines and national newspapers in the 1950s but also by the author of "Brighter Than A Thousand Suns", Robert Jungk. This is an authoritative and historical account of the development of the Atomic Bomb written by a respected author. The book itself, still available and published by Harcourt and Brace, received critical acclaim from Bertrand Russell, amongst others. A section of text on page 87 of the paperback edition states:

"The indifference of Hitler and those about him to research in natural sciences amounted to positive hostility. *" The accompanying footnote reads as follows:

"*The only exception to the lack of interest shown by authority was constituted by he Air Ministry [Reichs Luftfahrt Ministirium or RLM, TM]. The Air Force research workers were in a peculiar position. They produced interesting new types such as the Delta [Lippisch and Horten, TM] ..and flying discs, The first of these "flying saucers", as they were later called - circular in shape, with a diameter of some 45 yards - were built by the specialists Schriever, Habermohl and Miethe. They were first airborne on February 14th 1945, over Prague and reached in three minutes a height of nearly eight miles. They had a speed of 1250 mph which was doubled in subsequent tests. It is believed that Habermohl fell into the hands of the Russians. Miethe developed at a later date similar "flying saucers" at A.V Roe and Company for the United States".

This use of the original Schriever story is interesting if only because the author felt that the information was good and warranted exposure. Given the nature of the book, we might well ask whether the author had any other information that supported the claims made as to the characteristics of the circular aircraft. It is up to the reader to decide whether these claims make any sense at all and more importantly, how this might affect our understanding of flying saucer history...

Until recently, it would have been rather safer and perhaps more sensible to argue that although various prototype saucers existed in whatever form they were never tested. Safety is often the best policy given the shark infested waters of modern-day UFO research. However, thanks to three years of painstaking research by UK astronomy, aviation and photographic expert Bill Rose which included on-site research in Germany, Canada and America we now know a great deal more. Initially Rose felt, like many skeptics, that the evidence for German flying saucer (and UFO) reality was very shaky.

Nevertheless, and without reference to the UFO community in his personal quest for the truth, he was able to use his expert technical knowledge to follow up leads and to make significant progress.

First of all he was able to discover that Dr. Walter Miethe, whom all sources agree was involved with Schriever, Klaus Habermohl and Giuseppe Bellonzo (an Italian engineer) had been the Director of the saucer program at two facilities located outside Prague. In May 1945, after testing of the prototype had taken place, both Miethe and Schriever were able to flee in the direction of Allied forces. The other two men, Habermohl and Bellonzo, were captured by Soviet forces and Habermohl was spirited East where he ended up working on various aviation projects quite probably at facilities located outside Moscow.

It would seem that Klaus Habermohl was the man who developed the radial-flow jet engine, described in various articles as a system of "adjustable" nozzles, of great significance just ten years later. (Radial-flow allowed for VTOL performance and used the little-known "Coanda" effect.) Rose learned that not only had test flights taken place but that film footage of these had been taken. This had always been rumored and makes perfect sense given the Nazi fetish for keeping records on everything. The footage, of good quality, has subsequently been stored in a secure location and shown only to a handful of people. Rose was shown stills taken from the original film and given his expert photo-technical background concluded, after careful consideration, that this was real and historical footage. He calculated that the craft was around half the size claimed in Klein's report. The saucer, rather less contoured and sleek than postwar artists' impressions might suggest (and unlike Bob Lazar's S4 "Sports Model"!), was perhaps 75 ft in diameter. The saucer was shown in flight above the runway over the heads of a couple of observers.

Although this is in itself of the greatest significance other more contradictory evidence has emerged. One of the people that Rose met had good information about the February test flight and was able to confirm that several people had seen the test-flight - as we might expect. It was said that Schriever himself had piloted the test craft. This does seems sensible (and logical) given Schriever's background in the Luftwaffe - although it is at variance with his own account. One can only speculate as to why this may be,

It should be pointed out that the performance characteristics of this jet-powered aircraft have probably been exaggerated and although it might have been technically possible given further research and development to approach supersonic speeds, this was almost certainly not achieved in February 1945. Finally, it seems as if Klein himself was centrally involved in the saucer project and may indeed have had responsibilities for procurement.

We know a little more about Dr. Miethe. One of the important pieces of information came in the form of a rare group photograph showing various young German scientists in 1933. The photograph shows Werner von Braun and Walter Miethe. It would seem that these two knew each other well. During the War various lists of "wanted" German scientists were drawn up. One of these was the "Black List" used by Counter Intelligence Corps and Combined Allied Field Teams (CAFT) as they moved through Germany from 1944 in order to help them get hold of the important scientific personnel.

Dr. von Braun was certainly at the top of the list and if Miethe and he were old friends and had cooperated on Morehouse, in what could be called a collective, subconscious field, a realm for the initiated, to be sure, in which we all participate through the mysterious entity known as the Unconscious Mind.

In his book, Psychic Warrior, Morehouse describes how he and other operatives learned to consciously leave their physical bodies and collect intelligence beyond the veil of the material world, unencumbered by distance and even time. The DIA project, code named Sun Streak, and later called Star Gate, grew out of a government-funded program conducted at the Stanford Research Institute under the direction of high energy physicists Dr. Russel Targ and Harold Putthoff. The Soviets, Chinese and Czechs, Morehouse tells us, involve themselves steadily in similar projects.

Morehouse reveals what may well be the mother of all conspiracies. The ubiquitous they theorists blame when things go seriously wrong in life, what in simpler times were called the forces of darkness, exist in other dimensions, according to Morehouse's description of his monitored experiences, which took place over a period of years. In this other world, DIA operatives exploit what Morehouse calls the phantom body, a subtle etheric vehicle through which he transcended space and time in order to gather intelligence for the government.

The picture Morehouse paints of this realm is not an inviting one, although he does reveal a benevolent force at play, a being he calls his Angel, who understands that Morehouse must pass through necessary trials in the ether for his own betterment. But this realm is also fraught with peril and malevolence. One operative identifies what he calls the deceivers in this ether, individuals dedicated to subversion, manipulation and deception. And as Professor Mack reports, regarding those claiming to have been abducted by telepathic aliens, this ethereal landscape has a Pandora's box quality, where psychic forces take shape in forms congruent with an individuals subconscious vulnerabilities. Indeed, Morehouse's account sounds more like Carlos Castenada's Journey to Ixtlan than a report about intelligence operatives, where subconscious reality seems inextricably blended with, even responsible for, the existence of shape-shifting landscapes and evil spirits.

Morehouse alerts us that this out-of-body reality, while ultimately deeply rewarding in its sublime aspects, harbors mental, emotional and spiritual peril for those who are unprepared, as an individual becomes acutely aware of subversive forces within the collective unconscious. He describes a landscape as murky as, and perhaps identical to, the depths of human insanity, which emerges as a vast field of situations and circumstances unbound by time and space, rather than the contained record within the physical brain described by materialists.

In accounts of alien abduction, now so strangely prolific, we hear about a similar realm, where the individual subconscious seems merged with a greater landscape that appears subject to manipulation. Alien spacecraft, too, according to descriptions, oscillate between some other dimension and our own, thereby, like Morehouse and his colleagues, defying the so-called laws of time and space has thought impossible. The abductees themselves, with uncanny consistency and similarity of descriptions, claim to have been whisked through, once again, some sort of subconscious dimension where they are subject to paternalistic forms of hypnosis and mind control, all of which speaks of the subservience of our material reality to the power of the consciousness, and of a hidden they who interfere at subtle but powerful levels within the universal unconscious.

The Big Picture

If all this sounds too foreboding, Tibetan Buddhism provide a comforting over-all context for the existence of evil forces in the world, as do many of the world's spiritual traditions. The One Universal Mind, the llamas tell us, the one consciousness which all existence shares, and through which all evolves, interpenetrates and animates even the nastiest of dimensional hobgoblins, or angels for that matter. This one clear essence resides within all things, the reality upon which modern physics now draws a bead. In Tibetan Buddhist Psychiatry (yes, such a thing exists), patients and practitioners find that all experience, all good and evil, exists in a medium that is luminous, unconditioned and utterly liberating when consciously perceived, a reality Morehouse's Angel seemed to understand and implicitly trust as he showed the way. Even identity, ultimately, turns out to be a condition superimposed upon an infinitely elastic conscious medium, God, if you will, which does not bode well for the bad guys. Evil, then, in this profound context, arises as a reflection of one's own denied, subconscious reality, the unerring, benevolent process of the one mind consciously bringing all existence to ultimate truth and resolution.

Underground Bases & NWO

Aliens & New World Order Conspiracy
A Lecture By Phil Schneider: May 1995

Phil Schneider, a very brave man, recently lost his life due to what appeared to be a military-style execution in January 1996. He was found dead in his apartment with piano wire still wrapped around his neck. According to some sources, he had been brutally tortured repeated before being killed. Phil Schneider was an ex-government engineer who was involved in building underground bases. He was one of three people to survive the 1979 fire fight between the large Greys and U.S. intelligence and military forces at Dulce underground base.

In May 1995, Phil Schneider did a lecture on what he had discovered. Seven months later he was tortured and killed by those for whom he had previously worked. This man's final acts should not go unnoticed.

"It is because of the horrendous structure of the federal government that I feel directly imperiled *not* to tell anybody about this material. How long I will be able to do this is anybody's guess. However, I would like to mention that this talk is going to be broken up into four main topics. Each of these topics will have some bearing on what you people are involved in, whether you are patriots or not.

"I want you to know that these United States are a beautiful place. I have gone to more than 70 countries, and I cannot remember any country that has the beauty, as well as the magnificence of its people, like these United States.

"To give you an overview of basically what I am, I started off and went through engineering school, Half of my school was in that field, and I built up a reputation for being a geological engineer, as well as a structural engineer with both military and aerospace applications. I have helped build two main bases in the United States that have some significance as far as what is called the New World Order. The first base is the one at Dulce, New Mexico. I was involved in 1979 in a firefight with alien humanoids, and I was one of the survivors. I'm probably the only talking survivor you will ever hear. Two other survivors are under close guard. I am the only one left that knows the detailed files of the entire operation. Sixty-six secret service agents, FBI, Black Berets and the like, died in that firefight. I was there.

"Number one, part of what I am going to tell you is going to be very shocking. Part of what I am going to tell you is probably going to be very unbelievable, though, instead of putting your glasses on, I'm going to ask you to put your "scepticals" on. But please, feel free to do your own homework. I know the Freedom of Information Act isn't much to go on, but it's the best we've got. The local law library is a good place to look for Congressional Records. So, if one continues to do their homework, then one can be standing vigilant in regard to their country.

Deep Underground Military Bases & Black Budget

"I love the country I am living in more than I love my life, but I would not be standing before you now, risking my life, if I did not believe it was so. The first part of this talk is going to concern deep underground military bases and the black budget. The Black Budget is a secretive budget that garners 25% of the gross national product of the United States. The Black Budget currently consumes $1.25 trillion per year. At least this amount is used in black programs, like those concerned with deep underground military bases. Presently, there are 129 deep underground military bases in the United States.

"They have been building these 129 bases day and night, unceasingly, since the early 1940's. Some of them were built even earlier than that. These bases are basically large cities underground connected by high-speed magneto-leviton trains that have speeds up to Mach 2. Several books have been written about this activity. Al Bielek has my only copy of one of them. Richard Souder, a Ph.D architect, has risked his life by talking about this. He worked with a number of government agencies on deep underground military bases. In around where you live, in Idaho, there are 11 of them.

"The average depth of these bases is over a mile, and they again are basically whole cities underground. They all are between 2.66 and 4.25 cubic miles in size. They have laser drilling machines that can drill a tunnel seven miles long in one day. The Black Projects sidestep the authority of Congress, which as we know is illegal. Right now, the New World Order is depending on these bases. If I had known at the time I was working on them that the NWO was involved, I would not have done it. I was lied to rather extensively.

Development of Military Technology, Implied German Interest in Hyperspacial Technology, and More

"Basically, as far as technology is concerned, for every calendar year that transpires, military technology increases about 44.5 years. This is why it is easy to understand that back in 1943 they were able to create, through the use of vacuum tube technology, a ship that could literally disappear from one place and appear in another place. My father, Otto Oscar Schneider, fought on both sides of the war. He was originally a U-boat captain, and was captured and repatriated in the United States. He was involved with different kinds of concerns, such as the A-bomb, the H-bomb and the Philadelphia Experiment. He invented a high-speed camera that took pictures of the first atomic tests at Bikini Island on July 12, 1946. I have original photographs of that test, and the photos also show UFO's fleeing the bomb site at a high rate of speed. Bikini Island at the time was infested with them, especially under the water, and the natives had problems with their animals being mutilated. At that time, General MacArthur felt that the next war would be with aliens from other worlds.

"Anyway, my father laid the groundwork with theoreticians about the Philadelphia experiment, as well as other experiments. What does that have to do with me? Nothing, other than the fact that he was my father. I don't agree with what he did on the other side, but I think he had a lot of guts in coming here. He was hated in Germany. There was a $1 million reward, payable in gold, to anyone who killed him. Obviously, they didn't succeed. Anyway, back to our topic - deep underground bases.

The Fire Fight At Dulce Base

"Back in 1954, under the Eisenhower administration, the federal government decided to circumvent the Constitution of the United States and form a treaty with alien entities. It was called the 1954 Greada Treaty, which basically made the agreement that the aliens involved could take a few cows and test their implanting techniques on a few human beings, but that they had to give details about the people involved. Slowly, the aliens altered the bargain until they decided they wouldn't abide by it at all. Back in 1979, this was the reality, and the firefight at Dulce occurred quite by accident. I was involved in building an addition to the deep underground military base at Dulce, which is probably the deepest base. It goes down

seven levels and over 2.5 miles deep. At that particular time, we had drilled four distinct holes in the desert, and we were going to link them together and blow out large sections at a time. My job was to go down the holes and check the rock samples, and recommend the explosive to deal with the particular rock. As I was headed down there, we found ourselves amidst a large cavern that was full of outer-space aliens, otherwise known as large Greys. I shot two of them. At that time, there were 30 people down there. About 40 more came down after this started, and all of them got killed. We had surprised a whole underground base of existing aliens. Later, we found out that they had been living on our planet for a long time, perhaps a million years. This could explain a lot of what is behind the theory of ancient astronauts.

"Anyway, I got shot in the chest with one of their weapons, which was a box on their body, that blew a hole in me and gave me a nasty dose of cobalt radiation. I have had cancer because of that.

"I didn't get really interested in UFO technology until I started work at Area 51, north of Las Vegas. After about two years recuperating after the 1979 incident, I went back to work for Morrison and Knudson, EG&G and other companies. At Area 51, they were testing all kinds of peculiar spacecraft. How many people here are familiar with Bob Lazar's story? He was a physicist working at Area 51 trying to decipher the propulsion factor in some of these craft.

Govt Factions, Railroad Cars & Shackle Contracts

"Now, I am very worried about the activity of the federal government. They have lied to the public, stonewalled senators, and have refused to tell the truth in regard to alien matters. I can go on and on. I can tell you that I am rather disgruntled. Recently, I knew someone who lived near where I live in Portland, Oregon. He worked at Gunderson Steel Fabrication, where they make railroad cars. Now, I knew this fellow for the better part of 30 years, and he was kind of a quiet type. He came in to see me one day, excited, and he told me "they're building prisoner cars." He was nervous.

Gunderson, he said, had a contract with the federal government to build 107,200 full length railroad cars, each with 143 pairs of shackles. There are 11 sub-contractors in this giant project. Supposedly, Gunderson got over 2 billion dollars for the contract. Bethlehem Steel and other steel outfits are involved. He showed me one of the cars in the rail yards in North Portland. He was right. If you multiply 107,200 times 143 times 11, you come up with about 15,000,000.

This is probably the number of people who disagree with the federal government. No more can you vote any of these people out of office. Our present structure of government is "technocracy", not democracy, and it is a form of feudalism. It has nothing to do with the republic of the United States. These people are god-less, and have legislated out prayer m public schools. You can get fined up to $100,000 and two years in prison for praying in school. I believe we can do better. I also believe that the federal government is running the gambit of enslaving the people of the United States. I am not a very good speaker, but I'll keep shooting my mouth off until somebody puts a bullet in me, because it's worth it to talk to a group like this about these atrocities.

America's Black Program Contractors

"There are other problems. I have some interesting 1993 figures. There are 29 prototype stealth aircraft presently. The budget from the U.S. Congress five-year plan for these is $245.6 million. You couldn't buy the spare parts for these black programs for that amount. So, we've been lied to. The black budget is roughly $1.3 trillion every two years. A trillion is a thousand billion. A trillion dollars weighs 11 tons. The U.S. Congress never sees the books involved with this clandestine pot of gold. Contractors of stealth programs: EG&G, Westinghouse, McDonnell Douglas, Morrison-Knudson, Wackenhut Security Systems, Boeing Aerospace, Lorimar Aerospace, Aerospacial in France, Mitsubishi Industries, Rider Trucks, Bechtel, *I.G. Farben*, plus a host of hundreds more. Is this what we are supposed

to be living up to as freedom-loving people? I don't believe so.

Star Wars and Apparent Alien Threat

"Still, 68% of the military budget is directly or indirectly affected by the black budget. Star Wars relies heavily upon stealth weaponry. By the way, none of the stealth program would have been available if we had not taken apart crashed alien disks. None of it. Some of you might ask what the "space shuttle" is "shuttling". Large ingots of special metals that are milled in space and cannot be produced on the surface of the earth. They need the near vacuum of outer space to produce them. We are not even being told anything close to the truth. I believe our government officials have sold us down the drain - lock, stock and barrel. Up until several weeks ago, I was employed by the U.S. government with a Ryolite-38 clearance factor - one of the highest in the world. I believe the Star Wars program is there solely to act as a buffer to prevent alien attack - it has nothing to do with the "cold war", which was only a toy to garner money from all the people - for what? The whole lie was planned and executed for the last 75 years.

Stealth Aircraft Technology Use by U.S. Agencies and the United Nations

"Here's another piece of information for you folks. The Drug Enforcement Administration and the ATF rely on stealth tactical weaponry for as much as 40% of their operations budget. This in 1993, and the figures have gone up considerably since. The United Nations used American stealth aircraft for over 28% of its collective worldwide operations from 1990 to 1992, according to the Center for Strategic Studies and UN Report 3092.

The Guardians of Stealth and Delta Force Origins of the Bosnia Conflict

"The Guardians of Stealth: There are at least three distinct classifications of police that guard our most well-kept secrets. Number one, the Military Joint Tactical Force (MJTF), sometimes called the Delta Force or Black Berets, is a multi-national tactical force primarily used to guard the various stealth aircraft worldwide. By the way, there were 172 stealth aircraft built. Ten crashed, so there were at last count about 162. Bill Clinton signed them away about six weeks ago to the United Nations. There have been indications that the Delta Force was sent over to Bosnia during the last days of the Bush administration as a covert sniper force, and that they started taking pot shots at each side of the controversy, in order to actually start the Bosnia conflict that would be used by succeeding administrations for political purposes.

Thoughts on the Bombings in the United States

"I was hired not too long ago to do a report on the World Trade Center bombing. I was hired because I know about the 90 some- odd varieties of chemical explosives. I looked at the pictures taken right after the blast. The concrete was puddled and melted. The steel and

the rebar was literally extruded up to six feet longer than its original length. There is only one weapon that can do that - a small nuclear weapon. That's a construction-type nuclear device. Obviously, when they say that it was a nitrate explosive that did the damage, they're lying 100%, folks. The people they have in custody probably didn't do the crime. As a matter of fact, I have reason to believe that the same group held in custody did do other crimes, such as killing a Jewish rabbi in New York. However, I want to further mention that with the last explosion in Oklahoma City, they are saying that it was a nitrate or fertilizer bomb that did it.

"First, they came out and said it was a 1,000 pound fertilizer bomb. Then, it was 1,500. Then 2,000 pounds. Now its 20,000. You can't put 20,000 pounds of fertilizer in a Rider Truck. Now, I've never mixed explosives, per se. I know the chemical structure and the application of construction explosives. My reputation was based on it. I helped hollow out more than 13 deep underground military bases in the United States. I worked on the Malta project, in West Germany, in Spain and in Italy. I can tell you from experience that a nitrate explosion would not have hardly shattered the windows of the federal building in Oklahoma City. It would have killed a few people and knocked part of the facing off the building, but it would have never have done that kind of damage. I believe I have been lied to, and I am not taking it any longer, so I'm telling you that you've been lied to.

The Truth Behind the Republican Contract With America

"I don't perceive at this time that we have too much more than six months of life left in this country, at the present rate. We are the laughing stock of the world, because we are being hoodwinked by so many evil people that are running this country. I think we can do better. I think the people over 45 are seriously worried about their future. I'm going to run some scary scenarios by you. The Contract With America. It contains the same terminology that Adolph Hitler used to subvert Germany in 1931. I believe we can do better. The Contract With America is a last ditch effort by our federal government to tear away the Constitution and the Bill of Rights.

Some Statistics on the Black Helicopter Presence

"The black helicopters. There are over 64,000 black helicopters in the United States. For every hour that goes by, there is one being built. Is this the proper use of our money? What does the federal government need 64,000 tactical helicopters for, if they are not trying to enslave us. I doubt if the entire military needs 64,000 worldwide. I doubt if all the world needs that many. There are 157 F-117A stealth aircraft loaded with LIDAR and computer-enhanced imaging radar. They can see you walking from room to room when they fly over your house. They see objects in the house from the air with a variation limit of 1 inch to 30,000 miles. That's how accurate that is. Now, I worked in the federal government for a long time, and I know exactly how they handle their business.

Government Earthquake Device, AIDS as a Bioweapon Based on Alien Excretions

"The federal government has now invented an earthquake device. I am a geologist, and I know what I am talking about. With the Kobe earthquake in Japan, there was no pulsewave as in a normal earthquake. None. In 1989, there was an earthquake in San Francisco. There was no pulse wave with that one either. It is a Tesla device that is being used for evil purposes. The black budget programs have subverted science as we know it. Look at AIDs,

invented by the National Ordinance Laboratory in Chicago, Illinois in 1972. It was a biological weapon to be used against the people of the United States. The reason I know this is that I have seen the documentation by the Office of Strategic Services, which by the way is still in operation to this day, through the CDC in Atlanta. They used the glandular excretions of animals, humans and alien humanoids to create the virus. These alien humanoids the government is hobnobbing with are the worst news. There is absolutely no defense against their germs - none. They are a biological weapon of terrible consequence. Every alien on the planet needs to be isolated.

"Saddam Hussein killed 3.5 million Kurdish people with a similar biological weapon. Do we, the people of this planet, deserve this? No, we don't, but we are not doing anything about it. Every moment we waste, we are doing other people on the planet a disservice. Right now, I am dying of cancer that I contracted because of my work for the federal government. I might live six months. I might not. I will tell you one thing. If I keep speaking out like I am, maybe God will give me the life to talk my head off. I will break every law that it takes to talk my head off. Eleven of my best friends in the last 22 years have been murdered. Eight of the murders were called "suicides." Before I went to talk in Las Vegas, I drove a friend down to Joshua Tree, near 29 Palms. I drove into the mountains in order to get to Needles, California, and I was followed by two government E-350 vans with G-14 plates, each with a couple of occupants, one of which had an Uzi. I knew exactly who they were. I have spoken 19 times and have probably reached 45,000 people. Well, I got ahead of them and came to a stop m the middle of the road. They both went on either side of me and down a ravine. Is this what its going to take? I cut up my security card and sent it back to the government, and told them if I was threatened, and I have been, that I was going to upload 140,000 pages of documentation to the internet about government structure and the whole plan. I have already begun that task.

"Thank you very much.

End of May 1995 Lecture

R.A.F. Officer's UFO Experiences

My father-in-law, Gordon W. Cammell, was a bomber Captain in the Royal Air Force during WWII. He flew Lancasters, was shot down over Germany and spent 1 1/2 years in prison camp.

He remained an R.A.F. pilot for many years after the war, and he'd always told us stories about his UFO experiences while in the service. At my request, he wrote the following personal accounts. {Unlike U.S.A.F. personnel, Mr. Cammell is not subject to any repressive "national security" oaths}.

Subject: A Report of UFO Sightings
By: Gordon W. Cammell Royal Air Force, retired

On those occasions when the subject of UFO's has been discussed, I have recounted experiences, some personal, and some second hand, of which I have some knowledge. I have now been asked to record details of these incidents and although one of them occurred fifty years ago, they are still quite clear in my mind.

I am a retired Royal Air Force officer and spent a combined total of more than twenty years as a pilot in the Royal New Zealand Air Force and R.A.F. In May, 1943 I was the captain of a Lancaster bomber aircraft, and as we crossed the English Channel upon returning from a bombing raid over Germany, I and all of my crew saw what appeared to be a huge orange ball on or near the sea, seven or eight thousand feet below us. It appeared to be stationary as we observed it for about ten minutes, and its light intensity was bright and constant. We decided that it was not an aircraft or ship on fire, since we could not see flames or changing reflections on the water. After landing back at our base at R.A.F. East Wretham, Suffolk, England, we reported our sighting to the debriefing officer who also had no idea of what we had seen.

In 1953 I was based at R.A.F. Coltishall, Norfolk, England as a jet pilot flying Meteor night fighters. During a routine night flying exercise one of our crews, Captain, F/OJ. Allison, and radar operator, F/OI. Heavers, reported sighting a cigar- shaped UFO with internal green lights visible through windows. When this crew entered our flight room upon their return, they were both very excited and convinced that the object they had seen was extra terrestrial, because of its very high speed and unusual configuration. The next day we learned that the crew of another night fighter jet of number 85 Squadron, flying near their base at R.A.F. Maidstone, Kent (over one hundred miles from Coltishall) had reported an identical sighting only three minutes after our crew's encounter. Three minutes to cover a distance of 100 miles meant that the UFO was traveling at about two thousand m.p.h., which was well in excess of the capability of any aircraft in the U.K. at that time in history.

It was within the same general time frame of the above reported UFO sighting that during one afternoon, I was doing duty in the aircraft control tower as "Duty Pilot". Fog covered the area, giving very limited visibility on the ground for take- offs and landings, and so flying had ceased for the day. However, an order was received from the officer commanding the ground control interception radar site at R.A.F. Neatishead, to scramble two radar equipped Meteors, and the crews were instructed to climb to 30,000' and attempt to intercept and identify two

UFO's that appeared on the radar screens moving at a speed in excess of 1700 m.p.h., inland after crossing the Norfolk coast from the sea. However, well before our aircraft could reach their assigned altitude, the UFO's
turned and traveled back towards the European Continent and were no longer visible on the ground radar screens. Our aircrews did not see the UFO's visually or on their radar screens, since they were out of their range by the time they had completed their climbs.

For some years my wife and I owned a holiday home near Victoria, British Columbia, Canada, and spent two or three months there each summer. Our house commanded a wide unobstructed view over farmland to Horo Straight, 1 1/2 miles distant, which runs between Vancouver Island and the San Juan Islands of Washington State. This view was seen through a large picture window in the living room where we relaxed, especially during the evenings. Quite often we would not draw the drapes so that we could enjoy the rising of a full moon as it appeared over the island, and left an orange reflective glow on the sea in the foreground. We sometimes saw lights of different colors moving across the sky, and these at times would remain stationary for periods of time before moving on again. I have spend nine years as a pilot flying small and large helicopters. I believe that I would have recognized them as such. I was always intrigued by these lights, but as they didn't appear often, I didn't think too much about them.

However in the summer of 1991 when the sun had set, and it was quite dark, I saw two orange balls on or near the water in Horo Straight about two miles away. They were very large, at least fifty feet in diameter, and were immobile. I took my binoculars to view these objects, but could not make out any details in the orange glows. Initially, they were close together and could be seen within the focal width of the binocular lens. Then after some time, maybe fifteen or twenty minutes, they appeared to drift apart so that I could not observe both orange balls through the lens at the same time. While viewing this phenomena I remembered that I had seen something very similar to this in 1943 on or over the English Channel. As of then, I couldn't bring myself to believe that I was watching extra terrestrial vehicles, and felt that there had to be a logical explanation for them. After perhaps an hour, when nothing seemed to have changed and the orange balls appeared as they were when I first saw them, I felt tired and retired to bed. During the night I awoke and looked to see if the orange balls were still visible, but they had disappeared.

For the next day or two I studied our local newspapers to learn whether others had reported any unusual sightings on Horo Straight, but there was nothing. I asked some of our neighbors if they had seen anything unusual that night, but of those to whom I spoke, their drapes had been drawn and none had seen anything unusual.

Gordon N. Cammell
R.N.Z.A.F./R.A.F.
Retired

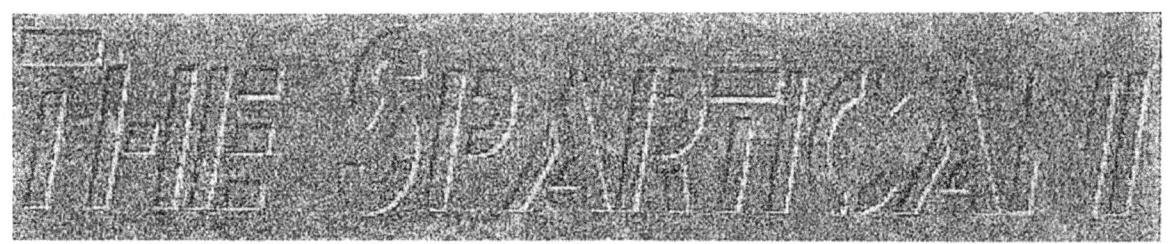

The Foo Fighter Mystery: Revised.

By Jeff A. Lindell
B.A., I.U. Folklore Institute
Electronic Warfare Systems Analyst, *USAF (Ret.)*

This study represents in total, an intense investigation into the backgrounds and experiences of 98 World War II night-time combat aviators, by means of recorded narratives, some 80+ hours were collected. These narratives were not collected according to belief or by the name "foo fighter" exclusively, but rather according to the similarity of the experiences. These experiences do not represent a solid, homogeneous, refutation of the reality of the foo fighters, but rather a panoramic survey of night flyer experiences. The organizing focus is centered around veterans who saw anomalous lights while flying in a night-time combat situation and what they believed them to be. The main division in the narratives resides in the interpretations of the events, bifurcating into opposing beliefs, supernatural and skeptical. The supernatural interpretations stick exclusively to contemporary beliefs concerning a "technological UFO," with the skeptical interpretations being drawn from secret-weapons lore current at the time and place of the individual sightings and traditional elaborations concerning mistaken identification of phenomena, i.e., St. Elmo's fire, ball lightning, the planet Venus, etc. The latter group has been the most influential in the formation of current etiologies refuting the existence of a "technological UFO." All of the "supernatural" interpretations are completely devoid of antiquated beliefs in ghosts, spooks or any non-corporal, ie., spiritual phenomena. But these experiences have been compared by some of the veterans as being similar to the Jack-o'-lantern or Will-o'-the-wisp lights. This is where a solution can be found. Here is a superb summary of the legendary qualities of this multi-talented mischief maker. Drawn from Pennsylvania Dutch belief traditions current in the 1890's, "Dragons" describes a very stable set of perceptual observations:

> This is a name that is sometimes applied to a phenomenon perhaps more frequently called Jack-o'-the-Lantern, or Will-o'-the-Wisp. It seems to be a ball of fire, varying in size from that of a candle-flame to that of a man's head. It is generally observed in damp, marshy places, moving to and fro; but it has been known to stand perfectly still and send off scintillations. As you approach it, it will move on, keeping just beyond your reach; if you retire, it will follow you. That these fireballs do occur, and that they will repeat your motion, seems to be established, but no satisfactory explanation has yet been offered that I have heard. Those who are little superstitious say that it is the ignition of the gases rising from the marsh. But how a light produced from burning gas could have the form described and move as described, advancing as you advance, receding as you recede, and at other times remaining stationary, without having any visible connection with the earth, is not clear to me."(Owens.p. 123.)

This version of the Jack-o-lantern was collected in 1968 by the folklorist Dr. Ronald L. Baker:

> One night at about three o'clock in the morning, one of my friends from Salem, who had been over to see his girl friend in Shoals, which is bout an hour and a half from Salem, was driving back to Salem. He reached a long strip of straight highway, and he was going about 90 miles an hour. He happened to look in his mirror, and there was a big ball of fire following the car. It was off the ground and right behind him. He went faster, and it kept following. He looked at the road for a second, and the next time he looked it was gone. He was so shook up that when he got home about 45 minutes later, he went in and woke up his dad and told him about it. His dad said it was probably a Jack-o'-lantern., he had seen one when he was a boy and lived in the country. (Baker, p.56.)

Let us proceed with the World War II version of this legend type. Early in October of 1944, pilots in the 422 Night Fighter Squadron (NFS), based out of Florennes, Belgium began to report "balls of light" pacing their fighters over Western Germany. By early November several 422nd pilots and Radar operators had reported encounters with Me 163 rocket fighters and Me262 jet fighters on night missions over the Reich. On the 7th of November of 1944 the Associated Press Corps in Paris released this statement:

New Aerial Weapon Used By Germans

> Paris (AP)-- The Germans are using jet and rocket propelled planes and various other 'newfangled' gadgets against Allied night fighters," Lt. Col. B. Johnson, Natchitoches, La., commander of a P-61 Black Widow group, said today." In recent nights we've counted 15 to 20 jet planes," Johnson said. "They sometimes fly in formations of four, but more often they fly alone." (The Day, New London, Connecticut, p.1)

Oris B. Johnson, commander of the 422nd NFS, reaffirmed that these sightings did occur, but admitted that the actual number was less than that originally printed in the AP release. The 422nd historical data, intelligence records and operations reports confirm that the pilots were reporting "jets" during night operations over the Ruhr Valley. On the 19th of January of 1945, Captain Edward S. Page, 5-2 Intelligence officer of the 422nd NFS filed this summary of the squadron's encounters with Me163 and Me262 aircraft to the Commanding General of the Ninth Air Force:

K. Enemy Aircraft Encountered

> c. Jets - have been unable to determine mission, as they -generally fly at altitudes in excess of 10,000 feet and make no effort to attack ground targets or our own aircraft, Possibly they are watching for mass RAF raids. (National Archives and Records Administration, Record Group 18, 422 NFS historical data.)

In an interview with Phillip Cuba, Assistant Intelligence officer of the 422 NFS, he states,

> Phillip. . . "At first we thought they (the pilots) were seeing things, and they kept saying that these things were chasing them around. Whether they actually identified.., not while I was on duty, they did not identify a jet as such. But I think that was the only conclusion we could reach... that was a jet. It could not have been a Will-o'-wisp or something like that. What they reported seeing was simply the exhaust, you see. They did mention that these guys (the jets) seemed to play around with them. They (the jets) never shot at them and I can't recall whether the Radar observer actually saw them on the screen. It was mostly visual in other words."

Jeff... "Really, what do you mean by Will-o'-wisp?"

Phillip..."Well it's sort of like a swamp fire, you know these things that keep going around... darting in and out. And they (the pilots) seemed mystified."

Meanwhile, the 415th N.F.S. based out of Dijon France began to report the "balls of fire" which they had affectionately dubbed, "foo fighters." On the 27th of November the first foo fighter was sighted over Western Germany by an Ed Schleuter and Don Meiers flying a Beaufighter, here is Don's account:

Donald J. Meiers: the first officially documented Flight Officer to ever use the term, "Foo Fighter."
(Gary Pape, 1992. *Queen of the Midnight Skies*, p.74)
Photo taken by: Robert Tierney, 422 NFS.

"A foo fighter picked me up at 700 feet and chased me 20 miles down the Rhine Valley," Meiers said. "I turned to starboard and two balls of fire turned with me. We were going 260 miles an hour and the balls were keeping right up with us. On another occasion when a foo fighter picked us up, I dived at 360 miles an hour. It kept right off our wing tips for awhile and then zoomed into the sky. When I first saw the things, I had the horrible thought that a German on the ground was ready to press a button and explode them. But they didn't explode or attack us. They just seem to follow us like the Will-o'-the-wisp. "(N.Y. Times, 2 Jan. 1945, p.1,4.)

Well, to complicate things even more, the 416th N.F.S. stationed in Pisa Italy also began to spot "foo fighters" in February of 1945. Here are some excerpts from the 416th NFS' historical data and operations records respectively:

17 February 1945: "Our crews are beginning to report mysterious orange-red lights in the sky near La Spezia and also inland. These "foo fighters" have been pursued, but no one has been able to make contact. G.C.I. and intelligence profess to be mystified by these ghostly apparitions. The hypothesis that the foo-fighters are a post-cognac manifestation has been disproved. Even the teetotalers have observed the strange and mysterious foo-fighters which have also been observed in France and in Belgium." (17 Feb. 1945, 416th historical data. U.S. Army.)

17 February 1945: "At 21:30 saw reddish white light going off and on in spurts about 6 or 8 miles away, near La Spezia at 10,000 ft. going NE. chased it at 280 MPH for 1 1/2 minutes. It took erratic course and faded out. At 21:40 saw some type of light 10 miles South of La Spezia and it went North and turned East of La Spezia at 9000'. Faded near La Spezia. Pilot came within 5 miles of La Spezia, suspected Ack Ack trap. At 21:55, 10 miles south of La Spezia chased another and it went across La Spezia and pilot followed. Faded 10 or 15 miles North of La Spezia. Our aircraft at 300 MPH couldn't catch it. No ack ack at La Spezia. At 22:50, 5 miles south of Pisa, saw same light from distance of 10

miles. Chased it for 2 or 2 1/2 minutes. It took north course, disappeared over mt. this light 10,000'. Light described as glow that alternates between weak and bright. No contacts on Al (radar). Apparently no jamming." (17 Feb. 1945. Daily Operations Report, 416th NFS, 12th AF-SCU-01.)

The above sighting was made by George Shultz and Frankie Robinson. These two persons had just arrived back at their unit after serving temporarily with the 425th N.F.S. in Etain France. In an interview with Frankie Robinson he confirmed that they had made a stop for a few days to visit and "Shoot the Bull" with friends of theirs who were pilots flying in the 415th N.F.S. based at Dijon France. It was at this time that Frankie and George learned of the foo fighters. This fact has been confirmed by both Frankie Robinson and George Shultz. After their return to Pisa, Italy on the evening of the 17th of February, 1945, Frankie and George spotted the 416th's first foo fighter.

These facts necessitate an investigation into the German Jet night fighter operations during the period of October 1944 to February of 1945. The only operational German Jet Night Fighter unit, 10/NJG/11 was only beginning operations in mid-December of 1944 just 50 miles south of Berlin. It was assigned with the task of defending Berlin, and Berlin only! Fritz Wendel, the chief test pilot of the Me262 paid a visit to 10/NJG11 at it's station in Burg bei Magdeburg. His report on the 19th of February of 1945 continues:

> "The NJG 11 (Night Fighter Squadron) has been stationed in Burg bei Magdeburg for the last few weeks, this unit belonging to Kommando Welter. Oberleutnant Kurt Welter is at the moment carrying out night flying operations using the method "Wilde San" with the Me262 (This night fighting method incorporated the use of a day fighter not equipped with air intercept radar and large detachments of ground searchlight batteries to illuminate Allied bombers.) He is using the standard Me262 type with some additions: a UV-light, map reading light and an emergency turn indicator. Welter is the only one flying this type of operation at this time, and using the said system has shot down five enemy aircraft. The other five pilots under his command at the moment are being retrained. The unit has six aircraft, and all should be operational within a few days."

Kurt Welter was appointed to form the first Me 262 Night Fighter test detachment (Erprobungs-Kommando) on 2 November of 1944. This was the only German Jet Night Fighting outfit in WWII and until the last week in February, Kurt Welter was the only pilot flying the Me 262 aircraft at night. Welter's detachment did not become operational until mid-December of 1944 with only two Me 262 A1-a's. His orders were to intercept the nightly assaults of Mosquito bombers hitting Berlin known as the "Berlin Express." This allows Welter very little time to organize, recruit, equip and fly all of the missions which Allied pilots claim were flown. (From Hugh Morgan's "Me262, Stormbird Rising")

This still leaves us with the question of the Me 163 rocket fighter. The Second Squadron of Jagdgeschwader (JG) 400, the first and only Me163 Combat Wing, was stationed at Venlo airfield in the Netherlands and saw limited action until it was withdrawn to the home wing in Brandis, south of Leipzig, in July of 1944. At Brandis, JG 400 saw it's peak of operational performance on the 28th of September of 1944 when it was able to scramble 9 Me163s in order to intercept an Allied day-light bombing raid. This rocket fighter was only used as a day interceptor for bombers, no records exist concerning the night testing of the Me 163 at the German experimental airfield, Estelle Rechlin, which is where all of the experimental aircraft were tested for night flying. (Morgon, Price, Ziegler.) Mano Zeigler who flew as one of the three chief test pilots assigned to Erprobungs-Kommando 16 and later a Rocket pilot in JG 400 commented on the practicability of flying such a nocturnal mission in a Me163, "Trying to land in the dark you'd spread yourself in small pieces around the countryside!" (Ziegler p.113) This aircraft also had an effective combat radius of no more than 25 miles under perfect visual conditions and thus limited JG 400's operations to the Leipzig area for the duration of the war.

This next sighting comes from the Pacific Theater of Operations. This was reported by a crew from the 500th Bomb Group, 20th A.F. on a raid on the Tachikawa aircraft plant, Tokyo, Mission No.# 38, 3-4 April 1945:"

> On this mission mysterious 'Balls of Fire' were observed by various crews during the course of the mission. Lt. Althoff and crew in Z Square 19 observed one near land's end at 9000 feet at about 0147. The 'Ball of Fire' was first seen at 5:00 level about 300 yards behind the B-29. As near as can be determined, the 'Ball of Fire' was about the size of a basketball. When evasive action was taken by the B-29 in the form of turns, the 'Ball of Fire' turned inside the B-29 and kept following. It appeared that each time the B-29 made a turn, the 'Ball of Fire' fell behind, but on the straightaway, it would catch up. The B-29 lost altitude, going down to 6000 feet, in order to gain speed and finally an airspeed of 295, at which speed the 'Ball of Fire' followed for about five or six minutes. One crew member thought that he was able to see a wing in connection with the 'ball,' and that the wing had an aviation light on at the tip." (4 April, 1945. Consolidated Mission Report, Mission no. #38, 500th Bomb Group.)

This report was funneled up to the 73rd Bomb Wing Intelligence, then to 20th A.F. Intelligence and then passed on to the Director of Intelligence, Army Air Forces, Pacific Ocean Areas. The resultant report published through this office on 7 April 1945 was titled:

"B-29s observed on 3 April 1945 a 'BALL OF FIRE' which was subject to some definite control. This is an attempt to describe the phenomenon and to define it with an eye toward the most recent Japanese fields of interest and development."

This is precisely what is occurring with all of the attempts to define the Will-o'-wisp phenomena, the interpretations are almost always drawn from their immediate context. Now read the conclusion of this report:

> "The three probabilities discussed are based on the interest the Japanese have held in the German development of jet units. It is impossible from the fragmentary evidence of an initial experience with this weapon to be more definite."

(note)

Unfortunately, this mild disclaimer was not circulated back to the Bomb Groups. The individual unit intelligence officers were sent detailed information on the Baka Bombs with pictures and diagrams of the Bakas captured on the Island of Okinawa. Several officers from the baka unit on Okinawa were captured and interrogated. These interrogation reports were redistributed and teletyped messages were received by the individual Bomb Groups. This report entitled "Another Rocket?" was dispatched to the Groups on 22 May 1945 from the Office of the Chief of Counter Intelligence, GHQ, Air Forces Pacific Command:

> "The probable existence of a second Japanese rocket-propelled plane has been disclosed in prisoner of war interrogation. The first was BAKA. The new plane is described as designed for interceptor duties, in particular to combat B-29s. It has an extraordinarily

high rate of climb, and is reputed to be capable of reaching 30,000 feet in approximately three minutes. This figure is matched only by the German Me163 rocket propelled interceptor. In general appearance the new plane is said to *resemble* BAKA, being approximately 20 feet long and 20 feet in wing span. Its weight is approximately 3,000 pounds. According to the POW two 20 mm cannon are fixed in the nose and propulsion is achieved by means of solid rockets, with the possibility that jet control is available to increase maneuverability. The plane is launched from the ground and is said to be airborne in about 100 feet. No landing gear or skids are fitted. Maximum flight time is limited to seven minutes, compared to 10-12 minutes for the Me163 at fill power." (Extract From Daily Intelligence Summary -22 May 1945, Office of the Chief of Counter Intelligence, GHQ, AFPAC.)

Throughout all of the Bomb Group records concerning the May 23rd and May 25th missions over Tokyo, none fail to mention the multitude of Bakas and "balls of light" sighted. In the 504th Bomb Group alone, 40 Bakas were sighted. In a post war interview with the director of Mitsubishi Heavy Industries, Yasujiro Okana laid out Japan's attempt to duplicate the German Me163. This was accomplished be receiving the German technical data for this rocket fighter and simply attempting a duplication. The result was two experimental aircraft, the J8M1 Shusui and the Ki-201. The J8M1 was flight tested without an engine on the 8th of January of 1945 with limited success. It was not until the 7th of July of 1945, however, that it was tested with a rocket engine. It crashed upon take-off, ending abruptly the rocket fighter program. (USSBS, Appendix 5, p.144.)

If the "jet" interpretation could suffice we are faced with the fact that these

sightings persisted after YE Day in the PTO. I offer the above incident from the 500th Bomb Group as a representative of the hundreds of officially documented accounts of this type. We do know for certain that the Japanese had no operational jets during the war, but they did have a rocket powered suicide bomb code-named "Baka bomb," or "crazy bomb." The Baka, Oka 11, was a modified glider equipped with three solid-fuel rockets with a 2,645 pound warhead. The effective range of the Oka 11 was virtually nil and had to be released by a parent bomber at an appropriate altitude and distance to allow the bomb to glide at a 50 degree glide-slope to it's target. It possessed virtually no ability to maneuver let alone engage in a night fighter role, The Oka 11 was designed by the Navy solely as a costal-defense (anti-ship) weapon and was first used in the Okinawa campaign where, "it quickly proved its ineffectiveness and production of the Oka 11 ceased in March

1945." (USSBS, p.81.)

There is a need to elaborate on the terror that the kamikazes inflicted in the minds of the Americans. This account is given concerning the experiences of the commander of "Southern Belle," Walt Sherrell , from the 498th Bomb Group, 874th Sq. 20th A.F.:

"He heard his co-pilot Orb Hall exclaim, 'Oh, my God!" Sherrell turned his head just in time to see a shadowy shape with a fiery tail hit a B-29, after which the B-29 went down flaming. Seeing a thin cloud layer ahead, he flew into it, seeking cover. He had barely emerged on the other side when one of the gunners reported a shadow trailing the right. Sherrell put "Southern Belle" into a screaming dive and, with his airspeed indicator reading well over 300 mph, pulled out after loosing about 3,000 feet of altitude. Another possible Baka was sighted, this time on the left. Sherrell racked the B-29, at full power, into a steep climbing turn to the right and into some clouds. After several more dives and climbs, they saw no more 'foofighters.'" (Kerr.p.242.)

I tracked down Walt Sherrell and all of the surviving members of "Southern Belle." The two side gunners and the tail gunner vividly recall the night of the 25th of May where this foo fighter chased their aircraft just after they had bombed Tokyo. All three gunners described this kamikaze as a "ball of fire" and saw nothing that could identify it as an aircraft. On the 27th of May the New York Times reported that the Japanese had begun to use the Baka against B-29 aircraft. Thus far, every account that I have collected concerning the Baka from 20th A.F. veterans concerns the sighting of a "ball of light" or a "ball of fire." I have found absolutely no documentation that can support the hypothesis that the Baka was ever used against any aircraft at all during the war. The Baka bomb is a traditional interpretation as is the jet interpretation in the ETO. These legends form the corpus of the Second World War's Secret-Weapons lore. So, what is a foo fighter? Because of the inherent ambiguity of the term and the lack of any clear guidelines encompassing the phenomenon of aerial encounters with anomalous lights, a wide variety of experiences are syncretically pulled together to form the corpus of the foo fighter mystery. David Hufford describes the usage of ambiguous terminology as, "where tradition has supplied a term to refer to

the experience, the term has developed a larger sphere of meaning. This is quite natural since phenomenological description is not a natural purpose in everyday speech." (Hufford p.15.) This process not only includes the foo fighters, but also jets, Bakas, St. Elmo's fire, ball lightning and even stories concerning the planet Venus. Remember, in order to objectively survey these experiences, the concept of "truth" must be set aside because of its highly subjective and biasing nature. The current trend is to assign the foo fighters to the "nearest" possible equivalent thus transforming a supernatural legend into a natural (believable) variant.

At this point it is of vital interest to relate the above terms with that of the concept of "aviator's vertigo." In May of 1946, Dr. W. E. Yinacke submitted the first ever report concerning folk beliefs among aviators concerning anomalous experiences associated with flying. In his report, "The Concept of Aviator's 'Vertigo,'" Yinacke states,

> "vertigo' is primarily a psychological problem. It appears to be associated with the mental hazards of flying, and with the 'mysterious' events which sometimes happen in an aircraft. There is thus a two-fold source of emotional loading in the term 'vertigo', i.e., dangerous conditions and unexplained, though actual, phenomena. (Vinacke .p.2.)

In the pursuit of fairness I have also interviewed the same pilots periodically and concerning various topics involving night flying. This effect has been significant. Pilots who never reported seeing foo fighters were asked if they had experienced vertigo. The vertigo stories could easily be classed as foo fighter stories. These persons tended to be either commanders or high ranking experienced night fighters. The point is that there are a wide variety of "conditions" in which a story can be recounted concerning an anomalous personal experience. Persons who had not seen foo fighters could offer no such similar experience other than a "mistaken identification" interpretation such as St. Elmo's fire, jets, Venus, etc. Persons who had experienced "visual-vertigo" in night flying offered experiences which are, for all practical purposes, identical to first hand experience narratives concerning foo fighters, baka bombs, jets, Venus, balls of fire and the Jack-o'-lantern. Edgar Vinacke writes,

> "Pilots do not have sufficient information about phenomena of disorientation, and, as a corollary, are given considerable disorganized, incomplete, and inaccurate information. They are largely dependent upon their own experience, which must supplement and

interpret the traditions about 'vertigo' which are passed on to them. When a concept thus grows out of anecdotes cemented together with practical necessity, it is bound to acquire elements of mystery. So far as 'vertigo' is concerned, no one really knows more than a small part of the facts, but a great deal of the peril. Since aviators are not skilled observers of human behavior, they usually have only the vaguest understanding of their own feelings. Like other naive persons, therefore, they have simply adopted a term to cover a multitude of otherwise inexplicable events." (Vinacke p.5.)

Therefore is a foo fighter a description of a class of events which one could label as vertigo? Possibly, but there are so many classes of events which are already grouped within this uncertain category. Perhaps the sub-set "visual-vertigo" would be more specific and confine the grouping of events a little more accurately. But the term "vertigo" still possess the connotation of disorientation with descriptions of these events including terms like, "imagination" "illusions" "hypnosis" "infatuation" "fatigue" and allusions to feelings that what is being seen is more akin to a hallucination or a "night time mirage." These connotations tend to differ from descriptions of disorientation such as dizziness, nausea or the swimming sensations of the head. Although vertigo is more akin to physiological symptoms associated with vestibular functions, it may not be totally divorced from visual-perceptual phenomena such as depth perception failure, autokinesis, gravical and rotary illusory-sensations, apparent parallactic movements of objects above horizons, etc. These visual sensations have been linked with vertigo for the very reason that it is believed that these false visual cues contribute to the onset of disorientation-vertigo syndromes. The most striking features concerning narratives about the foo fighters consist primarily of beliefs in the external (objective) reality of these objects, be they foo fighters, baka bombs or jets. In understanding these narratives offered by night time combat aviators one must realize that the process of identification of an objects movement immediately places this object in a priority threat classification. In a nighttime combat situation, aviators must distinguish hostile and non-hostile lights by means of their apparent movement, ie., a hostile light would possess apparent movement and a non-hostile light would appear to be stationary. This is, perhaps, virtually impossible. Anticipation or expectation of movement of a light is all the stimulus needed to trigger the autokinetic sensation of movement. This illusory sensation of movement can cause a chain reaction of reactions and further stimulations that can drastically enhance the illusory perception of movement.

A typical sequence of events inside an aircraft can unfoldin a like manner:

1) prior instruction concerning a warning about an unidentified aircraft,

2) one observer identifying a light as having perceptible movement,

3) second observer. verifying the perceived movement of a light thus forming a regenerative feedback loop reinforcing the first observer's belief that the light is indeed in motion,

4) the observers form a normative estimate of the degree and "purpose" of the lights movement and declare the object as hostile or non-threatening,

5) if the light (object) is assumed to be hostile, further reinforcement of the regenerative feedback loop will occur thus forcing a reaction from the crew in two general directions

    A) toward the light, or rather in a pursuit effort,

B) away from the light, retreat.
   6) both of the reactions require the pilot of an aircraft to dive, climb, turn etc., in order to accomplish the set goal.

These gravical and angular maneuvers can markedly offset the illusory sensations of movement of the light in question, further reinforcing the regenerative feedback loop.

These sensations are known as the oculargyral, oculargravic and ocularagravic illusions. These chains of events can form under a multitude of preconceived notions and may include any of the following combinations: three dimensional autokinetic movement; multiple-target autokinesis; depth perception failure; the illusory perception of color changes; real color changes; fluctuations in apparent brightness, both real and illusory, adding further to depth perception failure; diplopia, or rather, the splitting of images due to the failure of focusing properly, harmonic vibrations etc.; the apparent motion parallax, where stationary objects appear to move in contrast to a moving horizon, ie., the moon following your car.

Of major importance in further exploring the eyewitness accounts of the foo fighters is the fact that every single sighting happened while the aircraft were flying out of formations. With Night Fighters, all missions were flown without wing men or in formation. With the B-29 bombers over Japan, mass raids of up to 500 planes were flown with the major exception that all the aircraft flew in single file and staggered so as not to be in formation. All of the foo fighter, etc., stories involve isolated crews. I have found no instances where more than one aircraft has witnessed this phenomena in visual proximity of another friendly aircraft. This fact combined with the earlier stories concerning Jack-o'-lanterns involve isolation at night and is a constant and significant condition under which these experiences unfold. The dynamics of fear and ambiguity are offset and impacted by the migratory legends which warn us of the dangers of being alone at night, especially while attacking the enemy in his homeland. The talk of secret-wonder weapons which pilots and crew members chat about while anticipating the next horrendous mission have credible bearing upon the attitudes of the crews as they attack an enemy's homeland. Anticipation, fear, anxiety, scuttlebutt and isolation all combine to form the context for the interpretation of the ambiguous and "mysterious" events that occur aboard an aircraft which may never return from the present mission.

Italian News Story Validates Nazi Scientists Built Flying Saucers During WWII

This story featured in the Italian press shows original Nazi blue prints for flying saucers built and operated during the closing days of World War II. Is it possible our Stealth technology originated during this period?

Welt am Sonntag April 26, 1953

Nazi UFO Photo Files Of Alleged German-Made Craft

No documentation is available on the nature of these pictures or their origins, and thus they can only be provided for research purposes with this understanding.

Sie ist gelandet und wird entladen. Ein Hamburg-Kennwagen steht dabei

HAT DEUTSCHLAND WIEDER GEHEIMWAFFEN?

STRENG VERTRAULICH!

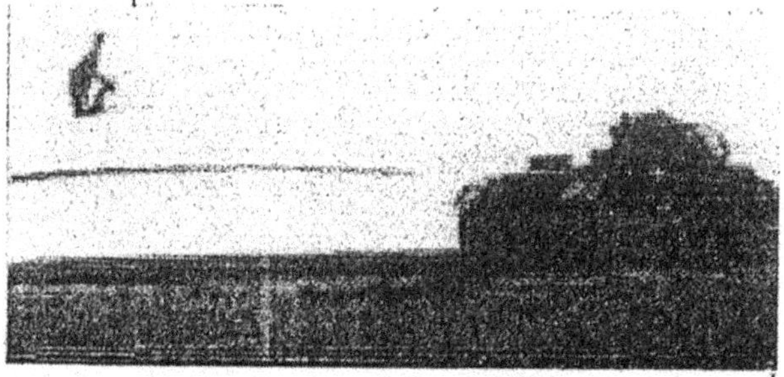

Pilot auf Flugscheibe neben deutschem Panzer

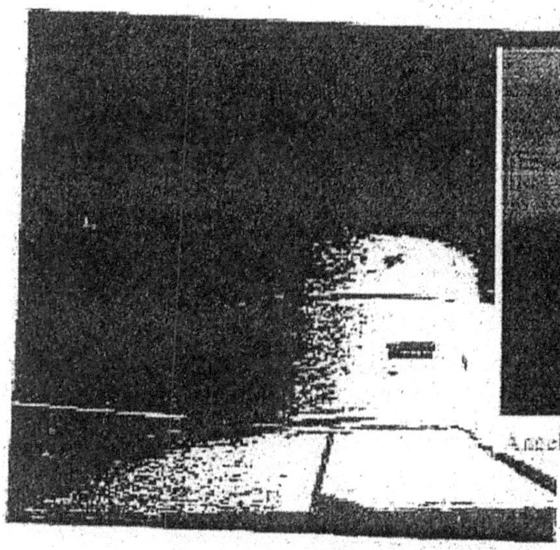

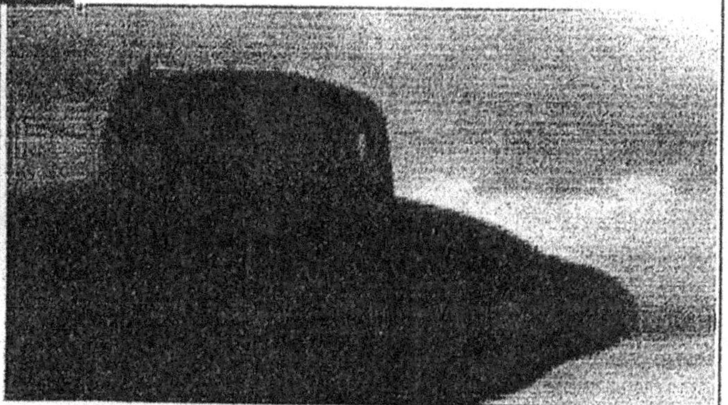

Angeblich Bundeswehr-Scheibe FU1 (Fliegende Untertasse 1)

BRD-UFO-Craft "FU-2"

Rheinland-Scheibe ist gestartet und steigt weiter auf

[illegible] Spaziergänger im Rheinland fotografiert [illegible]

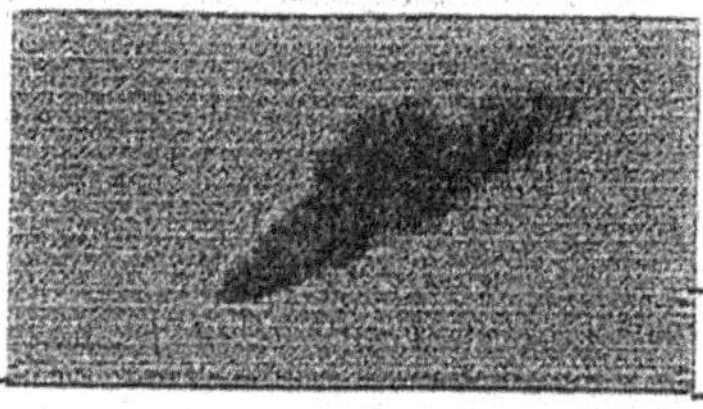

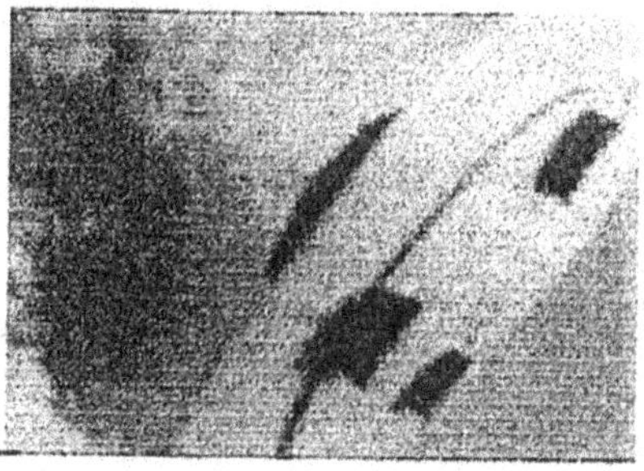

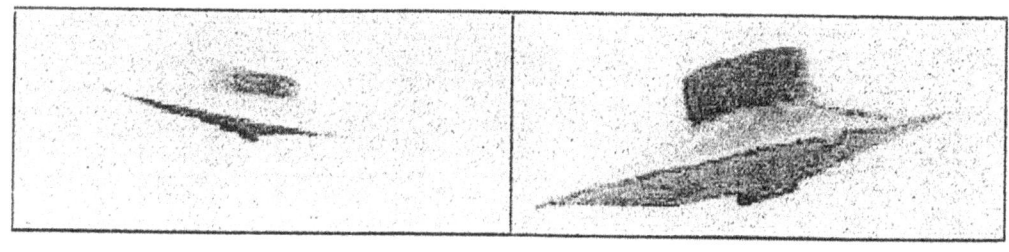

www.ingramcontent.com/pod-product-compliance
Lightning Source LLC
Chambersburg PA
CBHW080359170426
43193CB00016B/2762